W9-ALW-074

Practical Django Projects

James Bennett

Apress®

Practical Django Projects

Copyright © 2008 by James Bennett

All rights reserved. No part of this work may be reproduced or transmitted in any form or by any means, electronic or mechanical, including photocopying, recording, or by any information storage or retrieval system, without the prior written permission of the copyright owner and the publisher.

ISBN-13 (pbk): 978-1-59059-996-9

ISBN-10 (pbk): 1-59059-996-9

ISBN-13 (electronic): 978-1-4302-0868-6

Printed and bound in the United States of America 9 8 7 6 5 4 3 2 1

Trademarked names may appear in this book. Rather than use a trademark symbol with every occurrence of a trademarked name, we use the names only in an editorial fashion and to the benefit of the trademark owner, with no intention of infringement of the trademark.

Java™ and all Java-based marks are trademarks or registered trademarks of Sun Microsystems, Inc., in the US and other countries. Apress, Inc., is not affiliated with Sun Microsystems, Inc., and this book was written without endorsement from Sun Microsystems, Inc.

Lead Editors: Steve Anglin, Tom Welsh
Technical Reviewer: Russell Keith-Magee
Editorial Board: Clay Andres, Steve Anglin, Ewan Buckingham, Tony Campbell, Gary Cornell,
    Jonathan Gennick, Matthew Moodie, Joseph Ottinger, Jeffrey Pepper, Frank Pohlmann,
    Ben Renow-Clarke, Dominic Shakeshaft, Matt Wade, Tom Welsh
Project Manager: Richard Dal Porto
Copy Editors: Kim Benbow, Nicole Abramowitz
Associate Production Director: Kari Brooks-Copony
Production Editor: Kelly Gunther
Compositor: Dina Quan
Proofreader: Nancy Sixsmith
Indexer: Carol Burbo
Cover Designer: Kurt Krames
Manufacturing Director: Tom Debolski

Distributed to the book trade worldwide by Springer-Verlag New York, Inc., 233 Spring Street, 6th Floor, New York, NY 10013. Phone 1-800-SPRINGER, fax 201-348-4505, e-mail orders-ny@springer-sbm.com, or visit http://www.springeronline.com.

For information on translations, please contact Apress directly at 2855 Telegraph Avenue, Suite 600, Berkeley, CA 94705. Phone 510-549-5930, fax 510-549-5939, e-mail info@apress.com, or visit http://www.apress.com.

Apress and friends of ED books may be purchased in bulk for academic, corporate, or promotional use. eBook versions and licenses are also available for most titles. For more information, reference our Special Bulk Sales—eBook Licensing web page at http://www.apress.com/info/bulksales.

The information in this book is distributed on an "as is" basis, without warranty. Although every precaution has been taken in the preparation of this work, neither the author(s) nor Apress shall have any liability to any person or entity with respect to any loss or damage caused or alleged to be caused directly or indirectly by the information contained in this work.

The source code for this book is available to readers at http://www.apress.com. You may need to answer questions pertaining to this book in order to successfully download the code.

This book would not have been possible without the huge and supportive community that has grown up around Django in the past three years. The willingness of people all around the world to freely contribute their code, their ideas, and their time to improving the state of our art never ceases to amaze me.

This book also would not have been possible without Mr. Morgan, who instilled in me both the craft and the joy of writing. For that he has my deepest thanks.

Contents at a Glance

Contents

About the Author

 **JAMES BENNETT** is a web developer at the *Lawrence Journal-World* in Lawrence, Kansas, where Django was originally developed. He is both a regular contributor to and the release manager for the open source Django project.

About the Technical Reviewer

DR. RUSSELL KEITH-MAGEE has been a core developer on the Django project since January 2006. He is a cofounder of Django Evolution, a schema evolution framework for Django. He is an active participant on the Django Users and Django Developers mailing lists and is a mentor in the Google Summer of Code 2008.

In addition to his work with Django, Russell has worked at two startup companies—one very successful and one still in development. In those jobs, he has used his passion for good design, powerful tools, and automated testing to find elegant solutions to real-world problems faced by real-world users.

Russell lives with his wife, son, and two cats in Perth, Western Australia.

Introduction

The past few years have seen an explosion in the development of dynamic, database-driven web sites. Where many sites were once built using nothing but handwritten HTML, or a few CGI scripts or server-side includes, today database-backed web applications have become the norm for everything from personal blogs to online stores to the social networking sites that have revolutionized the way many people use the Web.

But this has come at a cost. Developing these applications, even for relatively simple uses, involves a significant amount of complex work, and much of that work ends up being repeated for each new application. Although web developers have always had access to libraries of code that could automate certain tasks, such as HTML templating or database querying, the process of bringing together all the necessary pieces for a fully polished application has largely remained difficult and tedious.

This has led to the recent development, and subsequent popularity, of "web frameworks," reusable collections of components that handle many of the common and repetitive tasks of application development in an integrated fashion. Instead of requiring you to obtain disparate libraries of code and find ways to make them work together, web frameworks provide all the necessary components in a single package and take care of the integration work for you.

Django is one of the most recent crop of web frameworks, growing out of the needs of a fast-paced online news operation. Django's original developers needed a set of tools that would not only help them quickly develop new and highly dynamic web applications in response to the rapidly evolving requirements of the news industry, but would also let them save time and effort by reusing pieces of code, and even entire applications, whenever possible.

In this book, you'll see how Django can help you achieve both of these goals—rapid application development and flexible, reusable code—through the tools it provides to you directly and the development practices that it makes possible. I'll guide you through the development of several example applications and show you how the various components and applications bundled with Django can help you to write less code at each stage of the development process. You'll also see firsthand a number of best practices for reusable code and learn how you can apply them in your own applications, as well as see how to integrate existing third-party libraries into Django-powered applications to minimize the amount of code you'll need to write from scratch.

I've written this book from a pragmatic viewpoint. The sample applications are all intended to be useful in real-world situations, and once you've worked through them, you'll have more than just a technical understanding of Django and its components. You'll have a clear understanding of how Django can help you become a more productive and more effective developer.

CHAPTER 1

■ ■ ■

Welcome to Django

Web development is hard, and don't let anybody tell you otherwise. Building a fully functional dynamic web application with all the features users will want is a daunting task with a seemingly endless list of things you have to get just right. And before you can even start thinking about most of them, there's a huge amount of up-front work: you have to set up a database, create all the tables to store your data, plan out all the relationships and queries, come up with a solution for dynamically generating the HTML, work out how to map specific URLs to different bits of the code, and the list goes on. Just getting to the point where you can add features your users will see or care about is a vast and largely thankless job.

But it doesn't have to be that way.

This book will teach you how to use Django, a "web framework" that will significantly ease the pain of embarking on new development projects. You'll be able to follow along and build real applications—code you can actually use in the real world—and at every step you'll see how Django is there to help you out. And at the end, you'll come to a wonderful realization— that web development is fun again.

What's a Web Framework and Why Should I Want One?

The biggest downside of web development is the sheer amount of tedium it involves. All those things I've listed previously—database creation and querying, HTML generation, URL mapping—and dozens more are lurking behind every new application you develop, and they quickly suck all the joy out of even the most exciting projects. Web frameworks like Django aim to take all that tedium away by providing an organized, reusable set of common libraries and components that can do the heavy lifting, freeing you up to work on the things that make your project unique.

This idea of standardizing a set of common libraries to deal with common tasks is far from new. In fact, in most areas of programming it's such an established practice that you'd get strange looks if you suggested somebody should just start writing code from scratch. And in enterprise web development, frameworks of various sorts have been in use for years. Most companies that routinely need to develop large-scale applications rely heavily on frameworks to provide common functionality and speed up their development processes.

But in the world of web development, frameworks have traditionally been, almost out of necessity, just as heavyweight as the applications they're used in. They tend to be written in Java or C#, targeted at large corporate development projects, and sometimes come with a price tag that only a *Fortune* 500 company could love. Django is part of a new generation of frameworks targeted at a broader audience: developers who don't necessarily have the weight of a multinational conglomerate's needs bearing down on their shoulders, but who still need to get things done quickly. Not to put too fine a point on it, developers like you and me.

The past couple of years have seen a number of these new web frameworks burst onto the scene, written in and for programming languages that are much more accessible to the average web developer (and, just as importantly, to the average web host): PHP, Perl, Python, and Ruby. Each one has a slightly different philosophy when it comes to things like code organization and how many "extras" should be bundled directly in the framework, but they all share a common baseline goal: provide an integrated, easy-to-use set of components that handle the tedious, repetitive tasks of web development with as little fuss as possible.

Say Hello to Django

Django began life as a simple set of tools used by the in-house web team of a newspaper company in a small college town in Kansas. Like anybody who spends enough time doing web development, they quickly got tired of writing the same kinds of code—database queries, templates, and the whole nine yards—over and over again, and extremely quickly, in fact, because they had the pressure of a newsroom schedule to keep up with. It wasn't (and still isn't) unusual to need custom code to go with a big story or feature, and the development timelines needed to be measurable in days, or even hours, in order to keep pace with the news.

In the space of a couple of years, they developed a set of libraries that worked extremely well together and, by automating or simplifying the common tasks of web development, helped them get their work done quickly and efficiently. In the summer of 2005, they got permission from the newspaper's management to release those libraries publicly, for free, and under an open source license so that anyone could use and improve them. They also gave it a snappy name, "Django," in honor of the famous gypsy jazz guitarist Django Reinhardt.

As befits its newsroom heritage, Django bills itself as "the web framework for perfectionists with deadlines." At its core is a set of solid, well-tested libraries covering all of the repetitive aspects of web development:

- An *object-relational mapper*, a library that knows what your database looks like, what your code looks like, and how to bridge the gap between them with as little hand-written SQL as possible.

- A set of HTTP libraries that knows how to parse incoming web requests and hand them to you in a standard, easy-to-use format and turns the results of your code into well-formed responses.

- A URL routing library that lets you define exactly the URLs you want and map them onto the appropriate parts of your code.

- A validation library for displaying forms in web pages and processing user-submitted data.

- A templating system that lets even nonprogrammers write HTML mixed with data generated by your code and just the right amount of presentational logic.

And that's just scratching the surface. Django's core libraries include a wealth of other features you'll come to love. A number of useful applications that build on Django's features are also bundled with it and provide out-of-the-box solutions for specific needs like administrative interfaces and user authentication. In the example applications used in this book, you'll see all of these features, and more, in action. So let's dive in.

Say Hello to Python

Django is written in a programming language called Python, so the applications you develop with it will also be written in Python. That also means you'll need to have Python installed on your computer before you can get started with Django. Python can be downloaded for free from `http://python.org/download/` and is available for all major operating systems. It's best to install the latest version of Python—Python 2.5.1 at the time of this writing—in order to have the latest features and bug fixes for the Python language.

ADMONITION: LEARNING PYTHON

If you don't know any Python, or even if you've never done any programming before, don't worry. Python is easy to learn (when I first started with Python, I learned the basics in a weekend by reading online tutorials), and you don't need to know much of it to get started with Django. In fact, many first-time Django users learn Python and Django at the same time.

Throughout this book, I'll call attention to important Python concepts when needed, but it would be a good idea to look at a Python tutorial before going very far into this book. The Python documentation index (available online at `http://python.org/doc/`) has a good list of tutorials and books (several of which are available for free online) to help you learn the basics of Python. (I'd recommend knowing at least how Python functions and classes work.) You'll be able to pick up the rest as you go along.

If you're looking for a good reference to keep handy as you're learning Django, *Beginning Python: From Novice to Professional* by Magnus Lie Hetland, and *Dive Into Python* by Mark Pilgrim (both from Apress) are good options.

Once you've installed Python, you should be able to open a command prompt (Command Prompt on Windows, Terminal on Mac OS X, or any terminal emulator on Linux) and enter the Python interactive interpreter by typing the command **python**. Normally, you'll be saving your Python code into files to be run as part of your applications, but the interactive interpreter will let you explore Python—and, once it's installed, Django—in a more freeform way: the interpreter lets you type in Python code, a line at a time, and see the results immediately. You can also use it to access and interact with code in your own Python files or in the Python standard libraries and any third-party libraries you've installed, which makes it a powerful learning and debugging tool.

When you first fire up the Python interpreter, you'll see something like this:

```
Python 2.5.1 (r251:54869, Apr 18 2007, 22:08:04)
[GCC 4.0.1 (Apple Computer, Inc. build 5367)] on darwin
Type "help", "copyright", "credits" or "license" for more information.
>>>
```

The >>> is Python's command prompt. You can type a line of Python code and press Enter, and if that code returns a result, you'll see it immediately. Let's test this with a simple line that just prints a line of text. At the Python interpreter prompt, type the following and press Enter:

```
>>> print "Hello, world!"
```

You'll see the result appear on the next line:

```
Hello, world!
>>>
```

Anything you can type into a file as part of a Python program can be typed directly into the interpreter, and there's also a full help system built in, which you can access at any time by typing **help()** and pressing Enter. When you're ready to exit the Python interpreter, press Ctrl+D, and it will shut down.

Installing Django

Now that you've got Python installed and working, it's time to install Django and start exploring its features. You can get a copy from the official Django web site; just visit www.djangoproject.com/download/ and follow the instructions for downloading the "development version" of Django.

ADMONITION: PACKAGED RELEASES VS. DEVELOPMENT CODE

Django is always being worked on and improved and, in addition to the official release, the current in-development code is available for download. The Django web site has instructions for installing this code on your computer, and you can follow that to obtain the development version of Django.

The advantage of using the development version is that new features are available as soon as they're added, so you can begin using them immediately instead of waiting for the next official release. In this book, I'll be assuming that you've installed the development version of Django, and several of the features we'll use are only available in the development version. This code will, in the near future, become Django's packaged 1.0 release, so starting out with it will minimize the amount of work you'll need to do to upgrade when that takes place. So when you download Django, be sure to follow the specific instructions for the development version found at www.djangoproject.com/documentation/install/#installing-the-development-version.

Once you've downloaded the Django code onto your computer, you can install it by typing a single command. On Linux or Mac OS X, open a terminal, navigate to the directory Django downloaded into, and you should see a file named setup.py. Type the following command, and enter your password when prompted:

```
sudo python setup.py install
```

On Windows, you'll need to open a command prompt with administrative privileges; then you can navigate to the Django directory and type the following:

```
python setup.py install
```

The `setup.py` script is a standard installation procedure for Python modules, and takes care of installing all of the relevant Django code into the correct locations for your operating system. If you're curious, Table 1-1 summarizes where the Django code will end up on various systems.

Table 1-1. *Django Installation Locations*

Operating system	Django location
Linux	/usr/local/lib/python2.5/site-packages/django
Mac OS X	/Library/Frameworks/Python.framework/Versions/2.5/lib/python2.5/site-packages/django
Windows	C:\Python\site-packages\django

Your First Steps with Django

You should now be able to verify that Django installed correctly on your computer. Next, start the interactive Python interpreter and type in the following:

```
>>> import django
>>> print django.VERSION
```

The result of this should be a set of numbers in parentheses, which represents the version of Django you're using. The Django 0.96 release, for example, will show (0, 96). Python software typically uses a *tuple*—a parenthesized, comma-separated list of numbers and/or words—to represent version numbers internally (which makes it easy for Python programs to automatically parse otherwise complex version numbers like "1.0 beta 3" or "2.4 prerelease").

Now you're ready to create your first Django project. A Django *project* is a wrapper of sorts, which contains settings for one or more Django-powered applications and a list of which applications it uses. Later on, when you're deploying your Django applications behind a real web server, you'll use projects to organize and configure them.

To set up your first project, create a directory on your computer where you'll keep your in-progress Django projects, and then navigate to it in a terminal or at a command prompt. It's often a good idea to have a single directory where you keep all of your own custom Python code. As you'll see a bit later on, doing so will simplify the process of telling Python how to find and use that code.

Now you can use the built-in Django management script, `django-admin.py`, to create your project. `django-admin.py` lives in the `bin/` subdirectory of the directory Django was installed into, and it knows how to handle various management tasks involving Django projects. The one you're interested in is called `startproject`, and it will create a new, empty Django project. In the directory where you want to create your project, type the following (refer to Table 1-1 for the correct path for your operating system):

```
/usr/local/lib/python2.5/site-packages/django/bin/django-admin.py startproject cms
```

This will create a new subdirectory called cms (you'll see why it's named that in the next chapter, when you start to work with this project) and populate it with the basic files needed by any Django project.

ADMONITION: PERMISSION ERRORS

If you're using Linux or Mac OS X, you may see an error message saying "permission denied." If this happens, you need to tell your operating system that the django-admin.py script is safe to run as a program. You can do this by navigating to the directory that django-admin.py is in and typing the command **chmod +x django-admin.py**. Then you can run the django-admin.py script as previously shown.

In the next section you'll see what each of the files in the project directory is for, but for now the most important one is called manage.py. Like django-admin.py, it's there to take care of common project and application management tasks for you. The manage.py script can start a simple web server that will host your project for testing purposes, and you can start it by going into your project directory and typing the following:

```
python manage.py runserver
```

Then you should be able to open up a web browser and visit the address http://127.0.0.1:8000/. The development web server, by default, runs on your computer's local "loopback" network address, which is always 127.0.0.1 and binds to port 8000. When you visit that address, you should see a simple page saying "It worked!" with some basic instructions for customizing your project (see Figure 1-1).

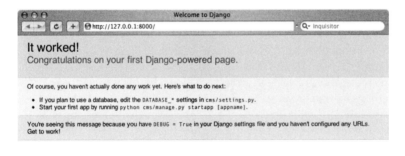

Figure 1-1. *Django welcome screen*

ADMONITION: CHANGING THE ADDRESS AND PORT

If something else is already using port 8000 on your computer, if you're not allowed to run programs that bind to that port, or if you want to view pages served by Django's development server from another computer, you'll need to manually specify the address and port to use when you launch the development server. The syntax for this is `python manage.py runserver ip_address:port_number`. So, for example, to listen on all of your computer's available IP addresses (so that other computers can view pages from the development server) and bind to port 9000 instead of 8000, you could type `python manage.py runserver 0.0.0.0:9000`.

You can stop the server by pressing Ctrl+C at the command prompt.

Exploring Your Django Project

The `startproject` command of `django-admin.py` created your project directory for you and automatically filled in a few files. Each one serves a specific purpose, and in future chapters you'll see what each one does, but for now here's a quick primer:

`__init__.py`: This will be an empty file. For now you don't need to put anything into it (and in fact, most of the time you won't need to). It's used to tell Python that this directory contains executable code. Python can treat any directory containing an `__init__.py` file as a Python module.

`manage.py`: As explained previously, this is a helper script that knows how to handle common management tasks. It knows how to start the built-in development web server, create new application modules, set up your database, and numerous other things that you'll see as you build your first Django applications.

`settings.py`: This is a Django *settings module*, which holds the configuration for your Django project. Over the next few chapters, you'll see some of the most common settings and how to edit them to suit your projects.

`urls.py`: This file contains your project's master URL configuration. Unlike some languages and frameworks that simply mimic HTML by letting you place code into the web server's public directory and access it directly by file name, Django uses an explicit configuration file to lay out which URLs point to which parts of your code, and this file defines the set of "root" URLs for an entire project.

You may notice that, after you started the built-in web server, one or more new files appeared in the project directory with the same names as those in the preceding list but with a .pyc extension instead of .py. Python can read the code directly out of your .py files, but it also can, and often does, automatically compile code into a form that's faster to load when a program starts up. This *bytecode*, as it's called, is then stored in identically named .pyc files, and if the original file hasn't changed since the last time a program used it, Python will load from the bytecode file to gain a speed boost.

Looking Ahead

In the next chapter, you'll walk through setting up your first real Django project, which will provide a simple content management system, or CMS. If you're ready to dive in, keep reading, but you should also feel free to pause and explore Python or Django a bit more on your own. Both the `django-admin.py` and `manage.py` scripts accept a `help` command, which will list all of the things they can do; and the Python interpreter's built-in help system can also automatically extract documentation from most Python modules on your computer, including the ones inside Django. There's also a special `shell` command to `manage.py` that you may find useful because it will launch a Python interpreter with a fully configured Django environment (based on your project's settings module) you can explore.

If you'd like, you can also take this opportunity to set up a database to use with Django. If you installed Python 2.5 or any later version, you won't have to do this right away. As of version 2.5, Python includes the lightweight SQLite database system directly, which you'll be able to use that throughout this book as you develop your first applications. However, Django also supports MySQL, PostgreSQL, and Oracle databases, so if you'd prefer to work with one of those, go ahead and set it up.

CHAPTER 2

■ ■ ■

Your First Django Site: A Simple CMS

One extremely common task in web development is building a simple content management system (CMS), which lets users create and edit pages on a site dynamically through a web-based interface. Sometimes called *brochureware* sites because they tend to be used in the same fashion as traditional printed brochures handed out by businesses, they're usually fairly simple feature-wise, but can be tedious to code over and over again.

In this chapter, you'll see how Django makes these sorts of sites almost trivially easy to build: I'll walk you through the setup of a simple CMS, and then in the next chapter, you'll see how to add a few extra features and provide room to expand it in the future.

Configuring Your First Django Project

In the last chapter, you created a Django project called cms. But before you can do much with it you'll need to do some basic configuration, so launch your favorite code editing program and use it to open up the settings.py file in your project.

ADMONITION: WRITING PYTHON

From here to the end of this book, you'll be writing Python code and the occasional template. If you haven't already looked at a Python tutorial to get a feel for the basics, now would be a good time. I'll explain some of the most important concepts as we go, but that's no substitute for a dedicated Python tutorial, which will cover them in depth.

And if you don't have an editing program suitable for working with programming code, you'll want to get one. Nearly all programmers' editors have support for Python (and other popular languages) built in, and this will make the process of writing code much easier.

Don't be daunted by the size of this file or the number of things you'll find in it. django-admin.py automatically filled in default values for a lot of them, and for now most of the defaults will be fine. Near the top of the file is a group of settings whose names all start with DATABASE. These settings tell Django what type of database to use and how to connect to it, and right now that's all you'll need to fill in.

Assuming you installed the latest version of Python, you'll already have a database adapter module that can talk to SQLite databases (Python 2.5 and later include this module in the standard Python library). SQLite stores the entire database in a single file on your computer and doesn't require any of the complex server or permissions setup of other database systems, so it's a great system to use when you're just starting out or exploring Django.

To use SQLite, you'll only need to change two settings. First, find the `DATABASE_ENGINE` setting and change it from this:

```
DATABASE_ENGINE = ''
```

to this:

```
DATABASE_ENGINE = 'sqlite3'
```

Now you'll need to tell Django where to find the SQLite database file. This goes into the `DATABASE_NAME` setting and can be anywhere on your computer's hard drive where you have permission to read and write files. You can even fill in a nonexistent file name, and the SQLite database engine will create the file for you automatically. Keeping the database file inside your project folder isn't a bad idea in this case, so go ahead and do that. I keep all of my Django projects in a folder called `django-projects` inside my home directory (on a laptop running Mac OS X), so I'll fill it in like so:

```
DATABASE_NAME = '/Users/jbennett/django-projects/cms/cms.db'
```

On other operating systems this will look a bit different, of course. On Windows it might be `C:\Documents and Settings\jbennett\django-projects\cms\cms.db`, for example, while on a Linux system it might be `/home/jbennett/django-projects/cms/cmd.db`.

I'm telling Django the SQLite database file should live inside the cms project directory and be named `cms.db`. The .db file extension isn't required, but it helps me to remember what that file is for, and so I'd recommend you use something similar.

ADMONITION: USING A DIFFERENT DATABASE

If you'd like to set up a MySQL, PostgreSQL, or Oracle database instead of using SQLite, consult the Django settings documentation online at `www.djangoproject.com/documentation/settings/` to see the correct values for the database settings. However, bear in mind that you will also need to install a Python adapter module for the database you're using—as of Python 2.5, SQLite is the only database system directly supported in the standard Python library.

If you're using a version of Python prior to 2.5, you'll need to install an adapter module for your database no matter which database you use. See the Django installation instructions for details at `www.djangoproject.com/documentation/install/#get-your-database-running`.

Finally, you'll probably want to change the `TIME_ZONE` setting. This tells Django which time zone to use when displaying dates and times from your database (which are typically stored in your database as UTC timestamps—Universal Time, Coordinated, which is the "base" time zone formerly known as Greenwich Mean Time, or GMT). Rather than using a country-specific time-zone name (like US Central Time) or a confusing UTC offset (like UTC-6), this setting uses names in zoneinfo format; *zoneinfo* is a standard format used by many computer operating systems and is also easy for humans to read. The default setting is

```
TIME_ZONE = "America/Chicago"
```

which is equivalent to the US Central time zone, six hours behind UTC. Full lists of zoneinfo time zone names are available online, and the official Django settings documentation at www.djangoproject.com/documentation/settings/ includes a link to one such list. You should change your TIME_ZONE setting to the zone in which you live.

ADMONITION: TIME ZONES ON WINDOWS

If you're using Microsoft Windows, you'll want to be careful with the TIME_ZONE setting. Because of quirks in Windows' operating environment, it's not possible to reliably use a time zone other than the one the computer as a whole is currently using. So for best results you'll want to specify TIME_ZONE to be the same as the time zone Windows is using.

You won't need to change it yet, but you'll also want to scroll down to the bottom of the settings file, where you'll see a setting called INSTALLED_APPS. As mentioned previously, a Django project is made up of one or more Django-powered applications, and this setting is how Django knows which applications are used by your project. The default value looks like this:

```
INSTALLED_APPS = (
    'django.contrib.auth',
    'django.contrib.contenttypes',
    'django.contrib.sessions',
    'django.contrib.sites',
)
```

Each of these is an application bundled with Django itself, and each one provides a useful piece of common functionality; django.contrib.auth, for example, provides a mechanism for storing data about users and for authenticating them, while django.contrib.sites provides an easy way to run multiple web sites from a single Django project and to specify which items in your database should be accessible to each site.

In time, you'll see examples of these applications in action, but for now it's best to leave the defaults as they are. They provide a "quick start" to your project by taking care of a lot of tasks right away, and you'll be building on their functionality in just a moment.

Now that you've provided some basic configuration data to Django, you can tell it to set up your database. Open up a terminal or command prompt, navigate to your project's directory, and type this command:

```
python manage.py syncdb
```

This command will create the database file if needed and then create the database tables for each application listed in the INSTALLED_APPS setting. You'll see several lines of output scroll by, and then, because the bundled user authentication application is being installed,

Django will ask if you'd like to create a "superuser" account for web-based administration. Type **yes**, and then enter a username, e-mail address, and password when prompted. You'll see shortly how you can use this account to log in to a Django administrative interface.

ADMONITION: WHAT GOES ON DURING SYNCDB

When you run `manage.py syncdb`, Django actually does several things in order, and the output on your screen shows each step. First, Django looks in each application module listed in `INSTALLED_APPS` and finds the *data models*. These are Python classes that define the different types of data the application uses, and Django knows how to automatically generate appropriate `CREATE TABLE` SQL statements from them. In Chapter 3, you'll write your first data model and see how Django generates the SQL for it.

Once the database tables have been created, Django looks for, and runs, any application-specific initialization code for each application. In this case, `django.contrib.auth` includes code that prompts you to create a user account.

Finally, Django finishes the database setup and installs any initial data you've provided. The default set of bundled applications doesn't use this feature, but later on you'll see how to supply an initial data file that can kick-start an application by giving it data to work with right away. You won't be providing any initial data with this application, but some of Django's bundled applications do provide data which will be inserted into the database when installed.

Putting Together the CMS

Most of the applications you'll build with Django will require you to write a fair amount of code on your own. Django will take care of the heavy lifting and the repetitive tasks, but it'll still be up to you to handle features unique to each specific application. Sometimes, though, features built in to Django or applications bundled with it will provide most or all of what you need. Django's contrib applications are designed with just this aim in mind: some types of applications are so common and so repetitive that it's best to just provide a single customizable version and reuse it from project to project.

A simple brochureware CMS is a good example of this, and you'll build it by relying heavily on two applications bundled with Django: django.contrib.flatpages and django.contrib.admin.

The first of these, django.contrib.flatpages, provides a data model for a simple page, with a title, content, and a few configurable options, such as custom templates or authentication. The other, django.contrib.admin, provides a powerful administrative interface that can work with any Django data model, letting you create a more or less "instant" web-based interface to administer a site.

The first step here is to add these applications to the INSTALLED_APPS setting. You'll remember that by default four applications were placed in the list, and now you can add two more:

```
INSTALLED_APPS = (
    'django.contrib.auth',
    'django.contrib.contenttypes',
    'django.contrib.sessions',
```

```
        'django.contrib.sites',
        'django.contrib.admin',
        'django.contrib.flatpages',
)
```

Once you've made that change and saved your settings file, run `syncdb` again:

```
python manage.py syncdb
```

You'll see the output scroll by as Django creates database tables for the data models defined in these applications. Now, open up the `urls.py` file in your project, which—as you saw in the previous chapter—contains the root URL configuration for your project. There's a line that says, "Uncomment this for admin:" followed by this line (the hash mark at the beginning indicates a Python comment and means the line will not be executed as code):

```
#     (r'^admin/', include('django.contrib.admin.urls')),
```

Uncomment that line and save the file. This will add a set of URLs, included in `django.contrib.admin`, to your project's URL configuration.

ADMONITION: HOW DJANGO URL CONFIGURATION WORKS

A Django URL configuration file, or `URLConf`, defines a list of URL patterns and indicates how they map to parts of your code. Each URL pattern has at least two parts: a regular expression that describes what the URL looks like and either a view (a Python function that can respond to HTTP requests) to map that URL to or an `include`, which points to a different `URLConf` module. The ability to include other `URLConf` modules makes it easy to define reusable and "pluggable" sets of URLs, which can be dropped into any point in your project's URL hierarchy.

A *regular expression*, in case you've never encountered that term before, is a common way to represent a particular pattern of text, and most programming languages have support for checking whether a given piece of text matches the pattern specified in a regular expression. Most introductory programming books cover regular expressions. *Dive Into Python* by Mark Pilgrim (Apress, 2004) has a good chapter that covers the basics.

Also, note that regular expressions are quite strict about matching. Ordinarily, a web server will be somewhat lax and treat, for example, `/admin` and `/admin/` as the same URL, returning the same result either way. But if you specify a regular expression that ends in a slash—as I'm doing here—you *must* include the slash on the end when you visit that address in your browser, or the pattern will not match and you'll get a "Page not found" error.

Now you'll be able to launch the built-in web server again and see the administrative interface:

```
python manage.py runserver
```

The URL pattern for the admin application is `^admin/`, which means that if you visit `http://127.0.0.1:8000/admin/` in your web browser, you'll see the login page. Enter the username and password you used when `syncdb` prompted you to create a user account, and you'll see the main admin index page, as shown in Figure 2-1. But note that URLs beginning with `admin/` are the only ones that will work right now; you haven't set up any other URLs yet.

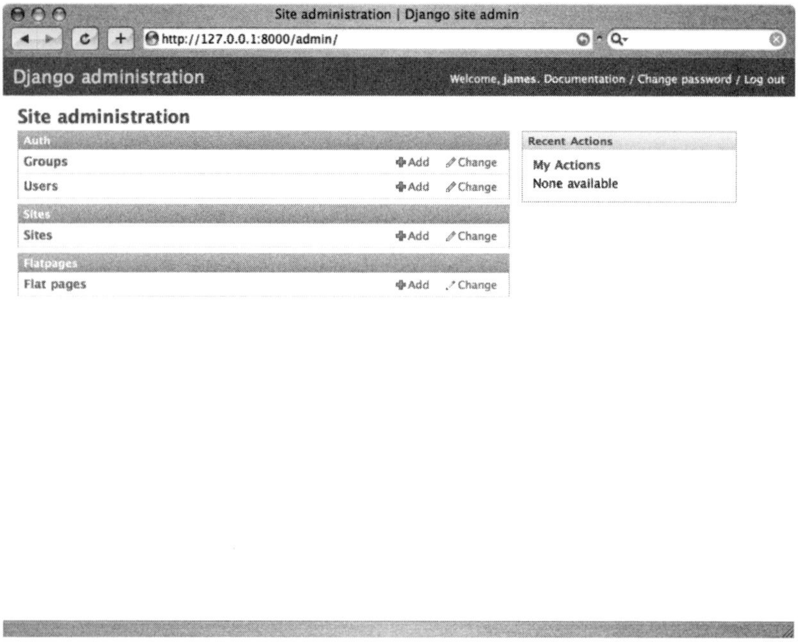

Figure 2-1. *Home page of the Django administrative interface*

Each item listed on the index page corresponds to a data model in one of the installed applications. They're grouped according to which application they belong to. The `auth` application, `django.contrib.auth`, provides models for users and groups; the `sites` application, `django.contrib.sites`, provides a model to represent a web site; and the `flatpages` application you just installed provides a "flat page" model. To the right of this list is a sidebar, which will report actions you've taken recently in the admin interface. Since you haven't done anything yet, it's empty, but as soon as you start making changes to site content it will show a summary of your actions. As a first step, click on the Sites link. You'll see a listing like the one shown in Figure 2-2.

As part of its initialization, `django.contrib.sites` created an example site "object" for you, which you can click to edit. Since the built-in web server is running on your computer's local loopback interface at port 8000, change the Domain Name field to **127.0.0.1:8000**, and change the Display Name field to **localhost**. Then click the Save button at the bottom right, and your changes will be saved to the database. If you go back to the main index of the admin interface, you'll see the sidebar now has an entry for that site, showing that you've changed it recently.

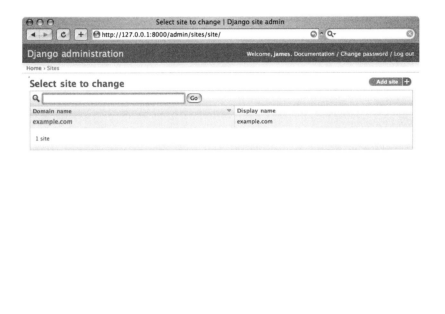

Figure 2-2. *The default site object created by Django*

You'll notice that the main admin page, next to each type of item, displays an Add link and a Change link; let's add a new flat page by clicking the Add link next to the Flat Page link. This will bring up a blank form, automatically generated from the appropriate data model. Enter the following values:

- In the URL field, enter **/first-page/**.

- In the Title field, enter **My first page**.

- In the Content field, enter **This is my first Django flat page**.

Then scroll down and click the Save and Continue Editing button. The new flat page will be saved into your database, and then the form will be redisplayed so you can edit the page. You'll also notice that two buttons have appeared above the form: History and View on Site. The History button will show a simplified history of this flat page (right now, nothing but the initial entry for it has been created). The View on Site button will let you see the flat page at its public URL. Click it, and you'll be redirected to `http://127.0.0.1:8000/first-page/`, which will, for the moment, display an error message like the one shown in Figure 2-3.

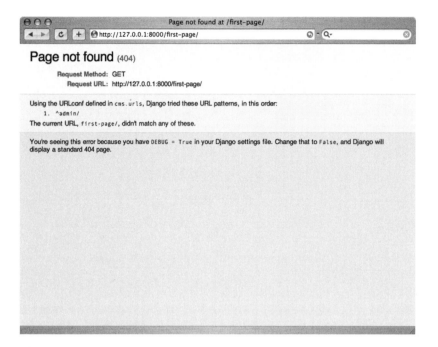

Figure 2-3. *A Django "Page not found" error*

This is a 404 "Page not found" error, but with a twist—every new Django project starts out in a debugging mode, which displays more helpful error messages to help you get up and running. In this case, Django shows you the URL patterns it found in your project's URLConf, and explains that the URL you tried to visit didn't match any of them, which makes sense because you haven't yet added anything that looks like the URL /first-page/. So let's fix that. Open up the urls.py file again and add the following line right below the one for the admin interface:

```
(r'', include('django.contrib.flatpages.urls')),
```

The pattern part of this is simply an empty string (''), which means it will actually match *any* URL. You could, if you wanted, go into urls.py and add a new line each time you add a flat page. In applications you'll develop later on, you'll mostly be defining individual URLs, but because django.contrib.flatpages lets you specify anything for the URL of a page, it's easiest in this case to simply place a "catch-all" URL pattern to handle it.

ADMONITION: ORDER OF URL PATTERNS

When Django is trying to match a URL, it starts at the top of the list of URL patterns and works its way down until it finds a match. This means that it's better to have more specific patterns like the ^admin/ line come first, and more general patterns like the catch-all for flat pages come last; otherwise, something like the catch-all might match a URL before Django gets to the more specific pattern you actually wanted.

This pattern, like the previous one for the admin, takes advantage of the "pluggable" URLs the include directive provides and says to use another URLConf module, django.contrib. flatpages.urls, for anything that matches the pattern. Save your urls.py and either refresh the page in your browser or navigate again to http://127.0.0.1:8000/first-page/. It's still going to display an error, but now you're closer to having the simple CMS working (see Figure 2-4).

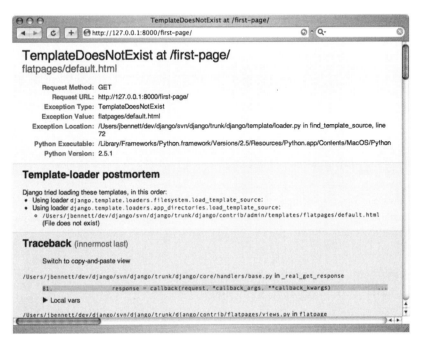

Figure 2-4. *A Django server error page*

This page looks a little scary, but it's actually not. Once again, Django's debugging mode is trying to give you as much information as it can. The top of the page shows a short summary of the error, followed by more detailed information, including a full *stack trace* (a copy of everything Python and Django were doing when the error happened), a listing of the incoming HTTP request, and your Django project's settings (with any sensitive settings, such as database passwords, blanked out for security reasons).

The problem here is that a flat page, like most output from Django, expects to be displayed using a template that will generate the correct HTML. django.contrib.flatpages, by default, looks for a template file named flatpages/default.html, and you haven't created that yet. The editing form in the admin interface will, if you go back and look for it, also show a field where you can input a different template file name on a per-page basis. So let's pause for a moment and take care of that.

A Quick Introduction to the Django Template System

Django includes a templating system (in the module `django.template`, if you've been exploring the Django codebase and want to take a look at it), which has two major design goals:

- Provide an easy way to express the logic needed for your application's presentation.

- As much as possible, avoid restricting the types of output you can generate.

Some template languages allow you to embed nearly any form of programming code directly in the templates. While this is sometimes handy, it also creates a tendency for your application's core programming logic to migrate slowly out of other parts of the code and into the templates, which really ought to confine themselves to the presentational aspects. And some templating languages force you to write XML or other specific types of markup, even if what you want to produce isn't XML at all. Django's template system does its best to avoid both of these pitfalls by keeping the allowed programming to a minimum and by not constraining you to specific markup languages. (I've used the Django template system to generate content for e-mail messages and even Excel spreadsheets, for example.)

Ultimately, a Django template file for a web page—in other words, a template whose output is HTML—doesn't end up looking all that different from a normal hand-written web page. The biggest distinction is in two features that the Django template system provides:

- **Variables**: Fed to the template by a *view*—the actual Python function that responds to an HTTP request—and are wrapped in double curly braces, like so: `{{ variable_name_here }}`. These are simply replaced with the actual value of the variable.

- **Tags**: Wrapped in a single curly braces and a percent sign, like this: `{% tag_name_here %}`. Tags can do almost anything, and the exact effect depends on the particular tag. You can also write and use your own custom tags in Django templates, so if there's something you need that isn't provided out of the box, you can add it.

Whenever Django needs a template file, it can look in any of several places, defined by configurable modules called *template loaders*. By default, Django looks in the following places:

- Inside any directories specified in your settings module by the setting `TEMPLATE_DIRS`

- Inside your installed applications, if any of them include a directory named `templates/`

This lets you provide a set of default templates with any given application, but also gives you the power to override those on a project-by-project basis by listing specific directories you'll put customized templates into. The administrative interface, for example, uses this to great effect: `django.contrib.admin` contains a `templates/` directory with the default templates, but if you need to customize the admin interface you can add your own templates in a project-specific template directory.

Go ahead and choose a directory where you'd like to keep the templates for the simple CMS application. The exact location doesn't matter, so long as it's someplace where you're allowed to create and read files on your computer. Next open up your project's `settings.py` file, scroll down until you see the `TEMPLATE_DIRS` setting, and add that directory to the list. Here's mine:

```
TEMPLATE_DIRS = (
    '/Users/jbennett/html/django-templates/cms/',
)
```

You'll note that I'm specifying a completely different directory from the one where the project's code is kept. This is often a good idea because it reinforces the idea that the particular presentation—in the form of a set of HTML templates—can and should be decoupled from the back-end code whenever possible. It's also a useful practice for any application you might end up reusing across multiple web sites. Different sites will obviously have different sets of templates, and so being able to switch them at will without needing to move lots of files in and out of a project-specific location is extremely handy.

ADMONITION: TRAILING COMMAS

As you may have already learned from a tutorial, Python offers two simple ways to represent sequences of items: lists and tuples. A tuple is usually wrapped in parentheses, as you've seen so far with the INSTALLED_APPS and now the TEMPLATE_DIRS settings, both of which accept tuples as legal values. But Python tuples require a comma after *every* item, even if there's only one item in the tuple, and leaving off the comma is a common annoyance for users who are getting used to the language. I've been writing Python for several years now, and I still sometimes forget to do that. Generally, I find it helpful to remember that in Python, the comma—and not parentheses, which technically aren't required—is what makes a tuple.

Now, inside the template directory you chose, create a subdirectory called flatpages/, and in that subdirectory create a new file called default.html. Refresh the flat page in your web browser, and you should see a blank white page. Now you have a template directory specified in your settings, and the file flatpages/default.html exists inside it, so there's no longer an error. But the template file is empty, and so it doesn't produce any output. Let's fix that by opening up the default.html file and adding some content:

```
<html>
    <head>
        <title>{{ flatpage.title }}</title>
    </head>
    <body>
        <h1>{{ flatpage.title }}</h1>
        {{ flatpage.content }}
    </body>
</html>
```

Now save the file and refresh the page in your web browser again. You should see something like what's shown in Figure 2-5.

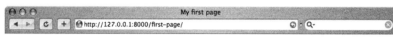

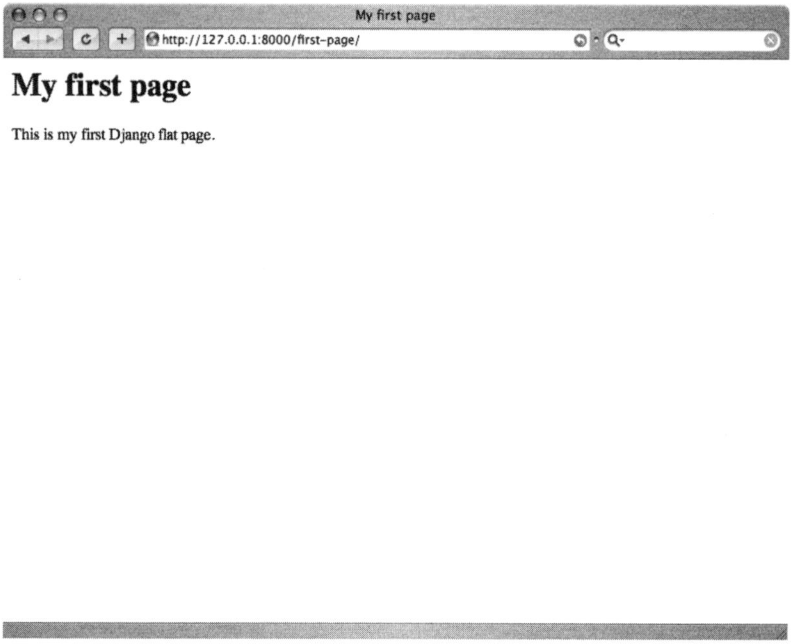

Figure 2-5. *Your first Django flat page*

You'll see that this template uses two variables—flatpage.title and flatpage.content—and no tags. Those variables actually come from a single source: a variable flatpage, which was passed to the template by a Python view function defined inside django.contrib. flatpages. The value of this variable is a FlatPage object, an instance of the data model for flat pages. This was created by querying the database for a row with a URL column that matched the URL /first-page/. It then used the data from that row to create a Python object with attributes named title and content, matching what you entered in the admin interface (along with other attributes—for example, url—which aren't as important for the presentational aspect of things).

ADMONITION: HOW DID DJANGO DO THAT?

Django includes a library called an object-relational mapper, or ORM. The ORM understands the structure of your data models (which are defined as simple Python classes) and the corresponding structure of your database. It provides a straightforward syntax for translating between rows and tables in your database and live Python objects in your code, usually without you having to write your own SQL queries. Throughout this book, you'll see examples of the Django ORM in action and get a feel for all of its features. You'll also see how you can bypass it in situations where you really want or need to roll your own query by hand.

With this template in place, you now have—literally—a simple dynamic content management system that will let you define as many pages as you'd like, title them, fill in content, and place them at any URL (except for URLs starting with admin/ because they'll be matched by the URL pattern for the admin interface). You could, if you wanted to, dress up the template with fancier HTML and a nice cascading style sheet (CSS), create a few more user accounts through the administrative interface, and deploy this onto a live web server for real-world use. But so far, you've only written a couple of lines of actual code: the URL pattern for the pages in your urls.py file, a few Django settings, and a little HTML.

Obviously, it won't always be quite this easy to get an application up and running with Django, but hopefully you've seen that taking advantage of Django's components can significantly cut down the amount of work you have to do.

Looking Ahead

Pause here for a few moments to play with the simple CMS and explore the Django administrative interface. Take particular note of the Documentation link that appears in the upper-right corner of each page in the admin. It provides automatically generated documentation for all of the data models, URL patterns, and template tags available in your Django project. Not all of it will be immediately understandable at this point, but click around in the documentation area and get a feel for what's in there. When you're developing or working with more complex applications, the admin documentation system will be an important resource for learning about and understanding the code you're using.

When you're ready to get back to work, the next chapter will be waiting for you with a guide to customizing this simple CMS and adding some useful features, including a search function.

CHAPTER 3

■ ■ ■

Customizing the Simple CMS

The simple CMS you put together in the last chapter is already in pretty good shape; it's something that most developers wouldn't mind showing to clients as an initial prototype, for example. But so far it's just using a few stock applications bundled with Django and hasn't added any extra features on top of that. In this chapter, you'll see how to take this simple project as a foundation and start adding your own customizations, like rich-text editing in the admin and a search system for quickly finding particular pages.

Adding Rich-Text Editing

The default administrative interface Django provides for the flatpages application is already production quality. Many Django-based sites already use it as is to provide an easy way to manage the occasional simple About page or to handle similar tasks. But it would be nice to make it just a little bit friendlier by adding a rich-text interface to it so that users of the web-based administrative interface don't have to type in raw HTML.

There are a number of JavaScript-based rich-text editors (RTEs), available with different features and configurations, but I'll be using one called TinyMCE. It's one of the most popular options and has roughly the best cross-browser support of any of the existing RTEs. (Due to differences in the APIs implemented by web browsers, there's no truly consistent cross-platform RTE at the moment.) TinyMCE is also free and released under an open source license. You can download a copy of the latest stable version from http://tinymce.moxiecode.com/.

Once you've unpacked TinyMCE, you'll see it contains a jscripts/ directory, inside which is a tiny_mce directory containing all the TinyMCE code. Make a note of where that directory is, and go to the project's urls.py file. In urls.py, add a new line so that it looks like the following:

```
from django.conf.urls.defaults import *

urlpatterns = patterns('',
    # Example:
    # (r'^foo/', include('foo.foo.urls')),

    # Uncomment this for admin:
    (r'^admin/', include('django.contrib.admin.urls')),
    (r'^tiny_mce/(?P<path>.*)$', 'django.views.static.serve',
                         { 'document_root': '/path/to/tiny_mce' },
)
```

Replace the /path/to/tiny_mce part with the actual location on your computer of the tiny_mce directory. For example, if it's at /Users/jbennett/javascript/TinyMCE/jscripts/ tiny_mce, you'd use that value.

ADMONITION: MEDIA FILES IN PRODUCTION VS. DEVELOPMENT

In production, you'll usually want to avoid having the same web server handle both Django and static media files, like style sheets or JavaScript. Because the web server process needs to keep a copy of Django's code and your applications in memory, it's a waste of resources to use that same process for the simple task of serving a file off the disk.

For now I'm using a helper function built into Django that can serve static files, but keep in mind this should only be used for development on your own computer. Using it on a live, deployed site will severely impact your site's performance. When you deploy a Django application to a live web server, consult the official Django documentation at www.djangoproject.com/documentation/ to see instructions for your specific server setup.

Now you just need to add the appropriate JavaScript calls to the template used for adding and editing flat pages. In the last chapter, when you filled in the TEMPLATE_DIRS setting, I mentioned that Django can also look directly inside an application for templates and that this lets an application author provide default templates while still allowing individual projects to use their own. That's precisely what we're going to take advantage of here. The admin application is not only designed to use its own templates as a fallback, but it also lets you provide your own if you'd like to customize it.

By default, the admin application will look for a template in several places, using the first one it finds. The template names it looks for are as follows, in order:

1. admin/flatpages/flatpage/change_form.html

2. admin/flatpages/change_form.html

3. admin/change_form.html

ADMONITION: CHOOSING FROM MULTIPLE TEMPLATES

Normally, when you write a Django view—the function that actually responds to an HTTP request—you'll set it up to use a single template for its output, and the applications you'll write in this book will typically only need to specify one template for each view. However, there is a helper function, django.template. loader.select_template, which takes a list of template names, searches for template files matching those names, and uses the first one it finds. The admin application makes use of this helper function to precisely enable the sort of customization we're making here. If you're ever writing an application where you need to do the same, keep that function in mind.

The admin application only provides the last template in this list—admin/change_form. html—and uses that for all adding and editing of items if you don't supply a custom template. But as you can see, there are a couple of other options. By using a list of possible template names, rather than a single prebuilt template, the admin application lets you override the interface for a specific application (in this case, the flatpages application, by supplying the template admin/flatpages/change_form.html) or for a specific data model (by supplying the template admin/flatpages/flatpage/change_form.html). Right now you only want to customize the interface for one specific model. So inside your templates directory, create an admin subdirectory. Then create a flatpages subdirectory inside of admin and a flatpage subdirectory inside of flatpages. Finally, copy the change_form template from django/ contrib/admin/templates/admin/change_form.html in your copy of Django into the admin/flatpages/flatpage/ directory you just created.

Now you can open up the change_form.html template in your template directory and edit it to add the appropriate JavaScript for TinyMCE. This template is going to look fairly complex—and it is, because the admin application has to adapt itself to provide appropriate forms for any data model—but the change you'll be making is pretty simple. On line 4 of the template, you'll see the following:

```
<script type="text/javascript" src="../../../jsi18n/"></script>
```

Immediately below that, add the following:

```
<script type="text/javascript" src="/tiny_mce/tiny_mce.js"></script>
<script type="text/javascript">
tinyMCE.init({
  mode: "textareas",
  theme: "simple"
});
</script>
```

This will make use of the URL you set up to serve the TinyMCE files. Now save the file and go back to your web browser. The form displayed for adding and editing flat pages will now have the basic TinyMCE editor attached to the text area for the page's content, as shown in Figure 3-1.

TinyMCE is extremely customizable. You can rearrange the editing toolbar, choose which of the many built-in controls should appear on it, add your own controls, and write new themes to change the way it looks. And if you'd like to use another rich-text editor or make other customizations to the admin interface, you can follow the same process.

Figure 3-1. *The flat pages admin form with rich-text editor*

Adding a Search System to the CMS

So far you've just been using the applications bundled with Django itself and making small customizations to the templates they use. Up to now that's accomplished a lot, but for most of your projects, you'll be writing your own applications in Python. So let's add a new feature— written in Python—to the simple CMS: a simple search system that will let users type in a query and get back a list of any pages whose titles or contents match.

It would be possible to add this directly to the flatpages application bundled with Django, but that's not really a good idea, for two reasons:

- It makes upgrading Django a hassle. You have extra Python code that didn't come with Django and the code needs to be preserved across the upgrade.

- A useful feature like a search system might need to be expanded later on to work with other types of content, in which case it wouldn't make sense to have it be part of the flatpages application.

So let's make this into its own application. Go to your project directory and type the following command:

```
python manage.py startapp search
```

Just as the `startproject` command to `django-admin.py` created a new, empty project directory, the `startapp` command to `manage.py` creates a new, empty application module. It will set up the `search/` directory inside your project and add the following files to it:

- `__init__.py`: Just like the one in the project directory, this `__init__.py` file starts out empty. Its job is to indicate that the directory is also a Python module.

- `models.py`: This file will contain any data models defined for the application. A little later in this chapter, you'll write your first model in this file.

- `views.py`: This is where the view functions, which respond to HTTP requests and do most of the work of user interaction, will go.

For now you'll just be writing a simple view, so open up the `views.py` file. The first step is to import the things you'll be using. Part of Python's (and Django's) design philosophy is that you should be able to clearly see what's happening with as little implicit "magic" as possible. So each file needs to contain Python `import` statements for things it wants to reference from other Python modules. To start with, you'll need three `import` statements:

```
from django.http import HttpResponse
from django.template import loader, Context
from django.contrib.flatpages.models import FlatPage
```

This gives you a solid foundation for writing your search view:

- `HttpResponse` is the class Django uses to represent an HTTP response. When an `HttpResponse` is given as the return value of a view, Django will automatically convert it into the correct response format for the web server it's running under.

- The `loader` module in `django.template` provides functions for specifying the name of a template file, which will be located (assuming it's in a directory specified in `TEMPLATE_DIRS`), read from disk, and parsed for rendering.

- `Context` is a class used to represent the variables for a template. You pass it a Python dictionary containing the names of the variables and their values. (If you're familiar with other programming languages, a Python dictionary is similar to what some languages call a *hash table* or *associative array*.)

- `FlatPage` is the model class that represents the pages in the CMS.

ADMONITION: PYTHON NAMING STYLE

Every programming language has a set of standard conventions for how to name things. Java, for example, tends to use *camel case*, where things are given NamesThatLookLikeThis, while PHP tends to favor underscores, or names_that_look_like_this.

The standard practice in Python is that classes should have capitalized names—hence Context—and use the camel-case style for multiword names like HttpResponse or FlatPage. Modules, functions, and normal variables use lowercase names and underscores to separate multiple words in a name. Following this convention will help Python programmers—including you—quickly understand a new piece of code when reading it for the first time.

If you're interested in learning more about standard Python style, you can read the official Python style guide online at www.python.org/dev/peps/pep-0008/.

Now you're ready to write a view function that will perform a basic search. Here's the code, which will go into views.py below the import statements you added:

```
def search(request):
    query = request.GET['q']
    results = FlatPage.objects.filter(content__icontains=query)
    template = loader.get_template('search/search.html')
    context = Context({ 'query': query, 'results': results })
    response = template.render(context)
    return HttpResponse(response)
```

Let's break this down line by line. First, you're defining a Python function using the keyword def. The function's name is search, and it takes one argument named request. This will be an HTTP request (an instance of the class django.http.HttpRequest), and Django will ensure that it's passed to the view function when needed.

Next, look at the HTTP GET variable q to see what the user searched for. Django automatically parsed the URL, so a URL like this:

```
http://www.example.com/search?q=foo
```

results in an HttpRequest whose GET attribute is a dictionary containing the name q and the value foo. Then you can read that value out of it just as you would access any Python dictionary.

The next line does the actual search. The FlatPage class, like nearly all Django data models, has an attribute named objects that can be used to perform queries on that model. In this case, you want to filter through all of the flat pages looking for those whose contents contain the search term, so you use the filter method and the argument content__icontains=query, storing the results in a variable named results. This will provide a list of FlatPage objects that matched the query.

ADMONITION: DJANGO DATABASE LOOKUP SYNTAX

As you'll see shortly, a Django data model has special attributes called *fields*, which usually correspond to the names of the columns in the database. When you use Django's object-relational mapper (ORM) to run a query, each argument in the query is made up of a combination of a field name and a lookup operator, separated by double underscores.

In this case, the field name is content because that's the field on the FlatPage model that represents the page's contents (each FlatPage also has fields named title, url, and so on). The lookup operator is icontains, which checks to see whether the value in that column contains the string you've passed to it. The "i" at the front means it's case-insensitive, so, for example, a query for "hello" would match both "hello" and "Hello". The Django ORM supports a large number of other lookup operators, many of which you'll see in action throughout this book.

Now that you have the query and the results, you need to produce some HTML and return a response; so the next line uses the get_template function of the loader module you imported to load a template named search/search.html. Next you need to give the template some data to work with, so create a Context containing two variables: query is the search query, and results contains the search results.

Next you use the template's render method, passing in the Context you created, to generate the HTML for the response. And finally, you'll return an HttpResponse containing the rendered HTML.

Now save the views.py file. You'll come back to it in a moment and make some improvements, but for now you need to create a template so that the search view can generate its HTML. Go into your templates directory, create a new subdirectory search, and create a file, search.html, inside it. Next you'll open up the search.html file and add the following to it:

```html
<html>
  <head>
    <title>Search</title>
  </head>
  <body>
    <p>You searched for "{{ query }}"; the results are listed below.</p>
    <ul>
      {% for page in results %}
        <li><a href="{{ page.get_absolute_url }}">{{ page.title }}</a></li>
      {% endfor %}
    </ul>
  </body>
</html>
```

This makes use of both the variables passed to it. It uses {{ query }} to display the query (remember, variables in Django templates can be output directly by wrapping their names in double curly braces), and loops over the results to display them in an unordered list.

Notice that I've also used a Django template tag, `for`, which lets you loop over a sequence of things and do something with each one. The syntax is pretty simple. In effect, it says, "for each page in the `results` variable, display the following HTML, filled in with the values from that page." You can probably guess that, within the `for` loop, `{{ page.title }}` refers to the `title` field of the current page in the loop, but `{{ page.get_absolute_url }}` is new. It's standard practice for a Django model class to define a method called `get_absolute_url()`, which will output a URL to be used for referring to the object, and the `FlatPage` model does so. (Its `get_absolute_url()` method simply returns the value of its `url` field; other models can and will have more complex ways of working out their URLs.)

> ### ADMONITION: CALLING AN OBJECT'S METHODS IN A DJANGO TEMPLATE
>
> The Django template system lets you access methods on Python objects in just the same way you access any other attributes: using a dot (.), `{{ page.get_absolute_url }}` calls the `get_absolute_url()` method. But note that in a template you *don't* use parentheses when calling a method, and you can't pass arguments to a method called in this way. This goes back to Django's philosophy of not allowing too much "programming" in templates—something that's complex enough to need arguments passed to it probably isn't purely presentational. The Django template system also forbids access to methods that alter the data in your database. Calls to those methods definitely belong in a view function and not in a template.
>
> You can also access values from a dictionary by using the same dot syntax. As with the lack of parentheses in method calls, this is different from how you would do it in Python code (where dictionary access uses brackets, as in `request.GET['q']`); but it has the advantage of making the Django template syntax extremely uniform and serves as a reminder that Django templates are not simply Python code and don't offer a full programming language.

Also, note that the `for` tag needs a matching `endfor` tag when you're done telling it what to do inside the loop. Most Django template tags that span over a section of the template will need an explicit end tag to declare when you're done with them.

Now open up your `flatpages/default.html` template and somewhere in it place the following HTML:

```
<form method="get" action="/search/">
  <p><label for="id_q">Search:</label>
  <input type="text" name="q" id="id_q" />
  <input type="submit" value="Submit" /></p>
</form>
```

This adds a search box that will submit to the correct URL with the correct GET variable (q) for the search query.

Finally, open up your project's `urls.py`, and—after the lines for the admin and the TinyMCE JavaScript, but *before* the catch-all pattern for the flat pages—add the following:

```
(r'^search/$', 'cms.search.views.search'),
```

Remember that since this regular expression ends in a slash, you'll need to include it when you type the address into your browser. Unlike the URL patterns you've set up previously, which used the `include` directive to pull in other `URLConf` modules, this one maps the URL `search/` to a single specific view: the search view you just wrote. Save the `urls.py` file, and now you should be able to type in a search query on any page in your CMS and get back a list of matching pages.

Improving the Search View

The search view works pretty well for something so short: it's only about a half dozen lines of code, plus a few `import` statements. But you can make it shorter, and it's a good idea to do so.

You'll notice that of the six lines of actual code in the search view, four are dedicated to loading the template, creating a `Context`, rendering the HTML, and returning the response. That's a series of steps you'll need to walk through on nearly every view you write, so Django provides a shortcut function, `django.shortcuts.render_to_response`, which handles that process all in one step. So edit the `views.py` file to look like the following:

```
from django.shortcuts import render_to_response
from django.contrib.flatpages.models import FlatPage

def search(request):
    query = request.GET['q']
    return render_to_response('search/search.html',
                              { 'query': query,
                                'results': FlatPage.objects.filter( ➥
content__icontains=query) })
```

The `render_to_response` function gets two arguments here:

1. The name of the template file, `search/search.html`.

2. The dictionary to use for the template's context.

Given that information, it handles the entire process of loading the template, rendering the output, and creating the `HttpResponse`. Notice also that you're no longer using a separate line to fetch the results. They're only needed for the template context, so you can do the query right there inside the dictionary, trusting that its result will be assigned properly to the `results` variable. You've also broken up the arguments, including the dictionary, over several lines. Python allows you to do this any time you're constructing a list or dictionary (as well as in several other situations), and it makes the code much easier to read than if all of this was sprawled out over one long line.

Save the `views.py` file, and then go back and search again. You'll notice that it works exactly the same way, only now the search view is much shorter and simpler and, importantly, doesn't have the repetitive "boilerplate" of the template loading and rendering process. There will be times when you'll want to do that manually (for example, if you wanted to insert some extra processing before returning the response), but in general you should be using the `render_to_response` shortcut whenever possible.

Another simple improvement would be to have the search view handle situations where it's accessed directly. Right now, if you just visit the URL `/search/` instead of accessing it through the search box on another page, you'll see an ugly error complaining that the key q wasn't found in the `request.GET` dictionary (because the q variable comes from performing a search). It would be much more helpful to simply display an empty search form, so let's rewrite the view to do the following:

```
def search(request):
    query = request.GET.get('q', '')
    results = []
    if query:
        results = FlatPage.objects.filter(content__icontains=query)
    return render_to_response('search/search.html',
                            { 'query': query,
                              'results': results })
```

Now you're using `request.GET.get('q', '')` to read the q variable. `get()` is a method available on any Python dictionary that lets you ask for the value for a particular key and specify a default to fall back to if the key doesn't exist. The default in this case is just an empty string, and then you can check the result to see whether there's a search query. If there isn't, you set `results` to an empty list to start with, and that won't be changed. This means you can rewrite the template like so:

```
<html>
  <head>
    <title>Search</title>
  </head>
  <body>
    <form method="get" action="/search/">
      <p><label for="id_q">Search:</label>
      <input type="text" name="q" id="id_q" value="{{ query }}" />
      <input type="submit" value="Submit" /></p>
    </form>
    {% if results %}
      <p>You searched for "{{ query }}"; the results are listed below.</p>
      <ul>
        {% for page in results %}
          <li><a href="{{ page.get_absolute_url }}">{{ page.title }}</a></li>
        {% endfor %}
      </ul>
    {% else %}
      {% if query %}
        <p>No results found.</p>
      {% else %}
        <p>Type a search query into the box above, and press "Submit"
            to search.</p>
      {% endif %}
    {% endif %}
  </body>
</html>
```

Now the `search.html` template will show a search box the same as all the other pages in the CMS, and you'll notice that a `value` attribute has also been added to the HTML for the search input box. This way, if there was a query, it will be filled in as a reminder of what the user searched for.

I'm also using another new template tag: `if`. The `if` tag works similarly to the `if` statement in Python, letting you test whether something is true or not, and then do something based on the result. It also takes an optional `else` clause, which I'm using to show a different message if the user hasn't searched for anything yet. Also, just as the `for` tag needed an `endfor` tag, `if` needs an `endif`. And, finally, notice that the `if` tag can be nested: inside the else clause I'm using another `if` tag to differentiate between the results being empty because there was no query and the results being empty because no pages matched the query.

ADMONITION: SECURITY CONSIDERATIONS

One of the most common types of security problems with web applications is vulnerability to a cross-site scripting attack, or XSS. This sort of vulnerability occurs when you blindly accept input from a user and display it in a page on your site, as I'm doing with the search query. The problem is that a hacker can send a search query that contains HTML and JavaScript, then lure someone into visiting a page for that query. The JavaScript will be executed as if it were part of your site and could be used to hijack a user's account.

There's also a risk of another form of attack, called SQL injection, where a hacker relies on a web site to include user input directly in a database query. For example, a hacker might send a search query containing the text "DROP DATABASE;" which could—if blindly executed—delete the entire database for the site.

Django provides some built-in protection from these types of attacks, however. Django templates automatically "escape" the contents of any variables you display (so that, for example, the < character becomes &lt, removing the ability for a variable to end up as HTML that's rendered by a web browser), and Django carefully constructs database queries so that SQL injection isn't possible.

However, you shouldn't let these mechanisms lull you into a false sense of invincibility. Any time you're dealing with user-submitted data, you need to carefully ensure that you're taking appropriate steps to preserve your site's security.

Improving the Search Function with Keywords

The search function you've just added to the CMS is pretty handy, but you can make it a little bit better by adding the ability to recognize specific keywords and automatically pull up particular pages in response. This will let the site's administrators provide helpful hints for users who are searching and also creates useful metadata that you might want to take advantage of later on.

To add this feature, you'll need to create a Django data model; models go in the `models.py` file, so open that up. You'll see that it already has an `import` statement at the top:

```
from django.db import models
```

This imports the module that contains all of the necessary classes for creating Django data models, and the `startapp` command automatically added it to the `models.py` file to help you get started. Below that line, add the following:

```
from django.contrib.flatpages.models import FlatPage


class SearchKeyword(models.Model):
    keyword = models.CharField(max_length=50)
    page = models.ForeignKey(FlatPage)

    class Admin:
        pass

    def __unicode__(self):
        return self.keyword
```

This is a simple Django model with two fields:

- keyword: This is a CharField, which means it will accept short strings. I've specified a max_length of 50, which means that up to 50 characters can go into this field. In the database, Django will turn this into a column declared as VARCHAR(50).

- page: This is a foreign key pointing at the FlatPage model, meaning that each SearchKeyword is tied to a specific page. Django will turn this into a foreign-key column referencing the table the flat pages are stored in.

There's also that short class Admin: declaration, which tells Django that you want the admin application to display an interface for adding and editing the keywords. The pass statement is Python's way of saying "don't do anything special here," and Django interprets that as indicating that the admin interface should use all of the default settings. You could add some statements here to configure the admin interface for keywords, but for now the defaults are fine.

Finally, there's one method on this model: __unicode__(). This is a standard method that all Django model classes should define, and it's used whenever a (Unicode) string representation of a SearchKeyword is needed. If you've ever worked with Java, this is like the toString() method on a Java class. The __unicode__() method should return something that can sensibly be used as a representation of the SearchKeyword, so it's defined to return the value of the keyword field.

ADMONITION: PYTHON'S TWO TYPES OF STRINGS

Python actually has two different classes that represent strings: str and unicode. (There's also a parent class, basestring, which can't be instantiated directly but does provide a useful way to check whether something is a string type.) Instances of str are sometimes called *bytestrings* because each one corresponds to a specific series of bytes in a specific character encoding. (The default for Python is ASCII, but you can easily create strings in other encodings.) Instances of unicode, meanwhile, are strings of Unicode characters, and need to be converted to a byte-based encoding, such as UTF-8 or UTF-16—Unicode itself is not an "encoding"—before being output.

Because of this, Python classes can define either of two specially named methods, `__str__()` or `__unicode__()__`, to provide string representations of themselves or, if necessary, they can define both. All of Django's internals are built to work with `unicode` strings, so it's best simply to define `__unicode__()`. Strings stored by Django models will be converted to `unicode` strings when they're retrieved from your database, and Django will automatically convert to appropriately encoded bytestrings when producing output for an HTTP response.

Be aware that not all Python software is written to handle `unicode` strings (or even non-ASCII-encoded bytestrings) properly. When you write applications that rely on third-party software, you will sometimes have to work around this by manually converting a string. Django provides a set of utility functions to make this easier, and in later chapters you'll see them in action.

Save the file, then open up the project's `settings.py`, and scroll down to the `INSTALLED_APPS` setting. Add `cms.search` to the list, and save the file. This will tell Django that the `search` application inside the `cms` project directory is now part of the project and that its data model should be installed. Next, run python `manage.py syncdb`, and Django will create the new table for the `SearchKeyword` model.

ADMONITION: WHY DID THE SEARCH VIEW WORK BEFORE?

You've probably noticed that I used the search view already without adding the `search` application to `INSTALLED_APPS`. This worked because you can take advantage of any Python code on your computer when routing URLs to view functions, regardless of whether they're in an application that's listed in `INSTALLED_APPS` or not. In fact, they don't have to be part of a Django application module at all. This means, if you really want or need to, you can keep standalone libraries of code on your computer and call on them from your Django projects.

Django does need to know exactly which applications to install data models for, however. So now that you've got a model, it's necessary to add the `search` application to `INSTALLED_APPS` so that Django will create the database table for it. There are some other features that require you to have an application and list it in `INSTALLED_APPS`. Most of the time you'll want to do that, regardless of whether it's strictly necessary (if for no other reason than to provide a quick reminder of what your project is using), but it's useful sometimes to know what requires this and what doesn't.

If you manually connect to your database and look at the table layout (consult the documentation for the specific database system you're using to see how to do this), you'll see that the new table was created with two columns corresponding to the fields on the `SearchKeyword` model. It also has a third column, `id`, which is declared as the primary key and is an auto-incrementing integer. If you don't explicitly mark any of the fields in a model to serve as a primary key, Django will do this for you automatically. Now you can fire up the development web server again, and you'll see the new model appear in the index. You can add and edit keywords just as you can add and edit instances of any of the models from the other installed applications. Unfortunately, this interface is a little bit clunky: the keywords are added on a separate page, and you have to explicitly choose which page to associate each keyword with, as shown in Figure 3-2.

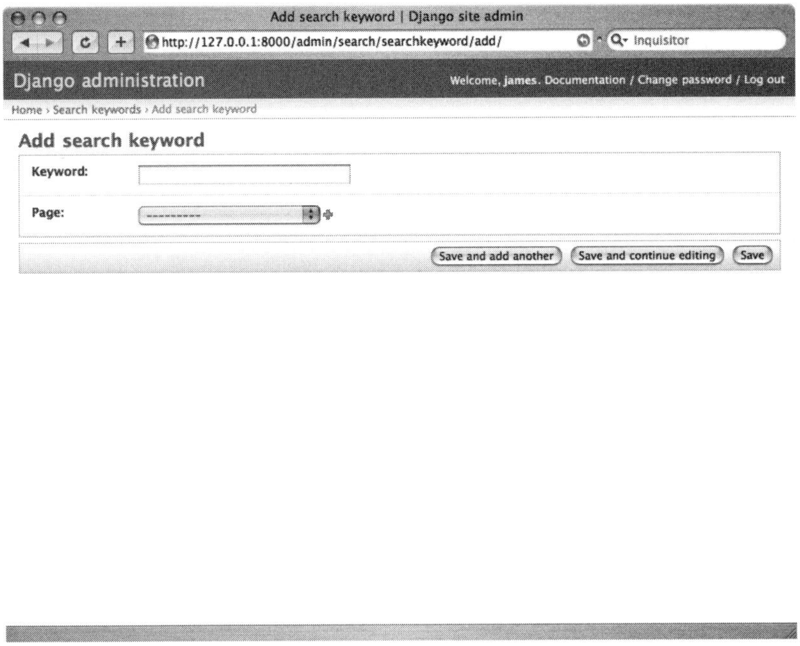

Figure 3-2. *The default admin form for a search keyword*

What you'd really like is to have the interface for the search keywords appear on the same page as the form for adding and editing pages. You can do that by making a small change to the SearchKeyword class so that it looks like this:

```
class SearchKeyword(models.Model):
    keyword = models.CharField(maxlength=50, core=True)
    page = models.ForeignKey(FlatPage, edit_inline=models.STACKED,
                             min_num_in_admin=3, num_extra_on_change=1)
```

Notice that I've added a couple of extra arguments to each field: keyword now has core=True, and page gained the edit_inline, min_num_in_admin, and num_extra_on_change arguments. Also, the class Admin: portion of the model has been removed.

Now save the models.py file. You'll notice that keywords no longer show up as their own item on the admin index page, but if you click to add or edit a flat page, you'll see something new, as shown in Figure 3-3.

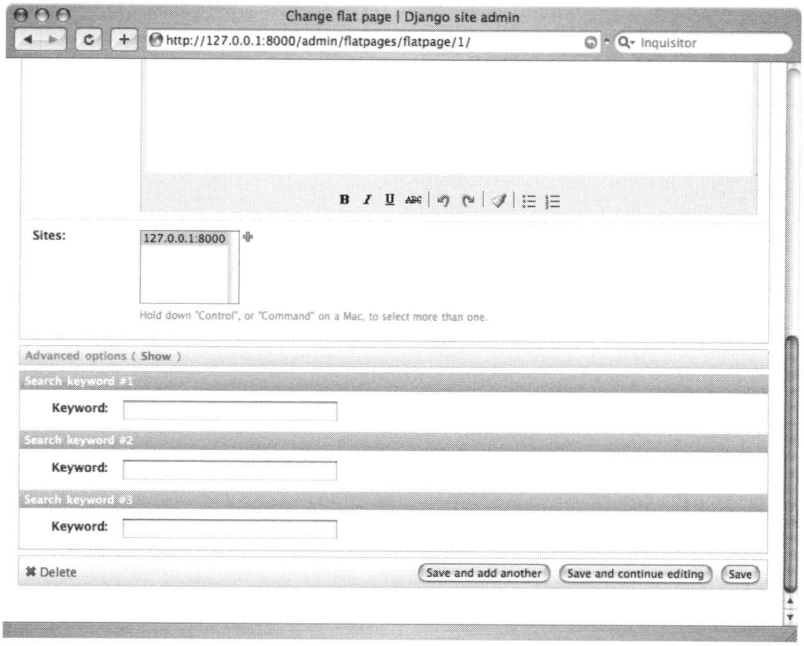

Figure 3-3. *Search keywords being edited inline, alongside a flat page*

The `edit_inline` argument means that the `SearchKeyword` model now gets displayed on the same page as the `FlatPage` model in the admin, and the arguments you've added control its presentation:

- `edit_inline=models.STACKED` means that multiple keywords will be displayed in a stacked interface. There's another option, `models.TABULAR`, which would instead display them in a table.

- `min_num_in_admin=3` and `num_extra_on_change=1` mean that form fields for at least three keywords will be displayed. And even if they're all filled in, at least one extra blank keyword will be displayed so that you can add more.

- The `core=True` argument on `keyword` solves an important problem. When this model had its own standalone pages in the admin, each one had a Delete button, but when editing inline, that's not displayed. Instead you can declare the core fields of the model, and if they're all left blank, Django will take that as a sign to delete that instance. In this case, if you clear the field for an existing keyword, it will be deleted when you click the Save button for its page.

Go ahead and add some keywords to the pages in your database; you'll want them to be available when you try out the improved keyword-based search.

Adding support for keywords in the search view is pretty easy. Just edit the view so that it looks like the following:

```
def search(request):
    query = request.GET.get('q', '')
    keyword_results = results = []
    if query:
        keyword_results = FlatPage.objects.filter( ➥
searchkeyword__keyword__in=query.split()).distinct()
        results = FlatPage.objects.filter(content__icontains=query)
    return render_to_response('search/search.html',
                              { 'query': query,
                                'keyword_results': keyword_results,
                                'results': results })
```

You've added a second query in the preceding code, which looks up pages whose associated search keywords match the query. Though it may look daunting at first, it's actually pretty simple.

First you're using a call to `filter`, just as in the other query. This one, though, is interesting. It's actually reaching "across" the foreign key from the `SearchKeyword` model and looking in the `keyword` field there. Any time you have a relationship like this between models, you can chain lookups across the relationship by using double underscores: `searchkeyword__keyword` translates to "the keyword field on the related `SearchKeyword` model." The lookup operator here is `__in`, which takes a list of things to match against. You're feeding it `query.split()`. The query variable, at this point, is a string, and Python provides a `split()` method which, by default, splits on spaces. This is exactly what you want—to be able to handle queries that contain multiple words.

Next, the call to `filter` is followed by `distinct()`. The nature of this query means that, if a single page has multiple keywords that match the search, multiple copies of that page will show up in the results. You only want one copy of each page, so you use the `distinct()` method, which adds the SQL keyword `DISTINCT` to the database query.

Finally, you add the `keyword_results` to the context you'll be using with the template. The template will need to update. Though it's getting a little bit more complex because of the multiple cases it has to handle, it's still fairly straightforward to follow:

```
<html>
  <head>
    <title>Search</title>
  </head>
  <body>
    <form method="get" action="/search/">
      <p><label for="id_q">Search:</label>
      <input type="text" name="q" id="id_q" value="{{ query }}" />
      <input type="submit" value="Submit" /></p>
    </form>
    {% if keyword_results or results %}
      <p>You searched for "{{ query }}".</p>
      {% if keyword_results %}
        <p>Recommended pages:</p>
```

```
    <ul>
      {% for page in keyword_results %}
        <li><a href="{{ page.get_absolute_url }}">{{ page.title }}</a></li>
      {% endfor %}
    </ul>
  {% endif %}
  {% if results %}
    <p>Search results:</p>
    <ul>
      {% for page in results %}
        <li><a href="{{ page.get_absolute_url }}">{{ page.title }}</a></li>
      {% endfor %}
    </ul>
  {% endif %}
  {% endif %}
  {% if query and not keyword_results and not results %}
    <p>No results found.</p>
  {% else %}
    <p>Type a search query into the box above, and press "Submit"
          to search.</p>
  {% endif %}
  </body>
</html>
```

The complexity really comes from the nested if tags to deal with the various cases, but this lets you cover every possibility. Also, notice the line that reads {% if keyword_results or results %}: the if tag lets you do some simple logic to test whether any or all of a set of conditions are met. In this case, it provides an easy way to handle the situation where there's *some* type of result, and then it tackles the different cases individually, as needed. If you've added some keywords to the pages in your database, try searching for those keywords now, and you'll see the appropriate pages show up in the search results.

Before I wrap up, let's add one more useful feature to the search view. If there's only one result that precisely matches a keyword, you'll redirect straight to that page and save the user a mouse click. You can accomplish this by using HttpResponseRedirect, a subclass of the HttpResponse class, which issues an HTTP redirect to a URL you specify. Open up views.py and add the following line at the top:

```
from django.http import HttpResponseRedirect
```

This is necessary because, again, Python requires you to explicitly import anything you plan to use. Now edit the search view like so:

```
def search(request):
    query = request.GET.get('q', '')
    keyword_results = results = []
    if query:
        keyword_results = FlatPage.objects.filter( ➥
searchkeyword__keyword__in=query.split()).distinct()
        if keyword_results.count() == 1:
```

```
            return HttpResponseRedirect(keyword_results[0].get_absolute_url())
        results = FlatPage.objects.filter(content__icontains=query)
    return render_to_response('search/search.html',
                                { 'query': query,
                                  'keyword_results': keyword_results,
                                  'results': results })
```

Up until now, you've been treating the results of database queries like normal Python lists, and, although they can be used like that, they're actually a special type of object called a QuerySet. QuerySet is a class Django uses to represent a database query. Each QuerySet has the methods you've seen so far—filter() and distinct()—plus several others, which you can "chain" together to build a progressively more complex query. A QuerySet also has a count() method, which will tell you how many rows in the database matched the query. (It does a SELECT COUNT to find this out, though for efficiency reasons, it can also take advantage of some other methods that don't require an extra query.)

ADMONITION: WHEN DOES DJANGO EXECUTE THE QUERY?

The single most important feature of QuerySet is that it's "lazy." Initially, it doesn't do anything except make a note of what query it's eventually supposed to execute in the database, which is why you can keep chaining extra things onto it to add filtering, a DISTINCT clause, or other conditions. The actual database query won't be executed until you do something that forces it to happen, like (in this case) counting or looping over the results.

By using count(), you can see whether a keyword search returned exactly one result and then issue a redirect. The URL you redirect to is keyword_results[0].get_absolute_url(), which pulls out the first (and, in this case, only) page in the results and calls its get_absolute_url() method to get the URL.

Go ahead and try this out. Add a new search keyword that's unique to one page, and then search for it. If you've set up the view as previously described, you'll immediately be redirected to that page.

Looking Ahead

In the last two chapters, you've gone from literally *nothing* to building a useful, functional content management system with an easy web-based administrative interface, adding rich-text editing to avoid the need to write raw HTML, and a search system that allows administrators to set up keyword-based results. Along the way, you've written fewer than a hundred lines of actual code. Django did most of the heavy lifting, and you just supplied the templates and a little bit of code to enable the search function.

Best of all, you now have a simple, reusable solution for a common web-development task: a brochureware-style CMS. Any time you need it, you can set up Django and walk through these same easy steps (or even just make a copy of the project, changing the appropriate settings in the process) to re-create it, saving you time and freeing you from the tedium of a fairly repetitive situation.

Feel free to spend some time playing around with the CMS: add some style to the templates, customize the admin pages a bit more, or—if you're feeling really adventurous—even try adding a few features of your own. If you'd like a homework assignment of sorts, check out the Django database API documentation (online at `www.djangoproject.com/documentation/db-api/`) and see if you can work out how to add an index view that lists all of the pages in the database.

When you're ready for a new project, start reading the next chapter, where you'll be starting on your first application from scratch: a Django-powered weblog.

CHAPTER 4

■■■

A Django-Powered Weblog

The simple CMS you built in the last two chapters was a good example of how Django's bundled applications can help you get a project off the ground quickly and without much code; but most of the time you'll probably be developing things that aren't covered quite so neatly by prebuilt applications included with Django itself. Django still has a lot to offer in these situations, mostly by taking the bulk of repetitive work off your shoulders. Over the rest of this book you'll be writing applications from scratch and seeing how Django's components can make that a much easier and much less painful process. Let's start with something that's quickly becoming a necessity for any organization that goes online: a weblog.

Feature Checklist

Real-world applications usually start with at least a rough specification of what they'll need to do, and I'll follow the same process here. Before you sit down and write the weblog application, you'll need to decide up-front what you want it to do. When I wrote a weblog app for my own personal use, this was the feature list I had in mind:

- It needs to provide an easy way to add and edit entries without writing raw HTML.

- It should support multiple authors and provide a way to separate entries according to author.

- Each entry should allow an optional short excerpt to be displayed when a summary is needed.

- The weblog's authors should be able to create categories and assign entries to them.

- Authors should be able to decide which entries will be displayed publicly and which will not (in order to, for example, mark an unfinished entry as a draft and come back to it later).

- Entries should be able to be "featured," and these entries should be easily retrievable (for display on the weblog's home page, for example).

- A link log should be provided, as well, to allow posting of interesting or notable links.

- Both entries and links should support *tagging*—adding arbitrary descriptive words to provide extra metadata or organization.

- The link log should integrate with del.icio.us or other popular link-sharing services so that links posted to the weblog automatically show up at the service as well.

- Visitors should be able to browse entries and links by date, by tag, or (in the case of entries) by category.

- Visitors to the blog should be able to leave comments on entries and links.

- Comments should be subject to some sort of moderation in order to avoid comment spam.

There are more features you could add here, but this list is enough to keep you busy for a while; it will make use of a broad range of Django's features. So let's get started.

Writing a Django Application

In the last chapter, when you added the `search` function and `SearchKeyword` model to the simple CMS, you built a simple Django application—initially created with the `manage.py startapp` command—to hold them. At the time I didn't spend much time detailing just what goes into a Django application. However, now that you're going to start doing more complex things, it's worth pausing for a moment to go over it, to understand how individual Django applications differ from a Django project.

Projects vs. Applications

As you've seen already, a Django *project* is configured by its settings module, which—among other things—specifies the database it will connect to and the list of applications it uses. In a way, the defining quality of a project is that it's the "thing" that holds the settings (including both the settings module and the root URLConf module, which specifies the project's base URL configuration).

A project can also contain other code if it makes sense for that code to be part of the project directly, but it's fairly rare for this to be needed. Generally, a project exists to provide a "container" for a set of Django applications to work together, and most projects won't ever need anything beyond the initial files created by `django-admin.py startproject`.

A Django *application*, on the other hand, is responsible for actually providing some piece of functionality and should try to focus on that functionality as much as possible. An application doesn't have a settings module—that's the job of any projects that use it—but it does provide several other things:

- An application can (and often does) provide one or more data models.

- An application usually provides one or more view functions, often related in some way to its data models.

- An application can provide libraries of custom template tags, which extend Django's template system with extra, application-specific features.

- An application can (and usually should) provide a URLConf module suitable for being "plugged in" to a project (via the `include` directive, as you've already seen in the case of the administrative interface and `flatpages` applications bundled with Django).

And, of course, an application should also provide any extra "utility" code needed to support itself, or it should have clear dependencies on other applications or on third-party Python modules, which provide that support.

Standalone and Coupled Applications

It is important to be aware of the distinction between two different ways of developing Django applications. One method, which I used in the last chapter, uses the `manage.py startapp` command to create an application module inside the project's directory. While this is easy and convenient, it does have some drawbacks, most notably in the fact that it "couples" the application to the project. Any other Python code that wants to access that application needs to know that it "lives" inside that particular project. (For example, to import the `SearchKeyword` model from a separate piece of code, you'd have to import it from `cms.search.models` instead of just `search.models`.) Any time you want to reuse the application, you need to either make a copy of the project or create a set of empty directories to emulate the project's directory structure.

The alternative is to develop a standalone application, which acts as an independent, self-contained Python module and doesn't need to be kept inside a project directory in order to work correctly. A standalone application is much easier to reuse and distribute, but it does involve a bit more work initially to set up: the `manage.py startapp` command can't create things automatically for you unless you're developing an application that's coupled to a particular project.

While there are cases where you'll develop one-off applications that don't need to be reusable or distributable (and in those cases, it's perfectly fine to develop them inside of, and coupled to, a particular project), in general, you'll get more benefit from developing standalone applications that can be reused in many different projects. That's how you'll be working for the rest of this book.

Creating the Weblog Application

Because this is going to be a standalone application, you'll need to create a Python module for it manually instead of relying on `manage.py startapp`, but that's not too hard. You may remember that all the `startapp` command really did was create a directory and put three files into it, and that's all you'll need to do to get started.

There are only two things you need to worry about when manually setting up a new application module: what to call it and where to put it. You can call an application by any name that's legal for a Python module. Python allows module names to be made up of any combination of letters and numbers and, optionally, underscores to separate words in the name (though the name must start with a letter). Because Django is named after a jazz musician, some developers like to continue the pattern by naming applications after famous jazz figures. (For example, the company I work for sells a CMS called Ellington—named for Duke Ellington—and there's a popular open source e-commerce application named Satchmo in honor of Louis Armstrong.) This isn't required, but it's something I like to do whenever there's not a more obvious name. So when I wrote my own weblog application, I named it Coltrane after John Coltrane. That seemed appropriate, given that Coltrane was known for composition and improvisation, two skills that also make a good blogger.

Where to put the application's code is a slightly trickier question to answer. So far you haven't run into this problem because Django's manage.py script, in order to make initial setup and development easier, somewhat obscures an important requirement for Python code: it has to be placed in a directory that's on the Python path. The *Python path* is simply a list of directories where Python will search whenever it encounters an import statement. So code that's meant to be imported (as your application will be, in order to be used as part of a Django project) needs to be on the Python path.

When you installed Python, a default Python path was set up for you, which included a directory called site-packages. When you installed Django, the setup.py installer script placed all of Django's code inside that directory. You can place your own code in site-packages if you like, but it's generally not a good idea to do so. The site-packages directory is almost always set up in a part of your computer's file system that requires administrative access to write to, and having to constantly jump through the hoop of authenticating to place things there isn't much fun. Instead, most Python programmers create a directory where they'll keep their own code and add it to the Python path, so let's do that. Since you've already created a directory to hold your Django projects, go ahead and add it to your Python path and place your stand-alone applications in it as well. This way you'll only need to add one directory to the Python path, and you won't be scattering code into multiple locations on your computer.

ADMONITION: HOW TO CHANGE YOUR PYTHON PATH

On Mac OS X, as well as most UNIX- or Linux-based systems, changing the Python path is easy. You can type a command like the following to add directories to the path:

```
export PYTHONPATH=/home/myuser/my-python-code:$PYTHONPATH
```

To avoid needing to type that over and over again, you can usually add it to a file called .profile or .bash_profile in your home directory. That way, it will be executed each time you open up a command line (but you may also need to add it to a .shrc or .bashrc file).

On Windows, the setup is a bit more involved, largely because Windows, unlike UNIX-based systems, isn't as friendly to command-line–based programs. In the Control Panel's System area, under the Advanced tab, you can set environment variables. The PYTHONPATH variable should already be set up with the initial value Python provided, and you can add new directories to it (directories in the list should be separated with semicolons).

Now, in the same directory where you created the cms project (in other words, alongside cms, not inside cms), create a new directory named coltrane. Inside that, create three empty files:

- __init__.py

- models.py

- views.py

This is all you'll need for now: the __init__.py file will tell Python that the coltrane directory is a Python module, and the models.py and views.py files will hold the initial code for the weblog application.

Designing the Models

You're going to need several models to implement all of the features in your list, and a couple of them will be moderately complex. However, you can start with a simple one: the model that will represent categories for entries to be assigned to. Open up the weblog application's models.py file, and add the following:

```python
from django.db import models


class Category(models.Model):
    title = models.CharField(max_length=250)
    slug = models.SlugField(unique=True)
    description = models.TextField()

    class Admin:
        pass

    def __unicode__(self):
        return self.title
```

Most of this should be familiar after your first foray into Django models in the last chapter. The import statement pulls in Django's models package, which includes the base Model class and definitions for the different types of fields to represent data. You've already seen the CharField (this one has a longer max_length in order to allow for long category names), the Admin class declaration to activate the admin interface, and the __unicode__() method (which, for this model, returns the value of the title field). But there are two new field types here: SlugField and TextField.

The meaning of TextField is pretty intuitive. It's meant to store a larger amount of text (in the database, it will become a TEXT column), and will be used here to provide a useful description of the category.

SlugField is a bit more interesting. It's meant to store a *slug*: a short, meaningful piece of text, composed entirely of characters that are safe to use in a URL and to be used in generating the URL for a particular object. This means, for example, that instead of having a URL like /categories?category_id=47, you could have /categories/programming/. This is useful to your site's visitors (because it makes the URL meaningful and easier to remember) and for search engine indexing. URLs that have a relevant word in the URL often rank higher in Google and other search engines than URLs that don't. The term *slug*, as befits Django's heritage, comes from the newspaper industry, where it is used in preprint production and sometimes in wire formats as a shorter identifier for a news story. Note that I've added an extra argument to SlugField: unique=True. Since the slug is going to be used in the URL and the same URL can't refer to two different categories, it needs to be unique. Django's administrative interface will enforce uniqueness for this field, and `manage.py syncdb` will create the database table with a `UNIQUE` constraint for that column.

It's useful when developing an application to stop every once in a while and actually try it out. So go back to the cms project, open up its settings file, and add `coltrane`—the new weblog application—to its `INSTALLED_APPS` setting:

```
INSTALLED_APPS = (
    'django.contrib.auth',
    'django.contrib.contenttypes',
    'django.contrib.sessions',
    'django.contrib.sites',
    'django.contrib.admin',
    'django.contrib.flatpages',
    'cms.search',
    'coltrane',
)
```

Because it's directly on the Python path, just adding `coltrane` will work. Next run python `manage.py syncdb` to install the table for the `Category` model and launch the development server. The admin index page will look like that shown in Figure 4-1.

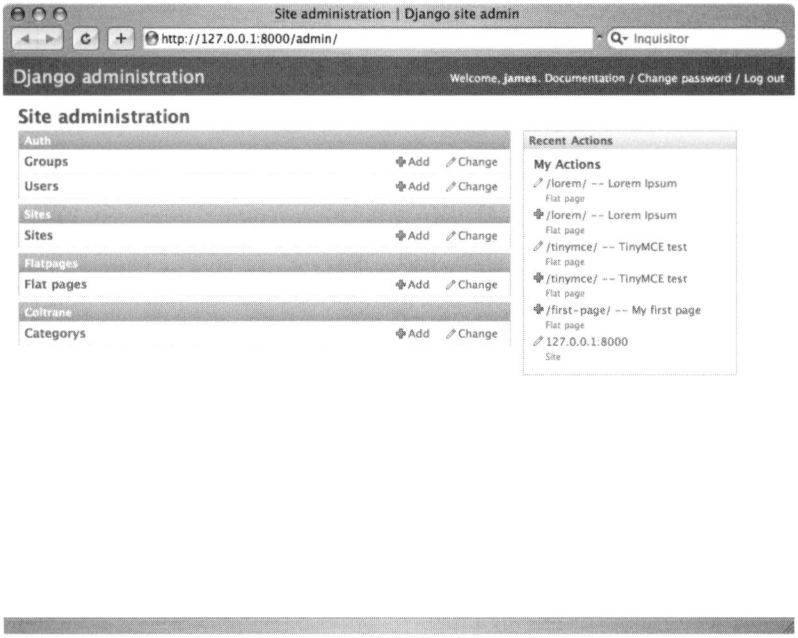

Figure 4-1. *The Django admin interface with the Category model*

You can see that the `Category` model shows up, but it's labeled "Categorys." That's no good. Django's admin interface generates that label from the name of the model class and tries to pluralize it by adding an "s," which works most of the time. It doesn't always work, though, and when it doesn't Django lets you specify the correct plural name. Go back to the weblog's `models.py` file and edit the `Category` model class to look like the following:

```python
class Category(models.Model):
    title = models.CharField(max_length=250)
    slug = models.SlugField(unique=True)
    description = models.TextField()

    class Meta:
        verbose_name_plural = "Categories"

    class Admin:
        pass

    def __unicode__(self):
        return self.title
```

Once you save the file and refresh the admin index page in your browser, you should see something similar to what's shown in Figure 4-2.

Figure 4-2. *The correct pluralization of the Category model*

Because you often need to provide extra meta-information about a model, Django lets you add an inner class, named `Meta`, which can specify a large number of common options. In this case, you're using an option called `verbose_name_plural`, which will return a pluralized name for the model class whenever it's needed. (There's also a `verbose_name` option, which can specify a singular version if it differs significantly from the class name, but you don't need it here.) You'll see a number of other useful options for the inner Meta class as you flesh out the weblog's models.

If you click in the admin interface to add a category, you'll see the appropriate fields in a nice form: title, slug, and description. But adding a category this way will reveal another shortcoming. Most of the time, the value for the slug field will probably be similar or even identical to the value for the title field (for example, a Programming category should probably have a slug like "programming"). Having to manually type the slug every time would be tedious, so why not have it automatically generated from the title, and then let the user manually change it if necessary? This is easy enough to do. Just change the definition of the slug field to look like this:

```
slug = models.SlugField(prepopulate_from=['title'], unique=True)
```

Then save the models.py file and add a category. The prepopulate_from argument will turn on a helpful piece of JavaScript in Django's administrative interface, and it will automatically fill in a suggested slug as you type a value into the title field. Note that prepopulate_from gets a list: this means you could specify multiple fields to try to draw the slug value from, which isn't common but is sometimes useful. The JavaScript that generates slugs is also smart enough to recognize, and omit, words like a, an, the, and so on. These are called *stop words* and generally aren't useful to have in a slug.

Also, note that when Django creates the database table for this model, it will add an index to the slug column. You can manually tell Django to do this with any field (by using the option db_index=True for the field), but SlugField will get one automatically, providing a performance boost in the common case of using a slug from a URL to perform database queries.

ADMONITION: SLUGS AND NORMALIZATION

If you're familiar with theories of database normalization—guidelines for designing relational databases so as to avoid duplicated information—you may be wondering why the slug gets its own column if it's just going to be generated from the title. This smells suspiciously like needless duplication, doesn't it?

The slug gets its own column mostly because it doesn't *necessarily* depend on the title. For some long category titles, for example, the slug might differ significantly in order to stay short and memorable. Also, normalized tables aren't an absolute rule. Deliberately denormalizing—so long as it's done carefully—can often yield important performance improvements, as you'll see when you write the model for entries.

While you're looking at categories in the admin interface, let's pause and add another useful feature—helpful hints that give the weblog application's users more information as they fill in the data. So edit the definition of the title field like so:

```
title = models.CharField(max_length=250, help_text='Maximum 250 characters.')
```

Next, save the models.py file and look at the admin form again (see Figure 4-3).

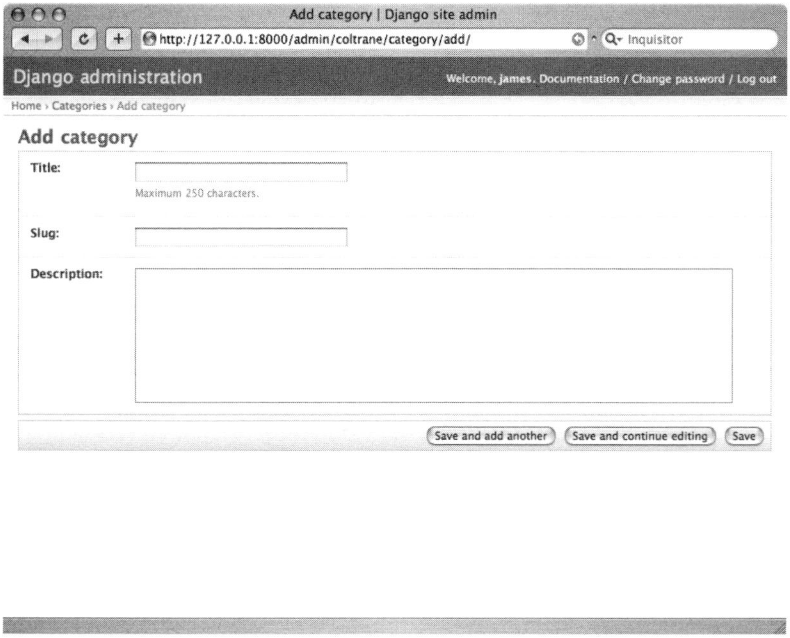

Figure 4-3. *The admin form for adding a category*

The string given in the `help_text` argument shows up underneath the text box for the `title` field, providing a useful hint about what can be entered there. You can add `help_text` to any field in your model, and it's generally a good idea to do so whenever there's something users should know while entering data. So let's add it for the `slug` field as well:

```
slug = models.SlugField(prepopulate_from=['title'], unique=True,
                        help_text="Suggested value automatically generated from➥
                                       title. Must be unique.")
```

Next save the `models.py` file and refresh the admin form again. You'll see that text show up under the `slug` field's text box, notifying users that a suggested value will be filled in and reminding them that the slug must be unique.

Before I move on, let's add one more improvement. If you try adding a couple of categories, you might notice that the admin page, which lists all of the categories, doesn't necessarily keep them in any order. It would be nice to have them displayed in an alphabetical list so that a user can scan through them quickly. Again, this is easy enough to do. The inner `Meta` class accepts an option to specify a default ordering for the model:

```
class Meta:
    ordering = ['title']
    verbose_name_plural = "Categories"
```

Save the `models.py` file, and the categories will be alphabetized. Unless you specifically override it on a per-query basis, Django will now append the clause `ORDER BY title ASC` to any database query for the categories table, which will get categories back in the correct alphabetical order. Notice that the value for ordering is a list. You can specify multiple fields here, and they'll be correctly placed into an ORDER BY clause for most queries. (The admin application only uses the first field in the ordering option when retrieving lists of objects.)

One more useful thing you can add is a special method called get_absolute_url(). In Chapter 2, you saw that this is the standard practice for a Django model that wants to specify its own URL, and every model that is intended to be used in a public-facing view should have a get_absolute_url() method. So let's add one:

```
def get_absolute_url(self):
    return "/categories/%s/" % self.slug
```

For now, just put this method at the bottom of the Category class (remember that it needs to be indented to be part of the class). You'll see a bit later on how to keep all the parts of a Django model class organized.

This will return a string with the value of the category's slug field interpolated into the correct place. Adding this method will also cause the admin interface to show a View on Site button for each category, though for now it won't be very useful because you haven't yet set up any URLs or views to actually display them.

ADMONITION: PYTHON STRING FORMATTING

While it's possible to create a string by *concatenation*—building up the pieces one at a time and using the plus sign (+) operator to join them together—that becomes extremely tedious if you need to include multiple variables or generated values in the final result. So most languages, Python included, provide a simpler way to interpolate variables and values into a string using special formatting characters.

The formatting characters (and, in many languages, the names of functions that build up strings in this fashion) come from the printf family of functions in the standard library of the C programming language. But Python doesn't use a function for this. Instead, you simply write out the string with the appropriate formatting characters, then follow it with a percent sign (%) and any values to be interpolated into the result.

The full specification of Python's string-formatting syntax, including a list of the formatting characters, is available in the Python documentation online at http://docs.python.org/lib/typesseq-strings.html.

The Entry Model

Now that you have categories to assign entries to, it's time to build the model for the weblog entries. Because it will really be the center of attention for this application, it'll also be the most complex model you'll need to build, so let's take it a bit at a time.

Basic Fields

First off, you need to have a few core fields to hold the title of the entry, the optional excerpt, the text of the entry, and the date the entry was published. So let's start with those. Open up the models.py file and, below the Category model class, start adding the new Entry model. (*Don't* run manage.py syncdb yet. You'll be adding more fields to this model, and it's best to wait until that's done before having Django create the database tables.)

```
class Entry(models.Model):
    title = models.CharField(max_length=250)
    excerpt = models.TextField(blank=True)
    body = models.TextField()
    pub_date = models.DateTimeField()
```

The first three fields are all of types you've seen before, but the last one—which will represent the entry's publication date—is new: DateTimeField. Compared to the field types you've seen so far, it's unique in several ways:

- When you store entries into or retrieve them from the database, this field will have as its value a Python datetime object (the datetime class is found in the datetime module, which is a standard part of Python), regardless of how it's actually stored in the database (different databases will, internally, handle it in slightly different ways). Django also provides separate field types, which store only a date or only a time, but DateTimeField handles both. This means you can track not only the date the entry was published, but also the time (so you can eventually display something like "Published on October 7 at 10:00 P.M.").

- The exact type of database column created for this field will vary from database to database. Up until now, you've seen fields that consistently become the same type of column (VARCHAR for CharField, for example) no matter what type of database you're using. However, because of variations in column types, Django will use different options as appropriate (on SQLite, this will become a DATETIME column while, in contrast, it will become a TIMESTAMP column in PostgreSQL).

- So far, each type of field you've worked with has translated directly into one form input in the administrative interface, usually a text box. A DateTimeField, however, becomes *two* form inputs: one for the date and one for the time. You'll see this when you start working with entries in the administrative interface.

There's also an option on the excerpt field that you haven't seen before: blank=True. So far the question of required fields hasn't really come up. You've been working with simple models where there's no need to have some things be optional, and so Django's default behavior—to make the field required when entering data through a form in the admin interface and to create a NOT NULL column in the database—has been fine. In this case, though, you need to make the excerpt field optional, and the blank=True option tells Django that it's okay not to enter anything for this field. You can add blank=True to any type of field in a Django model.

ADMONITION: BLANK FIELDS VS. NULL FIELDS

Django actually uses two separate options to handle required and nonrequired fields on models: `blank` and `null`. The `blank` option only affects forms displayed to users of a Django-powered application and will prevent the form from displaying a validation error if no value is entered. The `null` option, on the other hand, will set up the database to accept a NULL value. If you need to allow users to leave a field blank *and* have a NULL inserted into its column in the database, you'll need to specify both options.

If this seems strange, keep in mind that there are very common cases where you'll want to allow a user to leave a field blank in a form (or even hide a field entirely) but still prevent a NULL value from going to the database (by generating a value for that field if the user doesn't supply one). You'll see an example later in this chapter.

Also, it's important to note that for text-based field types (`CharField`, `TextField`, and others) Django will never insert a NULL. For these field types, a blank value will be inserted as an empty string. This is to avoid a situation where there are potentially two different blank values for the field (either an empty string or a NULL) and to ensure that code that checks for blank values can be kept simple. Because of this, you should generally avoid specifying `null=True` on text-based field types.

Slugs, Useful Defaults, and Uniqueness Constraints

Just as you added a slug for categories, it's a good idea to add one for entries and to set it up to populate a default from the entry's title. So add the following to the `Entry` model:

```
slug = models.SlugField(prepopulate_from=['title'])
```

With the `Category` model, you added `unique=True` to force the slug to be unique, but for entries it would be nice to have something slightly different. Most good weblog software builds URLs that include the publication dates of entries (so that they look like /2007/10/09/ entry-title/), which means that all you really need is for the *combination* of the slug and the publication date to be unique. Django provides an easy way to specify this, through an option called `unique_for_date`:

```
slug = models.SlugField(prepopulate_from=['title'],
                        unique_for_date='pub_date')
```

This will tell Django to allow a particular slug to be used only once on each date. The `unique_for_date` constraint is one of three date-based constraints supported by Django. The other two are `unique_for_month` and `unique_for_year`. Where `unique_for_date` allows a given value to be used only once per day, the other two constrain values to being used once per month and once per year, respectively.

It would also be nice to provide a sensible default value for the `pub_date` field. Most of the time, entries will be "published" on the same day they're entered, so defaulting to the current date and time would be convenient for the weblog's authors. Django allows you to specify a default value for any type of field by using the default option. The only question is how to specify a default of "right now."

The answer lies in Python's standard `datetime` module. This provides a function, `datetime.datetime.now()`, for obtaining the current date and time and returns the correct type of object (a Python `datetime`, as previously described) for filling in a `DateTimeField`. So at the top of the `models.py` file, add an `import` statement to make the `datetime` module available:

```
import datetime
```

and then edit the `pub_date` field to add the default:

```
pub_date = models.DateTimeField(default=datetime.datetime.now)
```

Notice that there aren't any parentheses there—it's `datetime.datetime.now`, *not* `datetime.datetime.now()`. When you're specifying a default, Django lets you supply either an appropriate value or a function, which will generate the appropriate value on demand. In this case, you're supplying a function, and Django will call it whenever the default value is needed. This ensures that the correct current `datetime` is generated each time.

ADMONITION: FUNCTIONS VS. RETURN VALUES

Python lets you refer to functions directly and pass them around as "first-class" objects the same way you can pass around any other type of value. The difference is simply that you leave off the parentheses, as you've done with the default value for the `pub_date` field. Understanding the difference between the function and the return value from calling the function is critical to using many parts of Django effectively. In this case, if the default had been specified as `datetime.datetime.now()`, it would have been called once—when the model was first loaded—and then never again, creating an apparently unchanging default value.

In general, Python programmers refer to this as passing a *callable*, a value that can be called as a function (though in some advanced uses of Python, you can encounter things that are callable but are not actually functions).

There are some other cases, some of which you'll see later in this book, where this distinction is important and can lead to unexpected and subtle bugs in your applications, so always be careful to leave off the parentheses in a situation where you want to pass a function and have it repeatedly called.

Authors, Comments, and Featured Entries

Because the weblog needs to support multiple authors, you need a way to mark the author of each entry. In the last chapter, when you implemented search keywords, you saw that Django provides the `ForeignKey` field for relating one model to another (and translates it into a foreign key in the database). The obvious solution is to have a model representing authors and a foreign key on each entry tying it to an author.

This is a case where Django will help you out immensely. The bundled application `django.contrib.auth` provides a `User` model. (This is the user account you created when running `manage.py syncdb` for the first time, which is stored in the database as an instance of the `User` model.) This model lives in the module `django.contrib.auth.models`, so you'll need to add an `import` statement in the weblog's `models.py` file. From `django.contrib.auth.models`, import `User`, and then add the foreign key to the `Entry` model:

```
author = models.ForeignKey(User)
```

ADMONITION: WHY NOT SPECIFY THE CURRENT USER AS A DEFAULT?

After going to the trouble of setting up slugs to automatically populate and the `pub_date` field to default to the current date and time, you might be wondering why I'm not using a default here to fill in the current user when an entry is being written. The primary reason is that, in the administrative interface, Django assumes you'll only grant access to people you trust and, therefore, that they'll fill in this sort of field correctly. Underlying this is a technical issue: Django's components are deliberately designed to require as little knowledge of each other as possible (a concept known as *loose coupling*) in order to make it easy to use them individually or, if necessary, to replace them with other components. Because of this, the Django object-relational mapper (ORM) has no knowledge of who the current user is in the authentication component.

Another feature that's easy to add is a per-entry way to allow or disallow comments. You haven't yet seen the code that will actually handle user-submitted comments (that will come a bit later); however, you will need something on the Entry model that allows you to check whether comments should be allowed. So let's add a field for it:

```
enable_comments = models.BooleanField(default=True)
```

A `BooleanField` has only two possible values—`True` or `False`—and in web-based forms will be represented by a check box. I give it a default value of `True` because most people will probably want comments on by default, but an entry's author will be able to uncheck the box in the admin interface to turn it off.

While you're looking at `BooleanField`, remember that one of the features on your list is the ability to mark entries as "featured" so that they can be singled out for special presentation. That's also easy to do with a `BooleanField`:

```
featured = models.BooleanField(default=False)
```

This time set the default to `False`, because only a few specific entries should be featured.

Different Types of Entries

You also need to support entries that are marked as "drafts," which aren't meant to be shown publicly. This means you'll need some way of recording an entry's status. One way would be to use another `BooleanField`, with a name like `is_draft` or, perhaps, `is_public`. Then you could just query for entries with the appropriate value, and authors could check or uncheck the box to control whether an entry shows up publicly.

But it would be better to have something that can be extended later on. If there's ever a need for even one more possible value, the `BooleanField` won't work. The ideal solution would be some way to specify a list of choices and allow the user to select from them; then if there's ever a need for more choices, they can simply be added to the list. Django provides an easy way to do this via an option called `choices`. Here's how you'll implement it:

```
STATUS_CHOICES = (
    (1, 'Live'),
    (2, 'Draft'),
)
status = models.IntegerField(choices=STATUS_CHOICES, default=1)
```

Here you're using IntegerField, which, as its name implies, stores a number—an integer—in the database. But you've used the choices option and defined a set of choices for it to use. The value passed to the choices option needs to be a list or a tuple, and each item in it also needs to be a list or a tuple with the following two items:

- The actual value to store in the database

- A human-readable name to represent the choice

You've also specified a default value: the value associated with the Live status, which will denote entries to be displayed live on the site using the weblog application.

You can use choices with any of Django's model field types, but generally it's most useful with IntegerField (where it can be used to provide meaningful names for a list of numeric choices) and CharField (where, for example, you can use it to store short abbreviations in the database, but still keep track of the full words or phrases they represent).

If you've used other programming languages that support enumerations, this is a similar concept. In fact, you could (and probably should) make it look a little bit more similar. Edit the Entry model so that it begins like so:

```
class Entry(models.Model):
    LIVE_STATUS = 1
    DRAFT_STATUS = 2
    STATUS_CHOICES = (
        (LIVE_STATUS, 'Live'),
        (DRAFT_STATUS, 'Draft'),
    )
```

Now instead of having to hard-code the integer values anywhere you're doing queries for specific types of entries, you can instead refer to Entry.LIVE_STATUS or Entry.DRAFT_STATUS and know that it'll be the right value. The status field can also be updated:

```
status = models.IntegerField(choices=STATUS_CHOICES, default=LIVE_STATUS)
```

And, just to show how easy it is to add new choices, let's throw in a third option: hidden. This is a common option offered by popular weblogging packages and covers situations where an entry isn't really a draft but also shouldn't be shown publicly. Now the relevant part of the Entry model looks like this:

```
LIVE_STATUS = 1
DRAFT_STATUS = 2
HIDDEN_STATUS = 3
STATUS_CHOICES = (
    (LIVE_STATUS, 'Live'),
    (DRAFT_STATUS, 'Draft'),
    (HIDDEN_STATUS, 'Hidden'),
)
```

And just as you can refer to Entry.LIVE_STATUS and Entry.DRAFT_STATUS, now you can also refer to Entry.HIDDEN_STATUS.

ADMONITION: BE CAREFUL WITH "MAGIC NUMBERS"

In general, any time you find yourself writing code that relies on a specific fixed value, like the status values for the Entry class, it's a good idea instead to create a variable that holds it and refer to that variable. (This is sometimes referred to as a *constant*, though Python doesn't have any special semantics for such a thing.) Then if the value (many programmers call these sorts of values "magic numbers") ever needs to be updated, you'll only need to make a single change in your code.

It's conventional in Python (and in many other programming languages) for these sorts of constants to be given names that are entirely uppercase in order to indicate that they have a meaning different from other variables. (You've already seen that Django's settings all use uppercase names; this is why.)

Categorizing and Tagging Entries

You'll remember that your feature list calls for two ways of grouping entries: categories (which you've already laid some groundwork for in the form of the Category model) and tags. Setting up the Entry model to use categories is easy:

```
categories = models.ManyToManyField(Category)
```

ManyToManyField is another way of relating two models to each other. Where a foreign key only allows you to relate to one specific object of the other model class, a ManyToManyField allows you to relate to as many of them as you'd like. In the admin interface, this will be represented as a list of categories presented in an HTML <select multiple> element.

ADMONITION: HOW MANY-TO-MANY RELATIONSHIPS WORK

At the database level, a ManyToManyField is actually represented by a separate *join table*. Each row in that table consists of two foreign keys: one to each side of the relationship. In this case, the table will be called coltrane_entry_categories, and each row will have one foreign key pointing to the entries table and one pointing to the categories table.

You probably won't ever need to refer to this join table explicitly. However, it's a good idea to know it's there and have an idea of how it works, if only to have a reminder that selecting or filtering on aspects of a many-to-many relationship will always involve joining the extra table (whereas queries based on a foreign key—depending on the exact parameters you're using to do the query—sometimes don't need to perform a join at all).

Tagging is a bit trickier because tags ultimately need to be applied to two different models: the Entry model you're writing now and the Link model you'll write (in the next chapter) to represent a link log. You could define two Tag models—one for entries and one for links—or set up multiple many-to-many relationships to allow a single Tag model to suffice for both, but Django provides a simpler solution in the form of a *generic relation*.

Generic relations actually involve two special field types (GenericForeignKey and GenericRelation), which allow one model to have relationships with any other model installed in your project. Because of the complexity necessary to make this work, they can be a bit tricky to set up and use. In this particular case you're lucky: there's an open source Django application available that implements tags via generic relations and has already done all the hard work.

The application is called django-tagging and can be downloaded at http://code.google. com/p/django-tagging/. Grab a copy and unpack it so that the tagging module it provides is on your Python path, then add tagging to your INSTALLED_APPS setting. To add tags to your Entry model, you'll need to import a custom field type defined in django-tagging, so add the following import statement in the weblog's models.py:

```
from tagging.fields import TagField
```

Next, add the following to the Entry model:

```
tags = TagField()
```

This may feel a bit strange, but actually it's the right way to handle tagging, for two reasons:

- Django provides a lot of built-in field types you can add to your models, but there's no way it could cover everything you might need to represent in a model class. So in addition to the built-in fields, Django also provides an API for writing your own custom field types. The TagField provided by django-tagging is simply an example of this.

- Encapsulating common types of functionality into reusable, "pluggable" applications is precisely what Django tries to encourage. The fact that, in this case, the application was written by someone else and isn't bundled in django.contrib shouldn't be a deterrent. As you work more with Django, you'll find that there's a large ecosystem of third-party applications you can take advantage of and will save you from having to reinvent the wheel with your own implementations of a lot of common functions.

ADMONITION: LEARNING MORE ABOUT GENERIC RELATIONS

I've intentionally left out the details of how generic relations work because they're somewhat complex and require a slightly deeper understanding of Django than you've developed so far. If you would like to find out more about them, the relevant code is in the django.contrib.contenttypes application bundled with Django and full details are available in the official Django documentation online at www.djangoproject. com/documentation/contenttypes/.

Writing Entries Without Writing HTML

The last important feature for the Entry model is the ability to write entries without having to compose them in raw HTML. Most popular weblogging applications allow users to write entries using a simpler syntax that will be automatically converted into HTML as needed.

There are a number of widely used systems that can take plain text with a little bit of special syntax and perform the conversion. Textile, Markdown, BBCode, and reStructuredText are the most popular.

One way you could handle this is with template filters. As you saw in the last chapter, Django's template system allows you to apply filters to variables in your templates (as you did when you used the escape filter to prevent cross-site scripting attacks). Django includes ready-made template filters for applying Textile, Markdown, and reStructuredText to any piece of text in a template, and that would be an easy solution. Unfortunately, it's also an *expensive* solution. Running a text-to-HTML converter every time you display an entry will needlessly eat up CPU cycles on your server, especially since the resulting HTML will be the same each time. A better solution would be to generate the HTML once—when the entry is saved to the database—and then retrieve it directly for display.

You could just store the generated HTML in the body and excerpt fields, but that would remove the benefit of using a simpler syntax for writing entries. As soon as you went back to edit an entry, you'd be presented with the HTML instead of the plain text it was generated from. So what you really need is a separate pair of fields that will store the HTML, as well as a bit of code to generate it whenever an entry is saved. If you were worried earlier about database normalization—the principle that information shouldn't be needlessly duplicated—this is a good example of where deliberate denormalization is useful. On most consumer-level web hosting, disk space is far more abundant than processor time, so accepting a bit of redundancy in the database in return for less processing on each page view is a good trade-off to make.

First, let's add the fields:

```
excerpt_html = models.TextField(editable=False, blank=True)
body_html = models.TextField(editable=False, blank=True)
```

Like their plain-text counterparts, these both use TextField. Both of them also use the blank option because you don't want users to have to enter anything in these fields. They also add the option editable=False. This tells Django not to bother displaying these fields when it generates forms for the Entry model, since you'll be automatically generating the HTML to put into them.

Generating the HTML whenever an entry is saved is actually fairly easy. The base Model class that all Django models inherit from defines a method named save(), and individual models can override that method to provide custom behavior. The only hard part is choosing a text-to-HTML converter to use. I like Markdown, so that's what I'll go with. There's an open source Python Markdown converter available, which you can download at https://sourceforge.net/projects/python-markdown/. It provides a module named markdown, which contains the markdown function for doing text-to-HTML conversion. This means you use one more import statement:

```
from markdown import markdown
```

The actual save() method inside the Entry model is fairly short:

```
def save(self):
    self.body_html = markdown(self.body)
    if self.excerpt:
        self.excerpt_html = markdown(self.excerpt)
    super(Entry, self).save()
```

This runs Markdown over the body field and stores the resulting HTML in body_HTML. It also does a similar conversion for the excerpt field (after checking to see if an excerpt was entered; remember that it's optional), and then saves the entry.

ADMONITION: USING super

Object-oriented languages that use subclassing typically need to provide a way to access features of a parent class, even if those features are being overridden. Conventions for this vary from language to language, but in Python the standard practice is to use super, as shown in the preceding code.

Finishing Touches

Now you have all the fields you'll need to handle your feature list for entries. It's taken a little while to cover the full list, but if you have a look at the Entry model, you'll notice that it's only around 30 lines of actual code. Django manages to pack a lot of functionality into a very small amount of code. Before moving on, though, let's add a few extra touches to this model to make it a bit easier to work with.

You've already seen with the Category model that Django will try to pluralize the name of the model when displaying it in the admin interface, sometimes with incorrect results. So let's add a plural name for the Entry model as well:

```
class Meta:
    verbose_name_plural = "Entries"
```

While you're at it, you can also add default ordering for the model. In this case, you want them ordered by date with the newest entries coming first, so you'll add an ordering option inside the inner Meta class:

```
ordering = ['-pub_date']
```

Now Django will use ORDER BY pub_date DESC when retrieving lists of entries.

Let's also go ahead and activate the default admin interface, adding a __unicode__() method so you can get a simple string representation of an entry:

```
class Admin:
    pass

def __unicode__(self):
    return self.title
```

It's also a good idea to add help_text to most of the fields. Use your judgment to decide which fields need it, but feel free to compare with and borrow from the full version of the Entry model included in this book.

Finally, let's add one more method: get_absolute_url(). Remember from Chapter 2 that it is standard convention in Django for a model to specify its own URL. In this case, you'll return a URL that includes the entry's publication date and its slug:

```
def get_absolute_url(self):
    return "/weblog/%s/%s/" % ➡
            (self.pub_date.strftime("%Y/%b/%d").lower(), self.slug)
```

Once again, you're using Python's standard string formatting. In this case, you're interpolating two values: the entry's pub_date (with a little extra formatting provided by the strftime() method available on Python datetime objects) and the entry's slug. This particular formatting string will result in a URL like /weblog/2007/oct/09/my-entry/. The %b character in strftime() produces a three-letter abbreviation of the month (which you force into lowercase with the lower() method in order to ensure consistently lowercase URLs). In general, I prefer that to numeric representations because it's a bit more readable. If you'd prefer the month to be represented numerically, use %m instead of %b.

The Weblog Models So Far

You've now got two of the three models you'll need. Only the Link model still needs to be written, and you'll deal with it in the next chapter. The rest of this chapter will cover the views and URLs for entries in the weblog. But before you move on to that, let's pause to organize the models.py file so it'll be easier to understand and edit later on.

I've mentioned previously that Python has an official style guide. It's a good idea to follow that whenever you're writing Python code because it will make your code clearer and more understandable to anyone who needs to read it (including you). There's also a (much shorter) style guide for Django, which also provides some useful conventions for keeping your code readable. The guideline for model classes is to lay them out in this order:

1. Any constants and/or lists of choices

2. The full list of fields

3. The Meta class, if present

4. The Admin class, if present

5. The __unicode__() method

6. The save() method, if it's being overridden

7. The get_absolute_url() method, if present

8. Any additional custom methods

For complex models, I also like to break up the field list into logical groups, with a short comment explaining what each group is. In general, it's easier to find things if you keep field names and options alphabetized whenever possible. So with that in mind, here's the full models.py file so far, organized and formatted so that it's clear and readable:

```
import datetime

from django.db import models
from django.contrib.auth.models import User
```

```python
from markdown import markdown
from tagging.fields import TagField


class Category(models.Model):
    description = models.TextField()
    slug = models.SlugField(prepopulate_from=['title'], unique=True,
                            help_text='Suggested value automatically generated ➥
                                                from title. Must be unique.')
    title = models.CharField(max_length=250,
                             help_text='Maximum 250 characters.')

    class Meta:
        ordering = ['title']
        verbose_name_plural = "Categories"

    class Admin:
        pass

    def __unicode__(self):
        return self.title

    def get_absolute_url(self):
        return "/categories/%s/" % self.slug


class Entry(models.Model):
    LIVE_STATUS = 1
    DRAFT_STATUS = 2
    HIDDEN_STATUS = 3
    STATUS_CHOICES = (
        (LIVE_STATUS, 'Live'),
        (DRAFT_STATUS, 'Draft'),
        (HIDDEN_STATUS, 'Hidden'),
    )


    # Core fields.
    title = models.CharField(max_length=250,
                             help_text="Maximum 250 characters.")
    excerpt = models.TextField(blank=True,
                               help_text="A short summary of the entry.➥
                                                Optional.")
    body = models.TextField()
    pub_date = models.DateTimeField(default=datetime.datetime.now)
```

```
# Fields to store generated HTML.
body_html = models.TextField(editable=False, blank=True)
excerpt_html = models.TextField(editable=False, blank=True)

# Metadata.
author = models.ForeignKey(User)
enable_comments = models.BooleanField(default=True)
featured = models.BooleanField(default=False)
slug = models.SlugField(prepopulate_from=['title'],
                        unique_for_date='pub_date',
                        help_text="Suggested value automatically generated➥
                                        from title.")
status = models.IntegerField(choices=STATUS_CHOICES,
                             default=LIVE_STATUS,
                             help_text="Only entries with 'Live' status ➥
                                    will be publicly displayed.")

# Categorization.
categories = models.ManyToManyField(Category)
tags = TagField(help_text="Separate tags with spaces.")

class Meta:
    ordering = ['-pub_date']
    verbose_name_plural = "Entries"

class Admin:
    pass

def __unicode__(self):
    return self.title

def save(self):
    self.body_html = markdown(self.body)
    if self.excerpt:
        self.excerpt_html = markdown(self.excerpt)
    super(Entry, self).save()


def get_absolute_url(self):
    return "/weblog/%s/%s/" % (self.pub_date.strftime("%Y/%b/%d").lower(),
                               self.slug)
```

Go ahead and run `manage.py syncdb` in the project directory. It'll add the new `Entry` model's table (and the join table for its many-to-many relationship to the `Category` model) and also a couple of tables for models from the tagging application you're using. Next use the administrative interface to add a couple of test entries to the weblog; you're about to start writing views for them, so you'll need some entries to work with.

Writing the First Views

Open up the `views.py` file you created inside the `coltrane` directory and add a couple of import statements at the top to include things that you'll need for these views:

```
from django.shortcuts import render_to_response
from coltrane.models import Entry
```

The first line you've seen already: `render_to_response()` is the `shortcuts` function that handles loading and rendering a template, as well as returning an `HttpResponse`. The second line imports the `Entry` model you just created, so you'll be able to retrieve entries from the database for display.

For your first view, start with a simple index that displays all of the "live" entries. Here's the code:

```
def entries_index(request):
    return render_to_response('coltrane/entry_index.html',
                              { 'entry_list': Entry.objects.all() })
```

Next create a `coltrane` directory in your `templates` directory (the directory you set up for the cms project's templates), and in it place an `entry_index.html` file. Add the following HTML in it:

```
<html>
    <head>
        <title>Entries index</title>
    </head>
    <body>
        <h1>Entries index</h1>
        {% for entry in entry_list %}
            <h2>{{ entry.title }}</h2>
            <p>Published on {{ entry.pub_date|date:"F j, Y" }}</p>
            {% if entry.excerpt_html %}
              {{ entry.excerpt_html|safe }}
            {% else %}
              {{ entry.body_html|truncatewords_html:"50"|safe }}
            {% endif %}
            <p><a href="{{ entry.get_absolute_url }}">Read full entry</a></p>
        {% endfor %}
    </body>
</html>
```

Note that you're using a filter to show the excerpt here. You'll remember that Django's template system automatically "escapes" the contents of variables to prevent cross-site scripting attacks. While you want to have that protection most of the time, you know that the contents of these variables are safe because they come from data that was entered into the admin interface by a trusted user. The `safe` filter lets you tell Django that you trust a particular variable and that it doesn't need any escaping.

Finally, you'll need to set up a URL. Open up the urls.py in the cms directory and, in the list of URL patterns, add the following before the catch-all pattern for the flat pages:

```
(r'^weblog/$', 'coltrane.views.entries_index'),
```

At that point, you should be able to visit http://127.0.0.1:8000/weblog/. You'll see all the entries you've created so far, displayed using the template you just created. There are a few things worth noting about the template:

- You're using a new filter: date. It's the first one you've seen that takes an argument, in this case a formatting string describing how to present a date. The syntax for this is similar to the syntax for the strftime() method, except that it *doesn't* use percent signs to mark formatting characters. This formatting string will produce a result like "October 10, 2007".

- You're using the if tag to test whether there's an excerpt on each entry. If there is, it's displayed. If not, the first 50 words of the entry's body will be displayed.

- When there is no excerpt, the entry's body is cut off using the truncatewords_html filter. This filter's argument tells it how many words to allow. When it's reached the limit, it ends the text fragment with ellipses (. . .), indicating to the reader that there's more text in the full entry. As the name implies, the truncatewords_html filter knows how to recognize HTML tags and doesn't count them as words. It also will keep track of open tags and close them if it cuts off the text before a closing tag. (A separate filter, truncatewords, simply cuts off at the specified number of words and pays no attention to HTML.)

Displaying an index of all the entries is a nice first step, but it's only the beginning. You'll also need to be able to display individual entries, and you'll need to query for them based on information you can read from the URL. In this case, the get_absolute_url() method on the Entry model will give a URL that contains the (formatted) pub_date and the slug of the entry. Before you write the view that retrieves the entry, let's take a look at the URL pattern for it. This gives a clue to how you'll get that information out of the URL:

```
(r'^weblog/(?P<year>\d{4})/(?P<month>\w{3})/(?P<day>\d{2})/(P?<slug>[-\w]+)/$',
                    'coltrane.views.entry_detail'),
```

This is quite a bit more complicated than the URL patterns you've seen so far. The regular expression is looking for several things and includes the strange ?P construct several times. So let's walk through it step by step.

First of all, in Python's regular-expression syntax, a set of parentheses whose contents begin with ?P, followed by a name in brackets and a pattern, matches a "named group"; any text that matches one of these parts of the URL will go into a dictionary, where the keys are the bracketed names and the values are the parts of the text that matched. This URL is looking for four named groups, then: year, month, day, and slug.

The actual patterns used in these named groups are fairly simple once that hurdle is cleared:

- The \d{4} for year will match four consecutive digits.

- The \w{3} for month will match three consecutive letters: the %b formatter you used in the get_absolute_url() method will return the month as a three-letter string like "oct" or "jun."

- The \d{2} for day will match two consecutive digits.

- The [-\w]+ for slug is somewhat tricky. It will match any sequence of consecutive characters where each character is either a letter or number, or a hyphen. This is precisely the same set of characters Django allows in a SlugField.

When a URL matches this pattern, Django will pass the named groups to the specified view function as keyword arguments. This means the entry_detail view will receive keyword arguments called year, month, day, and slug, which will make the process of looking up the entry much simpler. Let's look at how that works by writing the entry_detail view:

```
def entry_detail(request, year, month, day, slug):
    import datetime, time
    date_stamp = time.strptime(year+month+day, "%Y%b%d")
    pub_date = datetime.date(*date_stamp[:3])
    return render_to_response('coltrane/entry_detail.html',
                              { 'entry': Entry.objects.get(pub_date__year=➡
pub_date.year,

                                   pub_date__month=pub_date.month,
                                   pub_date__day=pub_date.day,
                                       slug=slug) })
```

The only complex bit here is parsing the date. First you use the strptime function in Python's standard time module, which takes a string representing a date or time, as well as a format string like the one passed to strftime(), and parses the result into a time tuple. All you need to do, then, is concatenate the year, month, and day together and supply the same format string used: get_absolute_url(). Then you can pass the first three items of that result into datetime.date to get a date object.

ADMONITION: UNDERSTANDING PYTHON FUNCTION ARGUMENTS

Functions and methods in Python can pass and receive arguments in two forms: *positional* arguments, where the meaning is determined by the order in which the arguments are passed, and *keyword* arguments, whose names are included directly with the values.

This corresponds quite neatly to Python's built-in list and dictionary types, and so two shortcuts are provided to make argument passing easier. Passing a list as an argument and prefixing it with a single asterisk (*) will cause each item of the list, in order, to be used as a separate positional argument. Passing a dictionary and prefixing it with two asterisks (**) will cause the keys of the dictionary to be used as names for separate keyword arguments and the dictionary's values to become the values of these arguments.

When a Python function needs to accept arbitrary sets of optional arguments, or to accept many different arguments based on different situations, it's common to define it like so:

```
def my_func(*args, **kwargs):
```

The function will then have access to a list named `args` containing all the positional arguments passed to it and a dictionary named `kwargs` containing all the keyword arguments passed to it. The function can then look at those variables to work out what it needs to do.

This is how the Django ORM is able to accept lookup arguments based on your model's fields. Its methods don't have fixed argument signatures, and instead accept arbitrary sets of keyword arguments defined as `**kwargs`, and then look at those arguments to work out which fields to query on.

Finally, you return a response where the template context will be the entry. The entry is retrieved using the lookup arguments, which look for entries matching the year, month, day, and slug from the URL.

Because you used `unique_for_date` on the `slug` field, this combination is enough to uniquely identify any entry in the database. The `get` method you're using here is also new. `filter` returns a `QuerySet` representing the set of all objects that match the query, but `get` tries to return one, and only one, object. (If no objects match your query, or if more than one object matches, it will raise an exception.)

Go ahead and create the template `coltrane/entry_detail.html` and fill it in any way you'd like. Next add the new URL pattern to the project's `urls.py` if you haven't already, reload the entries index page in your browser, and click the link to one of them to see the new view in action.

It's not perfect, though. If you try a properly formatted URL for a nonexistent entry (say, `/weblog/1946/sep/12/no-entry-here/`), you'll get an error message and a traceback. The exception is `Entry.DoesNotExist`, which is Django's way of telling you that there wasn't an entry matching your criteria. It would be nice to return an HTTP 404 "Page Not Found" error in this case. You could do that manually by wrapping the query in a `try` block, catching the `DoesNotExist` exception, and then returning an appropriate response. But that would be repetitive work. Trying to retrieve something that may or may not exist, and returning a 404 if it doesn't, is something you need to do a lot in web development. So instead of doing it manually, you can use a helper function Django provides for this exact purpose: `get_object_or_404()`. First, change the `import` statement at the top of `views.py` like so:

```
from django.shortcuts import get_object_or_404, render_to_response
```

Then you can rewrite the view like this:

```
def entry_detail(request, year, month, day, slug):
    import datetime, time
    date_stamp = time.strptime(year+month+day, "%Y%b%d")
    pub_date = datetime.date(*date_stamp[:3])
    entry = get_object_or_404(Entry, pub_date__year=pub_date.year,
                                     pub_date__month=pub_date.month,
                                     pub_date__day=pub_date.day,
                                     slug=slug)
```

```
        return render_to_response('coltrane/entry_detail.html',
                            { 'entry': entry })
```

The get_object_or_404() shortcut will use the same get() lookup you just tried, but it will catch the DoesNotExist exception and re-raise the exception django.http.Http404. Django's HTTP-processing code recognizes this exception and will turn it into an HTTP 404 response.

Using Django's Generic Views

So far you've only written two views—an index of entries and a detail view for them—but already it looks like this could get tedious and boring. You're going to need views for the latest entries; for browsing them by day, month, and year; and for browsing them by categories and tags. And, worse, a lot of it will be awfully repetitive: doing a query based on a date and returning one or more entries as a result. Wouldn't it be nice if you could avoid doing all that work by hand?

As it turns out, you can, by using Django's built-in generic views. There are several extremely common patterns of views that web applications need, regardless of the type of content they're presenting. So Django includes several sets of views, which are designed to work with any model and which take care of these common tasks. Broadly speaking, these tasks break down into four groups:

- Performing simple redirects and just rendering a template based on a URL

- Displaying lists of objects and individual objects

- Date-based archives

- Creation, updating, and deletion (sometimes called CRUD) of objects

The weblog will rely heavily on date-based archives, so I'll show you how that works. Go into the urls.py file and remove the pattern that routes to your entry_detail view. Replace it with this:

```
(r'^weblog/(?P<year>\d{4})/(?P<month>\w{3})/(?P<day>\d{2})/(?P<slug>[-\w]+)/$,
 'django.views.generic.date_based.object_detail', entry_info_dict),
```

This makes use of a variable named entry_info_dict, which you haven't defined. So above the list of URL patterns (but below the import statements), define it like this:

```
entry_info_dict = {
    'queryset': Entry.objects.all(),
    'date_field': 'pub_date',
}
```

Now, make one change to the entry_detail.html template. Anywhere there's a reference to the variable entry (which your view was supplying), change it to object. You can also delete the entry_detail view you previously wrote because it's no longer needed. Next go back and click through to an entry's URL in your browser. It will be retrieved properly from the database and displayed as specified in your template. URLs for nonexistent entries will return a 404, just as your entry_detail view did once you started using get_object_or_404().

How Did Django Do That?

The answer is actually pretty simple. The generic view wants to receive a couple of arguments that tell it what it needs to do, and from there it can rely on the fact that the Django database API and template system work the same way in all situations.

The `queryset` argument is the key here because (as you'll remember from Chapter 3) many of Django's database-querying methods actually return a special type of object called a `QuerySet`, which can be further filtered and modified before it performs its actual query. In this case, you pass it `Entry.objects.all()`, which is a `QuerySet` representing all the entries in the database. You also give it the argument `date_field`, which tells the generic view which field on the model represents the date you want to filter on. The remainder of the required arguments are all in the URL: `year`, `month`, `day`, and `slug` are received by the generic view the same way they were received by the `entry_detail` view, and it performs the same database query you were doing.

But since the generic view can be reused with different sets of arguments (particularly, with a different value for the `queryset` argument and possibly `date_field` and/or `slug_field`—used if the model's `slug` field isn't named `slug`—as needed), it can be used to create date-based archives for *any* model, saving you from writing all the repetitive code over and over. All you need to do is set up the right URL pattern and hand it the necessary set of arguments in a dictionary.

The date-based generic views all live in the module `django.views.generic.date_based`, and while there are seven of them total, you'll only need to use five for your weblog functionality:

- `object_detail`: As you've already seen, provides a view of an individual object.

- `archive_day`: Provides a view of all the objects on a given day.

- `archive_month`: Provides a view of all the objects in a given month.

- `archive_year`: Provides a list of all the months that have objects in them in a given year and, optionally, a full list of all the objects in that year. (This is optional because it might be an extremely large list.)

- `archive_index`: Provides a list of the latest objects.

So let's rewrite the `urls.py` file to use generic views for entries. It'll end up looking like the following code (but for simplicity's sake, I'm still using the `cms` project that's already been created):

```python
from django.conf.urls.defaults import *

from coltrane.models import Entry

entry_info_dict = {
    'queryset': Entry.objects.all(),
    'date_field': 'pub_date',
    }
```

```
    urlpatterns = patterns('',
        (r'^admin/', include('django.contrib.admin.urls')),
        (r'^search/$', 'cms.search.views.search'),
        (r'^weblog/$', 'django.views.generic.date_based.archive_index',
         entry_info_dict),
        (r'^weblog/(?P<year>\d{4}/$',
         'django.views.generic.date_based.archive_year',
         entry_info_dict),
        (r'^weblog/(?P<year>\d{4}/(?P<month>\w{3})/$',
         'django.views.generic.date_based.archive_month',
         entry_info_dict),
        (r'^weblog/(?P<year>\d{4}/(?P<month>\w{3})/(?P<day>\d{2})/$',
         'django.views.generic.date_based.archive_day',
         entry_info_dict),
        (r'^weblog/(?P<year>\d{4}/(?P<month>\w{3})/(?P<day>\d{2})/➡
(?P<slug>[-\w]+)/$',
         'django.views.generic.date_based.object_detail',
         entry_info_dict),
        (r'', include('django.contrib.flatpages.urls')),
    )
```

You'll need to create templates for each view. All of the generic views accept an optional argument to specify a custom template name to use (the argument, appropriately enough, is called template_name), but by default they'll use the following:

- archive_index will use coltrane/entry_archive.html.

- archive_year will use coltrane/entry_archive_year.html.

- archive_month will use coltrane/entry_archive_month.html.

- archive_day will use coltrane/entry_archive_day.html.

- object_detail will use coltrane/entry_detail.html.

ADMONITION: HOW THE TEMPLATE NAMES ARE DETERMINED

The default template names used by Django's generic views are all based on two pieces of information: the model the generic view is working with and the application that model lives in. In this case, the model is the Entry class, and the application is coltrane. For consistency purposes, Django lowercases both when generating the default template name.

The object_detail view, as you've already seen, makes the entry available in a variable named object. In the daily and monthly archive views, you'll get a list of entries as the variable object_list. In both cases, this is customizable by an optional argument called template_object_name. The yearly archive will—as previously explained—default to simply giving you a list of months in which entries have been published. This will be the variable date_list in the template. The `archive_index` view will supply its template with a variable called `latest`, which will contain the latest entries (up to a maximum of 15). You can use the `for` tag in the appropriate templates (just as you did previously in your hand-rolled entry index) to loop through these lists.

The daily, monthly, and yearly archives also give the template an extra variable representing the date or date range they're working with: day, month, and year, respectively. As you've seen already in the templates for the entry views you wrote by hand, you can use the date template filter to format them however you'd like.

ADMONITION: FILLING OUT THE ENTRY TEMPLATES

If you're interested in seeing a full set of (simple) example templates, they're included in the sample code you can download from the Apress web site for this book. Be aware that they do make use of some features that haven't been introduced yet, but enough has been covered that you should be able to understand most of what's going on in them.

Decoupling the URLs

At this point, between the models you've defined, Django's administrative interface, and the date-based generic views, you've got a pretty good weblog application. But already there's a big problem: it's really not reusable because its URLs are "coupled" to the particular setup you've put together:

- The set of URL patterns for the entries are sitting in the project's `urls.py`, which means you would need to copy them into any other project that needs a weblog.

- The URL patterns, and the `Entry` and `Category` models' `get_absolute_url()` methods (though you haven't set up views for categories yet) are all hard-coded and assume a particular URL layout for the site. It's a fairly sensible layout, but some users might want a different setup (for example, `/blog/` as the weblog root instead of `/weblog/`).

Let's fix that. First of all, you've already seen that Django offers the `include()` function for plugging in a set of URLs at a specific point in a project (as you've done with the administrative application). So let's create a reusable set of URLs that lives inside the weblog application. Go into its directory and create a file named `urls.py`, then copy the appropriate `import` statements and URL patterns into it:

```
from django.conf.urls.defaults import *

from coltrane.models import Entry

entry_info_dict = {
    'queryset': Entry.objects.all(),
    'date_field': 'pub_date',
    }
```

```
urlpatterns = patterns('',
    (r'^$', 'django.views.generic.date_based.archive_index', entry_info_dict),
    (r'^(?P<year>\d{4}/$', 'django.views.generic.date_based.archive_year',
     entry_info_dict),
    (r'^(?P<year>\d{4}/(?P<month>\w{3})/$',
     'django.views.generic.date_based.archive_month',
     entry_info_dict),
    (r'^(?P<year>\d{4}/(?P<month>\w{3})/(?P<day>\d{2})/$',
     'django.views.generic.date_based.archive_day',
     entry_info_dict),
    (r'^(?P<year>\d{4}/(?P<month>\w{3})/(?P<day>\d{2})/➥
(?P<slug>[-\w]+)/$',
     'django.views.generic.date_based.object_detail',
     entry_info_dict),
)
```

In the project's `urls.py`, you can remove the import of the `Entry` model and the `entry_info_dict` variable, as well as the URL patterns for the entries (the ones starting with `^weblog/`). They can all be replaced with one URL pattern:

```
(r'^weblog/', include('coltrane.urls')),
```

Notice that the URLConf module inside the weblog application doesn't include the `weblog/` prefix on any of its URL patterns. It's relying on the project to decide where to put this set of URLs.

You can also cut down on some repetitive typing here: all the views used in the weblog's URLConf start with `django.views.generic.date_based`, which isn't fun to type out over and over again. Meanwhile, there's a conspicuous empty string as the first thing in the list. That empty string isn't a URL. It's a special parameter that lets you specify a view prefix, in case all the view functions have identical module paths. Let's take advantage of that:

```
urlpatterns = patterns('django.views.generic.date_based',
    (r'^$', 'archive_index', entry_info_dict).
    (r'^(?P<year>\d{4}/$', 'archive_year', entry_info_dict),
    (r'^(?P<year>\d{4}/(?P<month>\w{3})/$', 'archive_month', entry_info_dict),
    (r'^(?P<year>\d{4}/(?P<month>\w{3})/(?P<day>\d{2})/$',
     'archive_day',
     entry_info_dict),
    (r'^(?P<year>\d{4}/(?P<month>\w{3})/(?P<day>\d{2})/(?P<slug>[-\w]+)/$',
     'object_detail',
     entry_info_dict),
)
```

Now Django will automatically prepend `django.views.generic.date_based` to all of these view function names before it tries to load them, which is much nicer.

Now you need to deal with the problem of the `get_absolute_url()` methods. On the `Entry` model, `get_absolute_url()` returns a URL with /weblog/ hard-coded into it, and that's no good. Somebody might plug these URLs into a different part of their site's URL layout. The solution is a pair of features in Django that let you give names to your URL patterns, and then specify that a function like get_absolute_url() should actually return a value by looking for URL patterns with particular names.

First, you need to make one more change to the weblog URLConf:

```
urlpatterns = patterns('django.views.generic.date_based',
        (r'^$', 'archive_index', entry_info_dict, 'coltrane_entry_archive_index'),
        (r'^(?P<year>\d{4}/$', 'archive_year', entry_info_dict, ➥
'coltrane_entry_archive_year'),
        (r'^(?P<year>\d{4})/(?P<month>\w{3})/$', 'archive_month', entry_info_dict, ➥
'coltrane_entry_archive_month'),
        (r'^(?P<year>\d{4})/(?P<month>\w{3})/(?P<day>\d{2}/)$', 'archive_day', ➥
entry_info_dict, 'coltrane_entry_archive_day'),
        (r'^(?P<year>\d{4})/(?P<month>\w{3})/(?P<day>\d{2})/(?P<slug>[-\w]+)/$', ➥
'object_detail', entry_info_dict, 'coltrane_entry_detail'),
        )
```

You've added a name to each one of these URL patterns. The names are made up of your application's name (so as to avoid name collisions with URL patterns in other applications) and a description of what the view is for.

Now you can rewrite the get_absolute_url() method on the Entry model:

```
def get_absolute_url(self):
    return ('coltrane_entry_detail', (), { 'year': self.pub_date.strftime("%Y"),
                                           'month': self.pub_date. ➥
                                           strftime("%b").lower(),
                                           'day': self.pub_date.strftime("%d"),
                                           'slug': self.slug })
get_absolute_url = models.permalink(get_absolute_url)
```

The get_absolute_url() method now returns a tuple, whose elements are as follows:

- The name of the URL pattern you want to use.

- A tuple of any positional arguments to be included in the URL (in this case, there aren't any).

- A dictionary of any keyword arguments to be included in the URL.

The last line is a new concept: a *decorator*. Decorators are special functions that do nothing on their own but can be used to change the behavior of other functions. The permalink decorator you're using here (which lives in django.db.models) will actually rewrite the get_absolute_url() function to do a reverse URL lookup. It will scan the project's URLConf looking for the URL pattern with the specified name, then use that pattern's regular expression to create the correct URL string and fill in the proper values for any arguments that need to be embedded in the URL.

Based on the URLConf you've set up for this project, it will find the /weblog/ prefix, then follow the include() to coltrane.urls, where it will find the pattern named coltrane_entry_detail and fill in the regular expression with the correct values. For an entry published on October 10, 2007, with the slug test-entry, this will generate the URL /weblog/2007/oct/10/test-entry/. If you changed the root URLConf to include the weblog URLs under blogs/ instead, it would generate /blogs/2007/oct/10/test-entry/.

ADMONITION: PYTHON DECORATOR SYNTAX

It's also possible to use a slightly different syntax for decorators in Python. They can be placed directly above the function or method's definition and prefixed with an at (@) symbol. In this case, that would have meant placing @models.permalink directly above:

```
def get_absolute_url(self):
```

This syntax was introduced in Python 2.4, so if you're using 2.4 or a later version, it will work. I generally avoid it in my Django applications, though, because Django also works with Python 2.3, where the only available syntax is to call the decorator below the function or method definition. In general, it's a good idea to write your code so that it's compatible with the largest possible number of Python versions.

And now you've completely decoupled the entry URLs from the project and from any assumptions about particular site URL layouts. These URLs can be plugged in to any project at any point in its URL hierarchy, and between include() and the permalink() decorator, the generated URLs will always be correct.

Looking Ahead

Once again, you've accomplished a lot without writing much actual code. The biggest hurdle in the weblog application so far has simply been getting a handle on the layout of a first "real" Django application and all of the assorted options Django provides to cut down on tedious and repetitive code. And it is flexible enough to be reused in any project where you need a blog.

At this point, you've got a large number of Django's most important concepts under your belt—the basic model/URL/view/template architecture, the syntax of each component, and the general principles of decoupling and code reuse (sometimes called DRY, short for "Don't Repeat Yourself," a software development guideline that says whenever possible you should have one, and only one, authoritative version of a piece of data or functionality). You might want to pause here and review what you've written so far because you're going to start picking up the pace and writing code much more quickly. Once you feel comfortable with the concepts and features introduced up to this point, move on to the next chapter. There you'll finish up the weblog models by writing the Link class, and then fill in the rest of the basic views. After that, you'll delve a bit deeper into Django's templating system and some more advanced features.

■ ■ ■
Expanding the Weblog

So far for your weblog you've written two models—Category and Entry—and set up views that will display the entries in the weblog. You still have some work to do to set up all the different views you'll want for the entries; however, before you do that, let's go back and finish up the weblog's data models by adding the final model class.

Writing the Link Model

Just as the fields on the Entry model logically broke down into groups according to how they would be used, the model you'll use to represent links—a class called Link—will need fields for several different purposes:

- **Core fields representing the link**: A title, a description and, of course, the URL to link to.

- **Metadata**: This includes the date the link was posted and the user who posted it as well as whether to allow comments for the link.

- **Categorization**: You'll accomplish this with tags.

- **Integration with an external link-posting service**: In this case, del.icio.us.

Let's begin with the basic core fields for the model (as with the Category and Entry models, this code goes in coltrane/models.py). Just as before, you'll build it up incrementally (so don't run syncdb yet):

```
class Link(models.Model):
    title = models.CharField(max_length=250)
    description = models.TextField(blank=True)
    description_html = models.TextField(blank=True)
    url = models.URLField(unique=True)
```

There's one new field type here: URLField. As the name suggests, it's meant to store a URL. In the database, it will simply be a VARCHAR column like most other text-based field types, but in automatically generated forms (like the ones displayed by the admin interface), additional validation will be performed for this field:

- The value entered will be checked against the syntax of an HTTP URL, so, for example, it must start with `http://` or `https://`.

- You won't be able to enter a nonexistent or "broken" URL. By default, Django will issue an HTTP request to the URL during validation and will refuse to accept the URL if it returns an HTTP error status (such as "404 Not Found" or "500 Internal Server Error"). This can be disabled by using the keyword argument `verify_exists=False` when setting up the `URLField`.

Also, note the keyword argument `unique=True`. As mentioned in Chapter 4, this will generate a `UNIQUE` constraint at the database level and will be enforced by Django as well. This will prevent the same link from being posted repeatedly.

Finally, the link description is optional—you might not always want to enter one—and uses two fields, just as the excerpt and body on the `Entry` model did. In a moment, you'll add a customized `save()` method to apply text-to-HTML conversion.

You already saw on the `Entry` model how to add a foreign key to a user to represent the person who posted an entry, and you can do the same with the `Link` model:

```
posted_by = models.ForeignKey(User)
```

Similarly, you can add a publication date and a slug:

```
pub_date = models.DateTimeField(default=datetime.datetime.now)
slug = models.SlugField(prepopulate_from=('title',), unique_for_date='pub_date')
```

You can add tagging just as you did with the `Entry` model:

```
tags = TagField()
```

and two Boolean fields: one for determining whether comments should be allowed and one for determining whether to post the link to an external service. In both cases, you'll default them to `True`:

```
enable_comments = models.BooleanField(default=True)
post_elsewhere = models.BooleanField('Post to del.icio.us', default=True)
```

I use del.icio.us as my link-aggregation service, so I've put that into the field's label; but later on, if you decide you want to use a different service, you should feel free to change it. When you write the custom `save()` method for this model, you'll see how to send the link to del.icio.us.

Finally, let's add a couple of more fields to get a little bit of extra metadata. It's fairly common to make a note of where you spotted a useful link, and you could use the description for that (e.g., you might enter "Link found via Slashdot"), but it's often handier to model that directly. So you'll add two more fields; one for storing the name of the person or site who pointed you to the link and one for storing the URL where you spotted the link. (Both of these are optional so that they don't have to be filled in when they're not applicable.)

```
via_name = models.CharField('Via', max_length=250, blank=True,
                            help_text='The name of the person whose site you➥
 spotted the link on. Optional.')
   via_url = models.URLField('Via URL', blank=True,
```

```
                           help_text='The URL of the site where you spotted the➡
link. Optional.')
```

You can also add a default ordering by the pub_date field and activate the admin interface

```
class Meta:
    ordering = ['-pub_date']

class Admin:
    pass
```

and a __unicode__() method so that each Link will have a useful string representation. Just as with entries, you'll use the title field for this:

```
def __unicode__(self):
    return self.title
```

And finally, you'll add a customized save() method, which needs to do two things:

- If anything was filled in for the description field, run Markdown over it and store the result in the description_html field.

- If the post_elsewhere field is True and this is the first time the link is being saved, post it to del.icio.us as well.

The first part is easy, and you can handle it in much the same way as you did the optional excerpt on entries:

```
def save(self):
    if self.description:
        self.description_html = markdown(self.description)
    super(Link, self).save()
```

The second part is a bit trickier. You'll need some way of communicating with the public link-posting API del.icio.us provides. Fortunately, there's an open source Python module available that can do this. It's called pydelicious and can be downloaded at http://code.google.com/p/pydelicious/.

ADMONITION: INSTALLING THIRD-PARTY PYTHON MODULES

Python provides a mechanism for packaging and installing modules so they can be easily distributed and reused. Most third-party Python modules and Django applications you'll encounter will work this way, so you'll be able to download a package, open it up, and, inside the resulting directory, type **python setup.py install** to install it.

The pydelicious module actually implements quite a few useful methods from the del.icio.us API, but the only one you need here is the one to publish a link. This is implemented in pydelicious as a function called add(), and that function takes five arguments:

- The del.icio.us username of the account to post the link to

- The del.icio.us password of the account to post the link to

- The URL of the link

- The title of the link

- The tags for the link, as a string with tags separated by spaces

It would be tempting to simply hard-code your own account information for the user-name and password parts, but that would cause problems down the line: you couldn't share the blog application with others (since they would get your username and password in the code), and you wouldn't be able to reuse the application with multiple blogs that post to dif-ferent del.icio.us accounts.

One good solution to that problem is to require a del.icio.us username and password to be placed in the Django settings file. This way, each site that uses the blog application can specify a different username and password and—since you won't be distributing your settings file anyway (because it has other sensitive information, like your database credentials)—there's no security fear. You'll call these settings `DELICIOUS_USER` and `DELICIOUS_PASSWORD` to make it clear what they mean.

So let's add a line at the top of `models.py` to import the Django settings you're using:

```
from django.conf import settings
```

ADMONITION: ACCESSING SETTINGS

You can access your Django settings file the same way you would access any other Python module by importing it from its location on your computer (e.g., `import cms.settings`). However, it's generally a better idea to use `from django.conf import settings`. This will enable a feature in Django that auto-matically supplies default values for many settings if you haven't filled them in.

If it feels weird to be making up new settings, don't worry. Defining and making use of additional settings is a perfectly normal and encouraged practice for Django applications (so long as each application documents any additional settings it requires); and keeping all con-figuration for a Django project in one place—the settings file—makes it easier to understand and manage a project than having "Django" settings and "application" settings spread out over multiple locations.

There's just one more thing I need to cover before you can write the finished `save()` method. The URL, title, and tags will be represented by Django as Unicode strings. Ordinarily, Django's practice of ensuring that strings stored in model fields are Unicode is a good thing: it removes a lot of the headaches of dealing with character encodings. But in this case, it's slightly problematic as well because Unicode strings don't translate directly into a series of binary bytes, so they aren't suitable to be sent out "over the wire" in a web-based API call.

So you'll need to convert the values of these fields into byte-based strings before passing them to the del.icio.us API. Django provides a helper function, `django.utils.encoding.smart_str()`, which will do this. In a lot of cases, you could probably also use Python's built-in str() and get away with it. However, Django's smart_str() can handle some situations that str() can't and also defaults to encoding the result in UTF-8 instead of ASCII (which is the default for most Python installations).

So now you can add the appropriate code to the save() method, and you're done:

```
def save(self):
    if self.description:
        self.description_html = markdown(self.description)
    if not self.id and self.post_elsewhere:
        import pydelicious
        from django.utils.encoding import smart_str
        pydelicious.add(settings.DELICIOUS_USER, settings.DELICIOUS_PASSWORD,
                        smart_str(self.url), smart_str(self.title),
                        smart_str(self.tags))
    super(Link, self).save()
```

The if not self.id and self.post_elsewhere are important to note because they work out all the logic to determine whether the link should be posted externally. The check for self.id is the key because that tells you whether the link is being saved for the first time or not (reposting the link over and over again every time it's saved wouldn't be useful). Remember that if you don't specify a primary key for a model, Django adds one automatically in a field named id, so if that field doesn't have a value, it must not have been saved to the database yet.

As a finishing touch to the Link model, you'll add a get_absolute_url() method. Just as you did with the Entry model, you'll use the permalink decorator to enable it to do a reverse look up in the project URLConf:

```
def get_absolute_url(self):
    return ('coltrane_link_detail', (), { 'year': self.pub_date.strftime('%Y'),
                                           'month': self.pub_date.strftime('%b')➥
.lower(),
                                           'day': self.pub_date.strftime('%d'),
                                           'slug': self.slug })
get_absolute_url = models.permalink(get_absolute_url)
```

You haven't yet defined any URL patterns for links, so there isn't a pattern named coltrane_link_detail. You'll add that in a moment.

At this point, you've got the Link model fully written, and you can run manage.py syncdb to install its database table. For reference, here's the full model definition with the fields neatly organized and some additional help_text mixed in, just as for the Entry model:

```
class Link(models.Model):
    # Metadata.
    enable_comments = models.BooleanField(default=True)
    post_elsewhere = models.BooleanField('Post to del.icio.us',
                                         default=True,
                                         help_text='If checked, this link will➥
 be posted both to your weblog and to your del.icio.us account.')
    posted_by = models.ForeignKey(User)
    pub_date = models.DateTimeField(default=datetime.datetime.now)
```

```
        slug = models.SlugField(prepopulate_from=('title',),
                                unique_for_date='pub_date',
                                help_text='Must be unique for the publication
date.')
        title = models.CharField(max_length=250)

        # The actual link bits.
        description = models.TextField(blank=True)
        description_html = models.TextField(editable=False, blank=True)
        via_name = models.CharField('Via', max_length=250, blank=True,
                                help_text='The name of the person whose site you➥
spotted the link on. Optional.')
        via_url = models.URLField('Via URL', verify_exists=False, blank=True,
                                help_text='The URL of the site where you spotted➥
the link. Optional.')
        tags = TagField()
        url = models.URLField('URL', unique=True)

        class Meta:
            ordering = ['-pub_date']

        class Admin:
            pass

        def __unicode__(self):
            return self.title

        def save(self):
            if not self.id and self.post_elsewhere:
                import pydelicious
                pydelicious.add(settings.DELICIOUS_USER,
                            settings.DELICIOUS_PASSWORD,
                            smart_str(self.url),
                            smart_str(self.title),
                            smart_str(self.tags))
            if self.description:
                self.description_html = markdown(self.description)
            super(Link, self).save()

        def get_absolute_url(self):
            return ('coltrane_link_detail', (),
                        { 'year': self.pub_date.strftime('%Y'),
                          'month': self.pub_date.strftime('%b').lower(),
                          'day': self.pub_date.strftime('%d'),
                          'slug': self.slug })
        get_absolute_url = models.permalink(get_absolute_url)
```

Views for the `Link` Model

You saw in the last chapter that Django's built-in generic views provide an easy way to handle common types of views. By passing the right parameters into a generic view, you can often save quite a bit of time and code when all you want is, for example, to display a list of model objects or a detail of a single object.

The situation is no different with the `Link` model. You want to have a detail view of each individual link and a date-based archive for browsing through all of the links in the database. So open up the `urls.py` file inside the weblog application, and change this line

```
from coltrane.models import Entry
```

to read

```
from coltrane.models import Entry, Link
```

Then, just as with the `Entry` model, you'll need to define a dictionary with arguments for the generic views:

```
link_info_dict = {
    'queryset': Link.objects.all(),
    'date_field': 'pub_date',
    }
```

Next you can add a new set of URL patterns to the existing list:

```
    (r'^links/$',
      'archive_index', link_info_dict,
      'coltrane_link_archive_index'),
    (r'^links/(?P<year>\d{4})/$',
     'archive_year', link_info_dict,
     'coltrane_link_archive_year'),
    (r'^links/(?P<year>\d{4})/(?P<month>\w{3})/$',
     'archive_month', link_info_dict,
     'coltrane_link_archive_month'),
    (r'^links/(?P<year>\d{4})/(?P<month>\w{3})/(?P<day>\d{2})/$',
     'archive_day', link_info_dict,
     'coltrane_link_archive_day'),
    (r'^links/(?P<year>\d{4})/(?P<month>\w{3})/(?P<day>\d{2})/➥
(?P<slug>[-\w]+)/$',
      'object_detail', link_info_dict,
      'coltrane_link_detail'),
```

When you used them for the `Entry` model, the template names for the views were (in order):

- `coltrane/entry_archive.html`

- `coltrane/entry_archive_year.html`

- `coltrane/entry_archive_month.html`

- coltrane/entry_archive_day.html

- coltrane/entry_detail.html

Now that you're also using generic views for the Link model, you'll need a slightly different set of templates:

- coltrane/link_archive.html

- coltrane/link_archive_year.html

- coltrane/link_archive_month.html

- coltrane/link_archive_day.html

- coltrane/link_detail.html

The variable names available in these templates will be the same as before, so it should be easy to work with them. For example, in the detail view, the Link object will be available in a variable named object. If you'd like to, go ahead and set up the templates for now, but in the next chapter you'll be taking a more detailed look at Django's template system and how it can greatly reduce the amount of repetitive work involved in writing templates.

Setting Up Views for Categories

At this point, you've got most of the weblog's features set up. The models are written, and thanks to generic views, you have an easy way to view date-based archives of entries and links, as well as individual Entry and Link objects on their own detail pages. But there are still two groups of views you need to handle:

- Views for browsing entries by categories

- Views for browsing entries and links by tags

Let's start with categories. You'll need two views for categories: one to display a list of all the categories in use and another to display the list of entries in a specific category. So open up the views.py file in the weblog application and add the following at the top, after the import statements that are already there:

```
from coltrane.models import Category
```

Writing the view that shows a list of categories is pretty easy. All you have to do is retrieve the list from the database and hand it off to the template. For the sake of consistency with how the generic views do things, you'll pass the list of categories to the template in a variable named object_list, and you'll use the template name coltrane/category_list.html (for reasons that will become clear in a few minutes):

```
def category_list(request):
    return render_to_response('coltrane/category_list.html',
                              { 'object_list': Category.objects.all() })
```

Displaying a list of entries in a particular category is only slightly more complex. Since each category has a SlugField suitable for use in a URL, you'll assume that the URL matches an argument called slug. You'll use that to look up the category (using get_object_or_404() to return a "404 Not Found" error if there isn't a category matching the slug given in the URL).

And once you have the Category object, accessing the list of entries is easy. Django knows about the relationship set up by the ManyToManyField on Entry, and it will ensure that each Category will have an attribute called entry_set, which can be used to access the entries that have been assigned to it. This attribute behaves much like the objects attribute on the Entry model. It has all the same methods—all() and filter(), for example—as Entry.objects, except it only returns entries assigned to that particular Category.

Following is the view, using coltrane/category_detail as the template name and, again, using the name object_list for the variable that holds the list of entries:

```
def category_detail(request, slug):
    category = get_object_or_404(Category, slug=slug)
    return render_to_response('coltrane/category_detail.html',
                              { 'object_list': category.entry_set.all(),
                                'category': category })
```

Next you can just add a couple of more patterns in the weblog application's urls.py file. The only tricky thing here is that you've already specified a prefix of django.views.generic. date_based for the URL patterns there, and these two views live in coltrane.views. You could remove the prefix and manually add django.views.generic.date_based to all those views again, but there's an easier way to solve this problem. Notice how the list of patterns begins:

```
urlpatterns = patterns('django.views.generic.date_based',
```

This is calling a function named patterns() (which, if you look up at the top of the file, is imported from django.conf.urls.defaults), which parses each pattern passed into it, and then returns a list of URL patterns in a standardized format Django can work with. That list ends up in a variable named urlpatterns. Since the end result is just an ordinary Python list, you can continue working with it. In this case, you're going to take advantage of the fact that Python lists can be added together with the plus sign (+) operator. You simply call patterns() a second time and add the result onto the urlpatterns variable you already have. However, this time you'll use a different prefix: coltrane.views.

So add the following code at the bottom of urls.py (you're actually using += instead of just + because it means a slightly shorter piece of code):

```
urlpatterns += patterns('coltrane.views',
    (r'^categories/$', 'category_list'),
    (r'^categories/(?P<slug>[-\w]+)/$', 'category_detail'),
)
```

Now you have views and URLs set up. You'll deal with templates for them in the next chapter. For now, let's focus on some ways you can improve what you've got here.

Using Generic Views (Again)

This is really more work than you need to do. You've already seen how generic views make it easy to set up date-based archives, and they're also pretty handy at handling non-date-based lists of objects. The module `django.views.generic.list_detail` contains two views, which produce non-date-based results:

- `object_list` simply takes the `queryset` argument you've already seen and fetches a list of objects.

- `object_detail` (which you won't be using in this application but is worth mentioning) takes the `queryset` argument, and either an `object_id` argument corresponding to an object's primary key or a combination of `slug_field` and `slug` arguments, and returns a `detail` view of a single object.

So you don't actually need the `category_list` view. The `object_list` generic view will do the same thing. Go back to the `urls.py` file and make one more change to the `import` statement that pulls in the weblog models. Change it from

```
from coltrane.models import Entry, Link
```

to

```
from coltrane.models import Category, Entry, Link
```

Then go back to the extra set of patterns you just added for the categories and change it to this:

```
urlpatterns += patterns('',
    (r'^categories/$',
     'django.views.generic.list_detail.object_list',
     { 'queryset': Category.objects.all() }),
    (r'^categories/(?P<slug>[-\w]+)/$',
     'coltrane.views.category_detail'),
)
```

The `object_list` generic view, by default, will use a template name of `coltrane/category_list.html` (which is why it was a good idea to choose that from the start for the original `category_list` view) and pass in the list of categories in a variable named `object_list`. This has the same effect as your manually written view (which can now be deleted).

You might be wondering at this point whether it's possible to use a generic view for the list of entries in a category. It doesn't seem as if there's any way to tell the generic view to also filter the entries based on the categories they belong to, since the exact filtering that needs to be done will vary according to which category you're looking at.

But there *is* a way to use a generic view here. The trick is to remember that, in Django, a view is simply a Python function that accepts an `HttpRequest` object (and potentially a set of additional arguments) and returns an `HttpResponse` object. This means that it's possible to write one view that imports and calls another view, as well as returns its response.

If that sounds confusing, here's how you could write a variation of the `category_detail` view that uses the `object_list` generic view:

```
from django.views.generic.list_detail import object_list

def category_detail(request, slug):
    category = get_object_or_404(Category, slug=slug)
    return object_list(request, queryset=category.entry_set.all(),
                       extra_context={ 'category': category }))
```

Let's break down what's happening here:

1. You import the `object_list` generic view from `django.views.generic.list_detail` (the other things you'll be using, like the `Category` model and the `get_object_or_404()` shortcut, have already been imported inside the `views.py` file).

2. You define your view function, `category_detail`, to accept the HTTP request and a slug.

3. You use `get_object_or_404()` to either get the `Category` corresponding to the `slug` argument or return a "404 Not Found" error.

4. You call the `object_list` generic view directly, passing along the HTTP request and setting its `queryset` argument to the set of entries in this specific category, and return the response directly.

5. You pass an extra argument, `extra_context`. Most of Django's generic views accept this argument, and it lets you specify extra variables and values to make available to the template. In this case, you're adding the `Category` object.

In effect, you're "wrapping" the generic view up inside another view function that does some preliminary work to filter the eventual `QuerySet` it will use.

Given how simple the original `category_detail` view was, this may seem like a strange way of doing things, and for this specific case it's probably not worth the effort of wrapping a generic view. But this is an *extremely* powerful pattern to keep in the back of your mind. There will be many times when you'll need something like a generic view, but with a little bit of extra filtering or processing. Using this sort of wrapper can, in more complex cases, often lead to a significant reduction in the amount of code you have to write by hand.

Views for Tags

You still need a set of views to handle browsing of entries and links by tags. As it turns out, though, you don't have to write them. The tagging application you're using provides a model, called `Tag`, to represent the tags, and you can simply use the `object_list` generic view to show a list of them.

Add one more import statement at the top of the `urls.py` file:

```
from tagging.models import Tag
```

And you'll add another set of URL patterns at the bottom:

```
urlpatterns += patterns('',
    (r'^tags/$',
     'django.views.generic.list_detail.object_list',
     { 'queryset': Tag.objects.all() }),
)
```

The tagging application also provides one view—written in the same general style as Django's built-in generic views—for showing all the objects from a particular model that have a particular tag. This view is tagging.views.tagged_object_list, and you need to give it three arguments:

- queryset_or_model: This will be the model class or QuerySet whose objects you want to view, and you'll pass it in directly in the URL pattern.

- tag: This can be either a Tag object or the name of a tag, and you'll set up the pattern so that it's read out of the URL.

- template_name: This is the name of the template the view will use. If it's not specified, it will default to tagging/tag_list.html, so you'll use something descriptive to make it easier to keep track of what's going on.

So all you need to do is add two more patterns: one for browsing entries by tag and one for browsing links by tag. You start with the pattern you already set up for the tag list:

```
urlpatterns += patterns('',
    (r'^tags/$',
     'django.views.generic.list_detail.object_list',
     { 'queryset': Tag.objects.all() }),
)
```

and add the two new patterns:

```
urlpatterns += patterns('',
    (r'^tags/$',
     'django.views.generic.list_detail.object_list',
     { 'queryset': Tag.objects.all() }),
    (r'^tags/entries/(?P<tag>[-\w]+)/$',
     'tagging.views.tagged_object_list',
     { 'queryset_or_model': Entry,
       'template_name': 'coltrane/entries_by_tag.html' }),
    (r'^tags/links/(?P<tag>[-\w]+)/$',
     'tagging.views.tagged_object_list',
     { 'queryset_or_model': Link,
       'template_name': 'coltrane/links_by_tag.html' }),
)
```

The tagged_object_list view is actually a wrapper around the object_list generic view, like the one you saw previously for the category_detail view but slightly more complex. (This is a case where wrapping a generic view *does* significantly reduce the amount of code.) Because of this, it will provide the list of objects to the template in a variable named object_list, making it nice and consistent with all of your other views.

Cleaning Up the URLConf

By this point, the `urls.py` file in the weblog application is starting to get unwieldy. Currently, it looks like the following:

```python
from django.conf.urls.defaults import *

from coltrane.models import Category, Entry, Link
from tagging.models import Tag

entry_info_dict = {
    'queryset': Entry.objects.all(),
    'date_field': 'pub_date',
    }

link_info_dict = {
    'queryset': Link.objects.all(),
    'date_field': 'pub_date',
    }

urlpatterns = patterns('django.views.generic.date_based',
    (r'^$', 'archive_index', entry_info_dict, 'coltrane_entry_archive_index'),
    (r'^(?P<year>\d{4})/$', 'archive_year',
     entry_info_dict,
     'coltrane_entry_archive_year'),
    (r'^(?P<year>\d{4})/(?P<month>\w{3})/$',
     'archive_month', entry_info_dict,
     'coltrane_entry_archive_month'),
    (r'^(?P<year>\d{4})/(?P<month>\w{3})/(?P<day>\d{2})/$',
     'archive_day',
     entry_info_dict,
     'coltrane_entry_archive_day'),
    (r'^(?P<year>\d{4})/(?P<month>\w{3})/(?P<day>\d{2})/(?P<slug>[-\w]+)/$',
     'object_detail',
     entry_info_dict,
     'coltrane_entry_detail'),
    (r'^links/$',
     'archive_index',
     link_info_dict,
     'coltrane_link_archive_index'),
    (r'^links/(?P<year>\d{4})/$',
     'archive_year',
     link_info_dict,
     'coltrane_link_archive_year'),
    (r'^links/(?P<year>\d{4})/(?P<month>\w{3})/$',
     'archive_month', link_info_dict, 'coltrane_link_archive_month'),
    (r'^links/(?P<year>\d{4})/(?P<month>\w{3})/(?P<day>\d{2})/$',
     'archive_day', link_info_dict, 'coltrane_link_archive_day'),
```

```
            (r'^links/(?P<year>\d{4})/(?P<month>\w{3})/(?P<day>\d{2})/➥
(?P<slug>[-\w]+)/$',
             'object_detail',
             link_info_dict,
             'coltrane_link_detail'),
    )

    urlpatterns += patterns('',
        (r'^categories/$',
         'django.views.generic.list_detail.object_list',
         { 'queryset': Category.objects.all() }),
        (r'^categories/(?P<slug>[-\w]+)/$',
         'coltrane.views.category_detail'),
    )

    urlpatterns += patterns('',
        (r'^tags/$', 'django.views.generic.list_detail.object_list',
         { 'queryset': Tag.objects.all() }),
        (r'^tags/entries/(?P<tag>[-\w]+)/$',
         'tagging.views.tagged_object_list',
         { 'queryset_or model': Entry,
           'template_name': 'coltrane/entries_by_tag.html' }),
        (r'^tags/links/(?P<tag>[-\w]+)/$',
         'tagging.views.tagged_object_list',
         { 'queryset_or_model': Link,
           'template_name': 'coltrane/links_by_tag.html' }),
    )
```

All together, you've got four models, two dictionaries of keyword arguments for generic views and three sets of URL patterns that get added together to make up the final set. This makes it a bit tricky to follow exactly what's going on, so let's reorganize a bit.

Inside the weblog application's directory, create a directory called urls, and inside it create five files:

- __init__.py (to signify that this will be a Python module)

- categories.py

- entries.py

- links.py

- tags.py

What you're going to do is break up the mess you currently have into four logical groups of URL patterns, each inside its own file. From there, you'll be able to use include() directives to add any or all of these URL patterns to any site that happens to be using the weblog application. Let's look at how this breaks down in each file.

In `categories.py`:

```python
from django.conf.urls.defaults import *

from coltrane.models import Category

urlpatterns = patterns('',
    (r'^$', 'django.views.generic.list_detail.object_list',
     { 'queryset': Category.objects.all() }),
    (r'^(?P<slug>[-\w]+)/$', 'coltrane.views.category_detail'),
)
```

Note that it's `urlpatterns = patterns('',` not `urlpatterns += patterns('',`. There will be only one set of patterns per file, so you don't need to add patterns together as you did when they were all in one file. Also, the URLs no longer have "categories/" in them. Because this is now intended to be accessed by an `include()` directive somewhere else, you can gain a little more flexibility by not requiring that the URLs contain the string "categories/".

In `entries.py`:

```python
from django.conf.urls.defaults import *

from coltrane.models import Entry

entry_info_dict = {
    'queryset': Entry.objects.all(),
    'date_field': 'pub_date',
    }

urlpatterns = patterns('django.views.generic.date_based',
    (r'^$', 'archive_index', entry_info_dict, 'coltrane_entry_archive_index'),
    (r'^(?P<year>\d{4})/$',
     'archive_year', entry_info_dict,
     'coltrane_entry_archive_year'),
    (r'^(?P<year>\d{4})/(?P<month>\w{3})/$',
     'archive_month',
     entry_info_dict,
     'coltrane_entry_archive_month'),
    (r'^(?P<year>\d{4})/(?P<month>\w{3})/(?P<day>\d{2})/$',
     'archive_day',
     entry_info_dict,
     'coltrane_entry_archive_day'),
    (r'^(?P<year>\d{4})/(?P<month>\w{3})/(?P<day>\d{2})/(?P<slug>[-\w]+)/$',
     'object_detail',
     entry_info_dict,
     'coltrane_entry_detail'),
)
```

In `links.py`:

```python
from django.conf.urls.defaults import *

from coltrane.models import Link

link_info_dict = {
    'queryset': Link.objects.all(),
    'date_field': 'pub_date',
    }

urlpatterns = patterns('django.views.generic.date_based',
    (r'^$', 'archive_index', link_info_dict, 'coltrane_link_archive_index'),
    (r'^(?P<year>\d{4})/$',
     'archive_year',
     link_info_dict,
     'coltrane_link_archive_year'),
    (r'^(?P<year>\d{4})/(?P<month>\w{3})/$',
     'archive_month', link_info_dict,
     'coltrane_link_archive_month'),
    (r'^(?P<year>\d{4})/(?P<month>\w{3})/(?P<day>\d{2})/$', 'archive_day',
     link_info_dict,
     'coltrane_link_archive_day'),
    (r'^(?P<year>\d{4})/(?P<month>\w{3})/(?P<day>\d{2})/(?P<slug>[-\w]+)/$',
     'object_detail',
     link_info_dict,
     'coltrane_link_detail'),
)
```

Just as with the category URLs, you've removed the `"links/"` bit from these patterns. And in `tags.py`:

```python
from django.conf.urls.defaults import *
from coltrane.models import Entry, Link
from tagging.models import Tag

urlpatterns = patterns('',
    (r'^$',
     'django.views.generic.list_detail.object_list',
     { 'queryset': Tag.objects.all() }),
    (r'^entries/(?P<tag>[-\w]+)/$',
     'tagging.views.tagged_object_list',
     { 'queryset_or_model': Entry,
       'template_name': 'coltrane/entries_by_tag.html' }),
    (r'^links/(?P<tag>[-\w]+)/$',
     'tagging.views.tagged_object_list',
     { 'queryset_or_model': Link,
       'template_name': 'coltrane/links_by_tag.html' }),
)
```

Again, as with categories and links, the "tags/" bit has gone away.

Once you've set up these files, you should delete the original urls.py from the weblog application's folder.

Now you can go back to the project's root URLConf, which had a pattern like this:

```
(r'^weblog/', include('coltrane.urls')),
```

and then pull in the individual bits where you want them:

```
(r'^weblog/categories/', include('coltrane.urls.categories')),
(r'^weblog/links/', include('coltrane.urls.links')),
(r'^weblog/tags/', include('coltrane.urls.tags')),
(r'^weblog/', include('coltrane.urls.entries')),
```

Although you now have several URLConf files inside the weblog application, and you need multiple include() directives to use them all, you've gained two big advantages.

- The weblog URLs are now much more manageable because they're broken up into small units that only contain sets of URLs that logically belong together.

- Because they're no longer jumbled together into one file, it's easy to use include() to put a specific group of patterns at any spot in a site's URL hierarchy. This means you're no longer tied to specific prefixes like "links/" or "tags/" if you don't want them.

As a general rule, any application whose URL patterns logically fall into related groups like these should have them broken up into multiple separate files for precisely these reasons. The benefits far outweigh the downside of having to deal with several files.

Handling Live Entries

Before you move on to the last part of the weblog—templating and comments, which I'll cover in the next chapter—let's solve one more missing feature.

You'll recall that when you set up the Entry model, you gave it a field called status, which allows entries to be marked as Live, Draft, or Hidden. At the moment, none of your views are taking that into account. If you add an entry with a status other than Live, you'll notice that it still shows up in all of the archive and detail views.

You've already seen that you can use the filter() method to get only the objects that match certain specific criteria. At first, that seems like an easy way to handle this. Anywhere you're using this:

```
Entry.objects.all()
```

you could just replace it with this:

```
Entry.objects.filter(status=Entry.LIVE_STATUS)
```

Remember that you defined named constants for the different status values to make these kinds of queries easier. But this is going to involve an awful lot of typing. You'll need to remember to type that extra query argument anywhere you're querying for entries. It would be much nicer if you could have a separate way of querying entries that only returns objects with the status field set to Live, maybe something like Entry.live.all() instead of Entry.objects. all(). This is actually pretty easy to do, but it requires the introduction of one more major feature of Django's model system: managers.

Up until now, I've been glossing over how Django actually does database queries. I've just been discussing things like Entry.objects.all() or FlatPage.objects.filter() without really talking about that special attribute called objects or where it comes from.

The objects attribute is an instance of a special class (django.db.models.Manager), which is meant to be "attached" to a particular model class, and which knows how to perform all sorts of database queries. In addition to the methods you've already seen—all() and filter()—it has a large number of other methods that can return single specific objects, return lists of objects, return other data structures corresponding to data stored by a model, change the ordering used to return results, and handle a variety of other useful tasks. Full documentation of the database API and all of its methods and options is available online at www.djangoproject.com/documentation/db-api/.

If you don't specify a manager for your model, Django adds one and calls it objects (this happens automatically for any class that subclasses django.db.models.Model). However, you're free to attach a manager with any name you like, and if you do, Django won't bother with the automatic default objects manager. For example, you could define a model like so:

```
class MyModel(models.Model):
    name = models.CharField(max_length=50)

    object_fetcher = models.Manager()
```

Then, instead of using, say, MyModel.objects.all(), you would use MyModel.object_ fetcher.all(). All of the standard querying methods will be there, just in an attribute with the name you've specified.

The most important thing about managers, however, is that you can easily define your own manager classes and give them customized behavior by writing a subclass of django.db. models.Manager and overriding the methods you want to customize. In this case you want to write a manager that, when attached to the Entry model, will only return entries whose status is Live. You can do this by writing a subclass of Manager and overriding one method, get_query_set(), which returns the initial QuerySet object that all(), filter(), and all the other querying methods will use. Doing this is surprisingly easy:

```
class LiveEntryManager(models.Manager):
    def get_query_set(self):
        return super(LiveEntryManager, self).get_query_set().filter(➥
status=self.model.LIVE_STATUS)
```

The only tricky bit here is that you're using self.model.LIVE_STATUS as the value to filter on. Every Manager that's been attached to a model can access that model class through the attribute self.model.

Place the preceding code in the weblog application's models.py file, somewhere *above* the definition of the Entry model. Then add the following lines inside the Entry model:

```
live = LiveEntryManager()
objects = models.Manager()
```

This gives the Entry model *two* managers. One is called objects and is just the standard manager every model normally gets. The other is an instance of the LiveEntryManager, which means you can now write

```
Entry.live.all()
```

and it will do precisely what you want it to do. Note that you have to define objects manually. When a model has a custom manager, Django doesn't automatically set up the objects manager for you.

Now you can simply perform a search and replace on the weblog code, changing any use of Entry.objects to Entry.live, and that will take care of any situations where you're querying for entries (only one so far, but if you had gone much further it could easily have been more).

There are two other places, though, where you'll need to worry about filtering for only live entries—when you retrieve entries for a specific category or tag. For categories, you can solve this fairly easily by adding a method on the Category model:

```
def live_entry_set(self):
    from coltrane.models import Entry
    return self.entry_set.filter(status=Entry.LIVE_STATUS)
```

And now, anywhere you used the entry_set attribute of a Category, you can simply replace it with a call to live_entry_set(). So, for example, the category_detail view will now look like this:

```
def category_detail(request, slug):
    category = get_object_or_404(Category, slug=slug)
    return render_to_response('coltrane/category_detail.html',
                              { 'object_list': category.live_entry_set() })
```

With tags it's a bit trickier, but you can still make it work. Remember that the argument the tagged_object_list view receives is called queryset_or_model. This means you can pass it either a model class, like Link, or a QuerySet. So where you're using the tagged_object_list view with the Entry model as an argument, change it to use Entry.live.all() instead.

Looking Ahead

The weblog application is almost complete now. There are only a couple of features left to add, and for them you'll be using applications bundled with Django plus a few customizations. I'll cover those in Chapter 7, but in the next chapter you'll take a much more detailed look at Django's template system, writing templates for the blog, and even writing a couple of custom template tags.

If you'd like to pause for a little while and play with the weblog application before moving on to Chapter 6, feel free to do so. Even without the comment system and template techniques you'll cover in the next chapter, this weblog application is already a pretty solid piece of software and offers a significant subset of the functionality of popular off-the-shelf weblog systems like Wordpress (but with significantly less code).

■■■

Templates for the Weblog

Your weblog application is almost complete. Over the last two chapters, you've implemented entries, links, and nearly all the attendant functionality you wanted to have with them. There are only two features left to implement—a comment system and syndication feeds—and Django is going to give you quite a bit of help with those, as you'll see in the next chapter.

But so far you've focused pretty exclusively on the "back end" of the site—the Python code that models your data, retrieves it from the database, lays out your URL structure, and so on—to the expense of the "front end," or the actual HTML you'll show to your site's visitors. You've seen how Django's generic views expose your database objects for use in templates (e.g., the `object_list` variable in the date-based archives). However, it's a big step from that to an attractive and usable weblog. Let's take a deeper look at Django's template system, and how you can use it to make the front end as easy as the back.

Dealing with Repetitive Elements: The Power of Inheritance

You're using Django's generic views to show both entries and links. Whether you're looking at the detail view of an `Entry` or of a `Link`, the actual Python code involved is the date-based `object_detail` generic view, which provides a variable named `object` to the template and represents the database object it retrieved. The biggest difference is that, for an `Entry`, the generic view will use a template named `coltrane/entry_detail.html` and for a `Link` it will use `coltrane/link_detail.html`.

Because the contexts are so similar, the templates will end up looking very much alike; for example, a simple `entry_detail` template might look like the following:

```
<!DOCTYPE html PUBLIC "-//W3C//DTD XHTML 1.0 Strict//EN"
                "http://www.w3.org/TR/xhtml1/DTD/xhtml1-strict.dtd">
<html xmlns="http://www.w3.org/1999/xhtml" lang="en" xml:lang="en">
<head>
<title>Weblog: {{ object.title }}</title>
</head>
<body>
<h1>{{ object.title }}</h1>
```

```
{{ object.body_html|safe }}
</body>
</html>
```

And a simple `link_detail` might look like this:

```
<!DOCTYPE html PUBLIC "-//W3C//DTD XHTML 1.0 Strict//EN"
                "http://www.w3.org/TR/xhtml1/DTD/xhtml1-strict.dtd">
<html xmlns="http://www.w3.org/1999/xhtml" lang="en" xml:lang="en">
<head>
<title>Weblog: {{ object.title }}</title>
</head>
<body>
<h1>{{ object.title }}</h1>
{{ object.description_html|safe }}
<p><a href="{{ object.url }}">Visit site</a></p>
</body>
</html>
```

Of course, for a finished site you'd want to do quite a bit more, but already it's apparent that there's a lot of repetition. There's all sorts of HTML boilerplate, which is the same in both templates, and even things like the `<title>` element and the `<h1>` heading have the same contents. Typing all of that over and over again is going to be awfully tedious, especially as the HTML gets more complex; and if you ever make changes to the HTML structure of a site, you'll have to make them in every single template. Django's been great so far at helping you avoid this sort of tedious and repetitive work on the Python side of things, so naturally it would be nice if it could do the same on the HTML side as well.

And it can. Django's template system supports a concept of *template inheritance*, which works in a way that's reminiscent of how subclassing works in normal Python code. Essentially, the Django template system lets you write a template with placeholders (called *blocks*) for sections of a page. These will vary from one template to the next, and then you'll write templates to "extend" that template and fill in the placeholders.

To see it in action, let's work through a simple example. Create a file in the root template directory for the project and name it `base.html`. This name isn't required, but it's a common practice and will help others to understand its purpose. In that file, put the following code:

```
<!DOCTYPE html PUBLIC "-//W3C//DTD XHTML 1.0 Strict//EN"
                "http://www.w3.org/TR/xhtml1/DTD/xhtml1-strict.dtd">
<html xmlns="http://www.w3.org/1999/xhtml" lang="en" xml:lang="en">
<head>
<title>Weblog: {{ object.title }}</title>
</head>
<body>
<h1>{{ object.title }}</h1>
{% block content %}
{% endblock %}
</body>
</html>
```

Now, edit the `coltrane/entry_detail.html` template so that it contains *nothing* but this:

```
{% extends "base.html" %}

{% block content %}
{{ object.body_html|safe }}
{% endblock %}
```

Next, edit `coltrane/link_detail.html` so that it contains nothing but this:

```
{% extends "base.html" %}

{% block content %}
{{ object.description_html|safe }}
<p><a href="{{ object.url }}">Visit site</a></p>
{% endblock %}
```

Finally, fire up the development server and visit a link or entry in the weblog, and then view the HTML source of the page. You'll see all the HTML boilerplate that's in `base.html`, and the area where `base.html` had an empty "content" block will be filled in by the appropriate results, according to whether you're looking at an entry or a link.

This is just a simple example. As your templates get more complex, the ability to factor out repetitive pieces like this is going to become a lifesaver. It'll cut down on both the time needed to put templates together and the time needed to change them later (since a change in a single "base" template will automatically show up in any templates that extend it).

How Template Inheritance Works

Template inheritance revolves around the two new tags seen in the previous example: `{% block %}` and `{% extends %}`. Essentially, the `{% block %}` tag lets you carve out a section of a template and give it a name, and possibly even some default content. The `{% extends %}` tag lets you specify the name of another template—which should contain one or more blocks—and then just fill in content for any blocks you want to use. The rest of the content, including default content from any blocks you didn't override, will automatically be filled in from the template you're extending. Additionally, within a block, you'll have access to the content that *would* have gone there if you weren't supplying your own. This is stored in a special variable named `block.super`. So if you had a base template that contained this:

```
{% block title %}My weblog:{% endblock %}
```

you could write a template that extended it, and fill in your own content:

```
{% block title %}My page{% endblock %}
```

Using `block.super`, you could access the default content from the parent block to get a final value of `My weblog: My page`:

```
{% block title %}{{ block.super }} My page{% endblock%}
```

Limits of Template Inheritance

As you start to work with inheritance in templates, there are a few caveats you'll want to keep in mind:

- If you use the {% extends %} tag, it must be the first thing in the template. Django needs to know up front that you're going to be extending another template.

- Each named block, if used, can appear only once in a given template. Just as HTML only permits you to have a single element with a given ID inside a single page, Django's template system only permits you to have a single block with a given name inside a single template.

- A template can only directly extend one other template—multiple uses of {% extends %} in the same template are invalid. However, the template being extended can, in turn, extend another template, leading to a chain of inheritance down through multiple templates.

This ability to "chain" inherited templates is key to a common pattern in template development. Often, a site will have multiple sections or areas that don't vary much from one another, so the templates end up forming a three-layered structure:

1. A single base template containing the common HTML of all pages.

2. Section-specific base templates that fill in appropriate navigation and/or theming, which extend the base template.

3. The "actual" templates that will be loaded and rendered by the views, which extend the appropriate template for their section.

In fact, this pattern is so common and so useful that you're going to use it for your blog's templates. Let's get started.

Defining the Base Template for the Blog

Building up a useful base template for a site largely consists of determining what the site's overall look and feel will be, writing out the appropriate HTML to support it, and then determining which areas will need to vary from page to page and turning them into blocks.

For this blog, let's go with a common visual layout—a header at the top of the page with room for a site logo, and two columns below it. One column will contain the main content of the page, the other a sidebar with navigation, metadata, and other useful information.

In HTML terms, this works out to three div elements: one for the header area, then one each for the content area and the sidebar. The structure looks like this:

```
<!DOCTYPE html PUBLIC "-//W3C//DTD XHTML 1.0 Strict//EN"
                "http://www.w3.org/TR/xhtml1/DTD/xhtml1-strict.dtd">
<html xmlns="http://www.w3.org/1999/xhtml" lang="en" xml:lang="en">
<head>
  <title></title>
</head>
<body>
```

```
    <div id="header"></div>
    <div id="content"></div>
    <div id="sidebar"></div>
  </body>
  </html>
```

Note that I've gone ahead and filled in some HTML id attributes on these div tags so that it'll be easy to set up the layout with cascading style sheets (CSS).

Now, one thing that jumps out is the fact that the title element is empty. This is definitely something that will vary, according to which part of the site you're in and what you're looking at, so let's go ahead and put a block there:

```
<title>My weblog {% block title %}{% endblock %}</title>
```

When you extend this template, you'll add more things here. The final effect will be to get a title like My weblog | Entries | February 2008, as you'll see in a moment.

Now, let's fill in the header. It's not something that's likely to change a lot, so you don't need a block here:

```
<div id="header">
  <h1 id="branding">My weblog</h1>
</div>
```

Again, I've added an id attribute to make it easy to style it later with CSS. For example, you could use an image-replacement technique to replace the text of the h1 with a logo.

Since the main content will vary quite a bit, you'll make it a block:

```
<div id="content">
  {% block content %}
  {% endblock %}
</div>
```

All that's left is the sidebar. The first thing you'll need there is a list of links to different things so that visitors can easily navigate around the site. You can do that easily enough (again, using id attributes to make it easy to come back later and style this):

```
<div id="sidebar">
  <h2>Navigation</h2>
  <ul id="main-nav">
    <li id="main-nav-entries">
      <a href="/weblog/">Entries</a></li>
    <li id="main-nav-links">
      <a href="/weblog/links/">Links</a></li>
    <li id="main-nav-categories">
      <a href="/weblog/categories/">Categories</a></li>
    <li id="main-nav-tags"><a href="/weblog/tags/">Tags</a></li>
  </ul>
</div>
```

But one thing stands out: you have hard-coded URLs here. They match what you've set up in your URLConf. But after you went to all the trouble to modularize and decouple them on the Python side, it would be a shame to just turn around and hard-code things in your templates.

A better solution is to use the {% url %} template tag, which—like the permalink decorator you used on the get_absolute_url() methods of your models—can perform a reverse lookup in your URLConf to determine the appropriate URL. This tag has quite a few options, but the one you care about right now is pretty simple: you can feed it the name of a URL pattern, and it will output the correct URL.

Using the {% url %} tag, you can rewrite your navigation list like so:

```
<ul id="main-nav">
  <li id="main-nav-entries">
    <a href="{% url coltrane_entry_archive_index %}">Entries</a>
  </li>
  <li id="main-nav-links">
    <a href="{% url coltrane_link_archive_index %}">Links</a>
  </li>
  <li id="main-nav-categories">
    <a href="{% url coltrane_category_list %}">Categories</a>
  </li>
  <li id="main-nav-tags">
    <a href="{% url coltrane_tag_list %}">Tags</a>
  </li>
</ul>
```

Now you won't have to make changes to your templates if you decide to shuffle some URLs around later.

While you're dealing with the navigation, let's add a block inside the body tag:

```
<body class="{% block bodyclass %}{% endblock %}">
```

A common technique in CSS-based web design is to use a class attribute on the body tag to trigger changes to a page's style. For example, you'll have a list of navigation options in the sidebar, representing different parts of the blog—entries, links, and so forth—and it would be nice to highlight the part a visitor is currently looking at. By changing the class of the body tag in different parts of the site, you can easily use CSS to highlight the correct item in the navigation list.

For the rest of the sidebar's content, it would be nice to have a little explanation of what a visitor is looking at, something like "An entry in my blog, published on February 7, 2008" or "A list of entries in the category 'Django.'" You can add a block for that as well:

```
<h2>What is this?</h2>
{% block whatis %}
{% endblock %}
```

You're done with the base template—for now. (You'll add a few things to it later on.) Here's what it looks like:

```
<!DOCTYPE html PUBLIC "-//W3C//DTD XHTML 1.0 Strict//EN"
                "http://www.w3.org/TR/xhtml1/DTD/xhtml1-strict.dtd">
```

```
<html xmlns="http://www.w3.org/1999/xhtml" lang="en" xml:lang="en">
<head>
  <title>My weblog {% block title %}{% endblock %}</title>
</head>
<body class="{% block bodyclass %}{% endblock %}">
  <div id="header">
    <h1 id="branding">My weblog</h1>
  </div>
  <div id="content">
    {% block content %}
    {% endblock %}
  </div>
  <div id="sidebar">
    <h2>Navigation</h2>
    <ul id="main-nav">
      <li id="main-nav-entries">
        <a href="{% url coltrane_entry_archive_index %}">Entries</a>
      </li>
      <li id="main-nav-links">
        <a href="{% url coltrane_link_archive_index %}">Links</a>
      </li>
      <li id="main-nav-categories">
        <a href="{% url coltrane_category_list %}">Categories</a>
      </li>
      <li id="main-nav-tags">
        <a href="{% url coltrane_tag_list %}">Tags</a>
      </li>
    </ul>
    <h2>What is this?</h2>
    {% block whatis %}
    {% endblock %}
  </div>
</body>
</html>
```

Section Templates

Now let's set up some templates that will handle the different main areas of the blog. You'll want one each for entries, links, tags, and categories. You'll call the template for entries base_entries.html, and all you really need to do is extend the base template and fill in a couple of blocks:

```
{% extends "base.html" %}

{% block title %}| Entries{% endblock %}

{% block bodyclass %}entries{% endblock %}
```

If you just used this template all by itself, you'd get the output from base.html, but with two changes:

- The title tag's contents would be My weblog | Entries.

- The body tag's class attribute would have a value of entries, which means it would be easy to cause the Entries item in the navigation to be highlighted.

The rest of the section templates are pretty easy to fill in. For example, you can write a base_links.html like so:

```
{% extends "base.html" %}

{% block title %}| Links{% endblock %}

{% block bodyclass %}Links{% endblock %}
```

You'll also need a base_tags.html and a base_categories.html, but you can just fill them in using the same pattern as described previously. These templates are slightly repetitive, and probably always will be, but the use of template inheritance means you've boiled down the repetitive bits to a bare minimum—you're only specifying the things that change, not the things that stay the same.

Archives of Entries

For displaying entries, you need five templates:

- The main, or home, page showing the latest entries

- A yearly archive

- A monthly archive

- A daily archive

- An individual entry

These correspond directly to the generic views you're using.

Entry Index

Let's start with the main index of entries. You'll recall that the generic view will look for the template coltrane/entry_archive.html and will provide a variable named latest containing a list of the latest entries. So you can fill in the template coltrane/entry_archive.html as follows (remembering to extend base_entries.html instead of base.html):

```
{% extends "base_entries.html" %}

{% block title %}{{ block.super }} | Latest entries{% endblock %}

{% block content %}
{% for entry in latest %}
```

```
<h2>{{ entry.title }}</h2>
<p>Published on {{ entry.pub_date|date:"F j, Y" }}</p>
{% if entry.excerpt_html %}
  {{ entry.excerpt_html|safe }}
{% else %}
  {{ entry.body_html|truncatewords_html:"50"|safe }}
{% endif %}
<p><a href="{{ entry.get_absolute_url }}">Read full entry. . .</a></p>
{% endfor %}
{% endblock %}

{% block whatis %}
<p>This is a list of the latest {{ latest.count }} entries published in
 my blog.</p>
{% endblock %}
```

Most of this should be pretty familiar. You're using the {% for %} tag to loop over the entries and display each one. And in the sidebar, you just have a short paragraph describing what's being shown on this page. It relies on the count() method of a Django QuerySet to find out how many entries were passed to the template in the latest variable.

There are a couple of new things here worth noting, though:

- The use of the date filter to format each entry's pub_date. This accepts a formatting string, similar to the strftime() method you've already seen, and outputs the date accordingly. In this case, it will print out in the form February 6, 2008.

- The use of the truncatewords_html filter. This filter takes a number as its argument and outputs that number of words from the variable it's applied to, adding an ellipsis (. . .) to the end. This is useful for generating a short excerpt when the entry doesn't have its excerpt field filled in.

Yearly Archive

The generic view that generates the yearly archive will provide two variables:

- year: The year being displayed.

- date_list: A list of Python datetime objects representing months in that year that have entries.

This generic view is going to look for the template coltrane/entry_archive_year.html, which you can fill in as follows:

```
{% extends "base_entries.html" %}

{% block title %}{{ block.super }} | {{ year }}{% endblock %}

{% block content %}
<ul>
  {% for month in date_list %}
```

```
    <li>
      <a href="/weblog/entries/{{ year }}/{{ month|date:"b" }}/">{{ month|➥
date:"F" }}</a>
    </li>
  {% endfor %}
</ul>
{% endblock %}

{% block whatis %}
<p>This is a list of months in {{ year }} in which I published entries in
 my blog.</p>
{% endblock %}
```

Here you're looping over the date_list and, for each month, showing a link to the archive for that month.

But there's a problem here: you can build up the URLs by using Django's built-in date filter, but once again you're hard-coding a URL. Previously, you got around that by using the {% url %} tag with the name of a URL pattern. You can do that again, but this time you'll need to supply some extra data: the year and month needed to generate the correct URL for a monthly archive. All you have to do is pass a second argument to the {% url %} tag, containing a comma-separated list of the values it needs, and you can even use filters to make sure they're correctly formatted:

```
<li><a href="{% url coltrane_entry_archive_month year,month|date:"b" %}">
  {{ month|date:"F" }}
</a></li>
```

With the current URL setup, this will correctly output URLs like /weblog/2008/jan/, /weblog/2008/feb/, and so on.

Monthly and Daily Archives

The generic views that generate the monthly and daily archives are extremely similar. Both will provide a list of entries in a variable named object_list, and the only real difference is that one will have a variable called month (representing the month for a monthly archive) and the other will have a variable called day (representing the day for a daily archive).

Here's the monthly archive template, which will be coltrane/entry_archive_month.html:

```
{% extends "base_entries.html" %}

{% block title %}
{{ block.super }} | Entries in {{ month|date:"F, Y" }}
{% endblock %}

{% block content %}
{% for entry in object_list %}
  <h2>{{ entry.title }}</h2>
  <p>Published on {{ entry.pub_date|date:"F j, Y" }}</p>
  {% if entry.excerpt_html %}
```

```
    {{ entry.excerpt_html|safe }}
  {% else %}
  {{ entry.body_html|truncatewords_html:"50"|safe }}
  {% endif %}
  <p><a href="{{ entry.get_absolute_url }}">Read full entry. . .</a></p>
{% endfor %}
{% endblock %}

{% block whatis %}
<p>This is a list of entries published in my blog in
  {{ month|date:"F, Y" }}.</p>
{% endblock %}
```

Except for a couple of changes to variable names and the use of the date filter to format the month (it will print in the form February, 2008), this isn't too different from what you've already seen. The daily archive template (coltrane/entry_archive_day.html) will be almost identical except for the use of the variable day and the appropriate formatting, so go ahead and fill that in. (You can find a full list of available date formatting options in the Django template documentation online at www.djangoproject.com/documentation/templates/.)

Entry Detail

The generic view that shows a single entry uses the template coltrane/entry_detail.html and provides one variable, object, which will be the entry. The first part of this template is easy:

```
{% extends "base_entries.html" %}

{% block title %}{{ block.super }} | {{ object.title }}{% endblock %}

{% block content %}
<h2>{{ object.title }}</h2>
{{ object.body_html|safe }}
{% endblock %}
```

The sidebar is a bit trickier. You can start out by showing the entry's pub_date:

```
{% block whatis %}
<p>This is an entry posted to my blog on
  {{ object.pub_date|date:"F j, Y" }}.</p>
```

Now, it would be nice to show the categories by saying something like, "This entry is part of the categories 'Django' and 'Python.'" But there are several things to take into account here:

- For an entry with one category you want to say "part of the category." But for an entry with more than one, it needs to be "part of the categories," and for an entry with no categories, you need to say, "This entry isn't part of any categories."

- For an entry with more than two categories, you'll need commas between category names and the word "and" before the final category. But for an entry with two categories, you don't need the commas, and for an entry with only one category, you don't need commas or the "and."

If there aren't any categories for an entry, `{{ object.categories.count }}` will be 0, which is `False` inside an `{% if %}` tag, so you can start with a test for that:

```
{% if object.categories.count %}
. . .you'll fill this in momentarily. . .
{% else %}
<p>This entry isn't part of any categories.</p>
{% endif %}
```

Now you need to handle the difference between "category" and "categories." Since this is a common problem, Django includes a filter, called `pluralize`, which can take care of it. The `pluralize` filter, by default, outputs nothing if applied to a variable that evaluates to the number 1, but outputs an "s" otherwise. It also accepts an argument that lets you specify other text to output. In this case, you want a "y" for the singular case and "ies" for the plural, so you can write:

```
{% if object.categories.count %}
<p>This entry is part of the
 category{{ object.categories.count|pluralize:"y,ies" }}
```

You'll get "category" when there's only one category and "categories" otherwise.

Finally, you need to loop over the categories. One option would be to join the list of categories using commas. In Python code, you'd write:

```
', '.join(object.categories.all())
```

And Django's template system provides a `join` filter, which works the same way:

```
{{ object.categories.all|join:", " }}
```

But you want to have the word "and" inserted before the final category in the list, and `join` can't do that. The solution is to use the `{% for %}` tag and to take advantage of some useful variables it makes available. Within the `{% for %}` loop, the following variables will automatically be available:

- `forloop.counter`: The current iteration of the loop, counting from 1. The fourth time through the loop, for example, this will be the number 4.

- `forloop.counter0`: Same as `forloop.counter`, but starts counting at 0 instead of 1. The fourth time through the loop, for example, this will be the number 3.

- `forloop.revcounter`: The number of iterations left until the end of the loop, counting down to 1. When there are four iterations left to go, for example, this will be the number 4.

- `forloop.revcounter0`: Same as `forloop.revcounter`, but counts down to 0 instead of 1.

- `forloop.first`: A boolean value—it will be `True` the first time through the loop and `False` the rest of the time.

- `forloop.last`: Another boolean—this one is `True` the *last* time through the loop and `False` the rest of the time.

Using these variables, you can work out the proper presentation. Expressed in English, the logic works like this:

1. Display a link to the category.

2. If this is the last time through the loop, don't display anything else.

3. If this is the next-to-last time through the loop, display the word "and."

4. Otherwise, display a comma.

And here it is in template code:

```
{% for category in object.categories.all %}
  <a href="{{ category.get_absolute_url }}">{{ category.title }}</a>
  {% if forloop.last %}{% else %}
  {% ifequal forloop.revcounter0 1 %}and {% else %}, {% endifequal %}
  {% endif %}
s  {% endfor %}
```

There are really two important bits here:

- {% if forloop.last %}{% else %}: This does absolutely nothing if you're in the last trip through the loop.

- {% ifequal forloop.revcounter0 1 %}: This determines whether you're in the next-to-last trip through the loop in order to print the "and" before the final category.

Here's the full sidebar block so far:

```
{% block whatis %}
<p>This is an entry posted to my blog on
 {{ object.pub_date|date:"F j, Y" }}.</p>

{% if object.categories.count %}
  <p>This entry is part of the
  category{{ object.categories.count|pluralize:"y,ies" }}
  {% for category in object.categories.all %}
    <a href="{{ category.get_absolute_url }}">{{ category.title }}</a>
    {% if forloop.last %}{% else %}
    {% ifequal forloop.revcounter0 1 %}and {% else %}, {% endifequal %}
    {% endif %}
  {% endfor %}
  </p>
{% else %}
  <p>This entry isn't part of any categories.</p>
{% endif %}
{% endblock %}
```

Handling tags will work much the same way. {{ object.tags }} will return the tags for the Entry, and a similar bit of template code can handle them. And with that, you have a pretty good entry detail template:

```
{% extends "base_entries.html" %}

{% block title %}{{ block.super }} | {{ object.title }}{% endblock %}

{% block content %}
<h2>{{ object.title }}</h2>
{{ object.body_html }}
{% endblock %}

{% block whatis %}
<p>This is an entry posted to my blog on
 {{ object.pub_date|date:"F j, Y" }}.</p>

{% if object.categories.count %}
  <p>This entry is part of the
  category{{ object.categories.count|pluralize:"y,ies" }}
  {% for category in object.categories.all %}
    <a href="{{ category.get_absolute_url }}">{{ category.title }}</a>
    {% if forloop.last %}{% else %}
    {% ifequal forloop.revcounter0 1 %}and {% else %}, {% endifequal %}
    {% endif %}
  {% endfor %}
  </p>
{% else %}
  <p>This entry isn't part of any categories.</p>
{% endif %}
{% endblock %}
```

Templates for Other Types of Content

The templates for displaying links in the blog aren't much different. They'll extend base_links.html, of course, but the variable names available in the various templates will be the same. The only difference is that the templates will have access to Link objects and so should display them based on the fields you've defined on the Link model. Here's an example of what coltrane/link_detail.html might look like:

```
{% extends "base_links.html" %}

{% block title %}{{ block.super }} | {{ object.title }}{% endblock %}

{% block content %}
<h2>{{ object.title }}</h2>
{{ object.description_html }}
<p><a href="{{ object.url }}">Visit site</a></p>
{% endblock %}
```

```
{% block whatis %}
<p>This is a link posted to my blog on {{ object.pub_date|date:"F j, Y" }}.</p>

{% if object.tags.count %}
  <p>This link is tagged with
  {% for tag in object.categories.all %}
    <a href="{{ tag.get_absolute_url }}">{{ tag.title }}</a>
    {% if forloop.last %}{% else %}
    {% ifequal forloop.revcounter0 1 %}and {% else %}, {% endifequal %}
    {% endif %}
  {% endfor %}
  </p>
{% else %}
  <p>This link doesn't have any tags.</p>
{% endif %}
{% endblock %}
```

Note that since links only have tags, not categories, this template just loops through the tags the same way coltrane/entry_detail.html loops through categories.

Similarly, the category and tag templates are easy to set up at this point. They just need to extend the correct template for the part of the site they represent and use the correct fields from the Category and Tag models, respectively (though remember that the detail view of categories and tags will actually return lists of Entry or Link objects for a particular Category or Tag). Full examples can be found in the sample code available from the Apress web site for this book.

Extending the Template System with Custom Tags

Right now, the only thing in the sidebar of your blog will be the list of navigation links and the short "What is this?" blurb for each page. While this is simple and usable, it would be nice to emulate what a lot of popular prebuilt blogging packages do and also display a list of, say, recent entries and recent links farther down in the sidebar so that visitors can quickly find fresh content.

But that poses a dilemma: it seems like you'd need to go back and rewrite every one of your views to also query for, say, the latest five entries and the latest five links, and then make them available to the template. That would be awfully cumbersome and repetitive, and it would get even worse if you ever wanted to change the number of recent items displayed or add new types of content to your blog. Once again, it feels like Django should provide some easy way to handle this without lots of repetitive code.

And it does. In fact, Django provides two easy ways to do this. One is a mechanism for writing a function—called a *context processor*—which can add extra variables to any template's context. The other way is to extend Django's template system to add the ability to fetch recent content using a custom template tag. Using this, you could simply use the appropriate tag in the base.html template, and all the other templates would have that automatic courtesy of template inheritance.

For this situation, let's go ahead and use a custom template tag to get a feel for how you can extend Django's template system when you need to add new features to it.

ADMONITION: SEPARATION OF CONCERNS

What you're about to do—write a template tag that retrieves items from the database for display—may feel strange, considering how cleanly Django separates major functions like data retrieval and HTML display from each other. However, it's not always a bad thing to blur that distinction a bit.

In this case, you want to retrieve these items solely for presentational purposes. You also want them to appear everywhere, so writing the functionality as an extension of Django's template system—which handles presentation of content—and taking advantage of template inheritance is a good way to handle it. Not everything is best done as an extension to the template system, though, so be careful to evaluate decisions like this one on a case-by-case basis as you're developing.

How a Django Template Works

Before you can dive into writing your own custom extensions to the template system, it's important to understand the actual mechanism behind Django's template system. Knowing how things work "under the hood" makes the process of writing custom template functionality much simpler.

The process Django goes through when loading a template works—roughly—like this:

1. **Read the actual template contents**: Most often this means reading out of a template file on disk, but that's not always the case. Django can work with anything that hands over a string containing the contents you want it to treat as a template.

2. **Parse through looking for tags and variables**: Each tag in the template, including all of Django's built-in tags, will correspond to a particular Python function defined somewhere (inside `django/template/defaulttags.py` in the case of the built-in tags). You'll see in a moment how to tell Django that a particular tag maps to a particular function. Typically this is referred to as the tag's *compilation function* because it's called while Django is compiling a list of the eventual template contents.

3. **For each tag, call the appropriate function, passing in two arguments**: One is the parsing class that is reading the template (useful for doing tricky things with the way the template gets processed), and the other is a string containing the contents of the tag. So, for example, the tag `{% if foo %}` results in a function (called `do_if()`, in Django's default tag library) being passed an object that holds the tag contents "if foo."

4. **Make a note of the return value of the Python function called for each tag**: Each function is required to return an instance of a special class—`django.template.Node`—or a subclass of it, and choosing an appropriate `Node` subclass based on the particular tag is primarily what these functions do.

The result is an instance of the class `django.template.Template`, and it contains a list of `Node` instances (or instances of `Node` subclasses). This is the actual "thing" that will be rendered to produce the output. Each `Node` is required to have a method named `render()`, which accepts a copy of the current template context (the dictionary of variables available to the template) and returns a string. The output of the template comes from concatenating those strings together.

A Simple Custom Tag

This can be a bit tricky to get the hang of at first, so let's start simply. You'll write a tag that fetches the latest five entries and puts them into a template variable named latest_entries.

To start with, you'll need to create a place for this tag's code to live. In the coltrane application directory, add a new directory called templatetags. In that, create two empty files: __init__.py (remember, this is necessary to tell Python that a directory contains loadable Python code) and coltrane_tags.py, which will be the file where your library of custom template tags lives. Next, inside coltrane_tags.py, add a couple of import statements at the top:

```
from django import template
from coltrane.models import Entry
```

Writing the Compilation Function

The custom tag is going to be called get_latest_entries—so that in templates you'll eventually be able to do {% get_latest_entries %}—but its compilation function (and its Node class) can be called by any name you like. It's generally a good idea to give the function a meaningful name for the tag it goes with, though, so call it do_latest_entries():

```
def do_latest_entries(parser, token):
```

The two arguments to this function are the template parser (which you won't be using here, but in a later chapter you'll write a tag that uses the template parser to implement more advanced features) and a token. This is an object representing part of the template that's being parsed. You also won't need that just yet, but later in this chapter when you expand this tag's functionality, you'll use it to work out the arguments passed to the tag from the template.

The only thing this function is required to do is return an instance of django.template. Node, or a subclass of Node. You'll define the Node for this tag in a moment, but it's going to be called LatestEntriesNode, so go ahead and fill that in:

```
def do_latest_entries(parser, token):
    return LatestEntriesNode()
```

Writing the Node

Next, you need to write the LatestEntriesNode class. This must be a subclass of django. template.Node, and it must have a method named render(). Django places two requirements on this method:

- It must accept a template context—the dictionary of variables available to the template—as an argument.

- It must return a string, even if the string doesn't contain anything. For tags that produce their output directly, the returned string is how their output gets into the final template output.

So you can start writing your Node as follows:

```
class LatestEntriesNode(template.Node):
    def render(self, context):
```

This tag will simply fetch the five latest entries and add them to the context as the variable latest_entries, so it doesn't have any direct output. All it does is add the new item to the context dictionary, then return an empty string (even when a tag doesn't directly output anything, the render() method of its Node *must* return a string):

```
class LatestEntriesNode(template.Node):
    def render(self, context):
        context['latest_entries'] = Entry.live.all()[:5]
        return ''
```

Registering the New Tag

Finally, you need to tell Django that the compilation function should be used when the {% get_latest_entries %} tag is encountered in a template. To do this, you create a new library of template tags and register your function with it, like so:

```
register = template.Library()
register.tag('get_latest_entries', do_latest_entries)
```

The syntax for this is simple. Once you create a new Library, you just call its tag() method and pass in the name you want to give your tag and the function that will handle it.

Here's what the full coltrane_tags.py file looks like now:

```
from django import template
from coltrane.models import Entry

def do_latest_entries(parser, token):
    return LatestEntriesNode()

class LatestEntriesNode(template.Node):
    def render(self, context):
        context['latest_entries'] = Entry.live.all()[:5]
        return ''

register = template.Library()
register.tag('get_latest_entries', do_latest_entries)
```

Using the New Tag

Now your new tag is ready for use. Open up the base.html template and go to the sidebar portion of it, which still looks like this:

```
<div id="sidebar">
  <h2>Navigation</h2>
  <ul id="main-nav">
    <li id="main-nav-entries">
      <a href="{% url coltrane_entry_archive_index %}">Entries</a>
    </li>
    <li id="main-nav-links">
```

```
      <a href="{% url coltrane_link_archive_index %}">Links</a>
    </li>
    <li id="main-nav-categories">
      <a href="{% url coltrane_category_list %}">Categories</a>
    </li>
    <li id="main-nav-tags">
      <a href="{% url coltrane_tag_list %}">Tags</a>
    </li>
  </ul>
  <h2>What is this?</h2>
  {% block whatis %}
  {% endblock %}
</div>
```

You're going to add the list of latest entries just below the "What is this?" block, and you do it like so:

```
{% load coltrane_tags %}
<h2>Latest entries in the weblog</h2>
<ul>
  {% get_latest_entries %}
  {% for entry in latest_entries %}
  <li>
    <a href="{{ entry.get_absolute_url }}">{{ entry.title }}</a>,
    posted {{ entry.pub_date|timesince }} ago.
  </li>
  {% endfor %}
</ul>
```

Here's what's going on:

- The {% load coltrane_tags %} tag tells Django you want to load a custom template tag library named coltrane_tags. When it sees this, Django will go looking through all of your installed applications for a templatetags directory containing a file named coltrane_tags.py, and it will load any tags defined there.

- Once your tag library has been loaded, the {% get_latest_entries %} tag can be called, and it creates the new template variable, latest_entries, containing the five latest entries.

- Then you just loop through latest_entries using the {% for %} tag, displaying a link to each and showing when it was posted. You're using a new filter here, called timesince, which is built in to Django and formats a date and time according to how long ago it was. The result (with the word "ago" added afterward) will be something like "3 days, 10 hours ago," and will give a visitor an idea of how recently the blog has been updated.

Writing a More Flexible Tag with Arguments

Now, you also want to show the latest links posted in the blog. You could do this by writing a new {% get_latest_links %} tag and having it add a latest_links variable to the template context. However, that's the start of a long and tedious path of writing a new tag every time you add a new type of content to your site, so it would be better to turn your existing {% get_latest_entries %} tag into a slightly more generic {% get_latest_content %} tag, which can fetch any of several types of content.

And while you're at it, it would be nice to add a bit more flexibility to the tag by letting it take arguments to specify how many items to retrieve, as well as the name of the variable to put them in. That way, you could have several lists of recent content that don't trample all over each other's variables. What you're going to end up with is a tag that works like this:

```
{% get_latest_content coltrane.link 5 as latest_links %}
```

which will, as the syntax indicates, fetch the five most recently published Link objects in the coltrane application and place them in a template variable named latest_links.

Writing the Compilation Function

You can start out the same as before, by defining a compilation function for your tag:

```
def do_latest_content(parser, token):
```

But now you'll need to read some arguments out of the tag. The full contents will be in token.contents and will be a string of the form get_latest_content coltrane.link 5 as latest_links. So you can use Python's built-in string-splitting function, which defaults to splitting on spaces, to turn this into a list of arguments:

```
def do_latest_content(parser, token):
    bits = token.contents.split()
```

Now the variable bits contains a list that looks like ["get_latest_content", "coltrane.link", "5", "as", "latest_links"]. If the tag was called properly (that's five items in all), you can check this and raise a template syntax error if you don't find the right number of arguments:

```
def do_latest_content(parser, token):
    bits = token.contents.split()
    if len(bits) != 5:
        raise template.TemplateSyntaxError("'get_latest_content'➥
 tag takes exactly four arguments")
```

This ensures that you never try to render a malformed use of the tag. Note that it says "four arguments," not "five arguments." Though bits has five items in it, the first item is the name the tag was called with, not an argument. (Sometimes it's useful to write a single compilation function and register multiple times under different names, allowing it to represent a family of similar tags and tell them apart by the tag name it receives.)

Next you want to return a Node. It will be called LatestContentNode, and you'll need to pass some information to it: the model to retrieve content from, the number of items to retrieve, and the variable name to store the results in. When you write `LatestContentNode` in a moment, you'll set up its constructor to accept this information:

```
def do_latest_content(parser, token):
    bits = token.contents.split()
    if len(bits) != 5:
        raise template.TemplateSyntaxError("'get_latest_content'➥
 tag takes exactly four arguments")
    return LatestContentNode(bits[1], bits[2], bits[4])
```

Note that because Python lists have indexes starting at 0, the model name—though it's the second item in `bits`—is `bits[1]`, the number of items is `bits[2]`, and so on.

ADMONITION: HOW MUCH ERROR CHECKING IS TOO MUCH?

You could also add a test to ensure that the fourth item in `bits` is the word "as," and raise a syntax error if you don't see it. But in this case, it's okay not to. For a simple tag like this, just checking the number of arguments is usually fine, and checking for the "as" would just add more code that probably won't be needed. For more complex tags, however, it's a good idea to write your compilation function to ensure the tag was used properly before trying to return anything from it.

Determining the Model to Retrieve Content From

In the original `{% get_latest_entries %}` tag, you simply imported the `Entry` model and referenced it directly. Your new tag, however, is going to get an argument like `coltrane.link` or `coltrane.entry`, and so you will need to import the correct model class dynamically.

Python provides a way to do this (through a special built-in function named `__import__()`, which takes strings as arguments), but loading a model class dynamically is a common enough need that Django provides a helper function to handle it more concisely. The function is `django.db.models.get_model()`, and it takes two arguments:

- The name of the application the model is defined in, as a string.

- The name of the model class, as a string.

It's customary to make both of these strings entirely lowercase because Django maintains a registry of installed models with the names normalized to lowercase. If you want to, you can pass mixed-case names to `get_model()`, but since they'll just be lowercased anyway, it's often easier to start with them that way.

To see how `get_model()` works, go to your project directory and run the command `python manage.py shell`. This will start a Python interpreter. In it, type the following:

```
>>> from django.db.models import get_model
>>> entry_model = get_model('coltrane', 'entry')
```

The get_model() function will go and retrieve the Entry model from the coltrane application and assign it to the variable entry_model. From there, you can query against it just the same as if you'd imported it normally. To verify this, type in the following:

```
>>> entry_model.live.all()[:5]
```

You'll see that it returns the latest five live entries.

Let's go ahead and change the compilation function to use this and retrieve the model class. One obvious way to do this would be as follows:

```
from django.db.models import get_model

def do_latest_content(parser, token):
    bits = token.contents.split()
    if len(bits) != 5:
        raise template.TemplateSyntaxError("'get_latest_content'➥
 tag takes exactly four arguments")
    model_args = bits[1].split('.')
    model = get_model(model_args[0], model_args[1])
    return LatestContentNode(model, bits[2], bits[4])
```

This has a couple of problems, though:

- If the first argument isn't an application name/model name pair separated by a dot (.), or if it has too few or too many parts, this might get the wrong model or no model at all.

- If the arguments you pass to get_model() don't actually correspond to any model class, it will return the value None, and that will trip up the LatestContentNode when it tries to retrieve the content.

So you need a little bit of error checking. You want to verify the following:

- When split on the dot (.) character, the first argument becomes a list of exactly two items.

- That these items, when passed to get_model(), do indeed return a model class.

You can do that in only a few lines of code:

```
model_args = bits[1].split('.')
if len(model_args) != 2:
    raise template.TemplateSyntaxError("First argument to➥
 'get_latest_content' must be an 'application name'.'model name' string")
model = get_model(*model_args)
if model is None:
    raise template.TemplateSyntaxError("'get_latest_content'➥
 tag got an invalid model: %s" % bits[1])
```

If you're wondering about this line:

```
model = get_model(*args)
```

remember that the asterisk (*) is special Python syntax for taking a list (the result of calling split()) and turning in a set of arguments to a function. Here's the finished compilation function:

```python
def do_latest_content(parser, token):
    bits = token.contents.split()
    if len(bits) != 5:
        raise template.TemplateSyntaxError("'get_latest_content'➥
 tag takes exactly four arguments")
    model_args = bits[1].split('.')
    if len(model_args) != 2:
        raise template.TemplateSyntaxError("First argument to➥
 'get_latest_content' must be an 'application name'.'model name' string")
    model = get_model(*model_args)
    if model is None:
        raise template.TemplateSyntaxError("'get_latest_content'➥
 tag got an invalid model: %s" % bits[1])
    return LatestContentNode(model, bits[2], bits[4])
```

Writing the `LatestContentNode`

You already know that LatestContentNode needs to accept three arguments in its constructor:

- The model to retrieve items from

- The number of items to retrieve

- The name of a variable to store the items in

So you can start by writing its constructor (remember that a Python object's constructor is always called __init__()) and simply storing those arguments as instance variables:

```python
class LatestContentNode(template.Node):
    def __init__(self, model, num, varname):
        self.model = model
        self.num = int(num)
        self.varname = varname
```

Notice that you force num to be an int here. All the arguments to the tag came in as strings, so before you can use this to control the number of items to retrieve, it needs to be converted to an actual number. Here's a simple way the render() method could be written:

```python
def render(self, context):
    context[self.varname] = self.model.objects.all()[:self.num]
    return ''
```

At first, this looks fine, but it's got a hidden problem. When you call it like so:

```
{% get_latest_content coltrane.entry 5 as latest_entries %}
```

the query it performs will be the equivalent of

```
Entry.objects.all()[:5]
```

which isn't what you want. This will return *any* entry, including entries that aren't meant to be publicly displayed. What you want is for it to do the equivalent of the following:

```
Entry.live.all()[:5]
```

You could write special-case code to see when you're working with the Entry model, but that's not good practice. If you later need to use this tag on other models with similar needs, you'll have to keep adding new pieces of special-case code.

The solution is to ask Django to use the model's default manager. The first manager defined in a model class is given special status. It becomes the default manager for that model, in addition to the name it was defined with. It will also be available as the attribute _default_manager, so you can actually write this as:

```
def render(self, context):
    context[self.varname] = self.model._default_manager.all()[:self.num]
    return ''
```

Because the live manager was defined first in the Entry model, this will do the right thing.

ADMONITION: USING DEFAULT MANAGERS

Whenever you don't know in advance which model you'll be working with (as in this case, and in most cases when you're using get_model()), it's a good idea to use _default_manager. When a model has multiple managers, or defines a single custom manager that's not named objects, trying to query through the objects attribute can be dangerous. That might not be the manager queries should go through (as in the case of Entry with its special live manager), and, in fact, objects might not even exist. Remember that when a model has a custom manager, Django doesn't automatically set up the objects manager on it, so trying to access objects may raise an exception.

Registering and Using the New Tag

Now you can simply register your new tag, and it's ready to go. The final coltrane_tags.py file looks like this:

```
from django.db.models import get_model
from django import template

def do_latest_content(parser, token):
    bits = token.contents.split()
    if len(bits) != 5:
        raise template.TemplateSyntaxError("'get_latest_content'➥
 tag takes exactly four arguments")
```

```
        model_args = bits[1].split('.')
        if len(model_args) != 2:
            raise template.TemplateSyntaxError("First argument to➥
'get_latest_content' must be an 'application name'.'model name' string")
        model = get_model(*model_args)
        if model is None:
            raise template.TemplateSyntaxError("'get_latest_content'➥
tag got an invalid model: %s" % bits[1])
        return LatestContentNode(model, bits[2], bits[4])

    class LatestContentNode(template.Node):
        def __init__(self, model, num, varname):
            self.model = model
            self.num = int(num)
            self.varname = varname

        def render(self, context):
            context[self.varname] = self.model._default_manager.all()[:self.num]
            return ''

    register = template.Library()
    register.tag('get_latest_content', do_latest_content)
```

And so you can rewrite the sidebar in the base.html template, like so:

```
    <div id="sidebar">
      <h2>Navigation</h2>
      <ul id="main-nav">
        <li id="main-nav-entries">
          <a href="{% url coltrane_entry_archive_index %}">Entries</a>
        </li>
        <li id="main-nav-links">
          <a href="{% url coltrane_link_archive_index %}">Links</a>
        </li>
        <li id="main-nav-categories">
          <a href="{% url coltrane_category_list %}">Categories</a>
        </li>
        <li id="main-nav-tags">
          <a href="{% url coltrane_tag_list %}">Tags</a>
        </li>
      </ul>
      <h2>What is this?</h2>
      {% block whatis %}
      {% endblock %}
      {% load coltrane_tags %}
      <h2>Latest entries in the weblog</h2>
      <ul>
        {% get_latest_content coltrane.entry 5 as latest_entries %}
```

```
    {% for entry in latest_entries %}
    <li>
      <a href="{{ entry.get_absolute_url }}">{{ entry.title }}</a>,
      posted {{ entry.pub_date|timesince }} ago.
    </li>
    {% endfor %}
  </ul>
  <h2>Latest links in the weblog</h2>
  <ul>
    {% get_latest_content coltrane.link 5 as latest_links %}
    {% for link in latest_links %}
    <li>
      <a href="{{ link.get_absolute_url }}">{{ link.title }}</a>,
      posted {{ link.pub_date|timesince }} ago.
    </li>
    {% endfor %}
  </ul>
</div>
```

This will ensure that every page has the list of the latest five entries and links, and it offers two big advantages over the original {% get_latest_entries %} tag:

- When you add new types of content to the blog (in the next chapter you'll add comments), you don't have to write a new tag. You can just reuse get_latest_content with different arguments.

- If you decide to change the number of entries or links to show, or the variables you want to use for them, it's just a matter of sending different arguments to the {% get_latest_content %} tag. You won't have to rewrite the tag to change this.

Looking Ahead

In the next chapter, you'll wrap up the weblog by adding comments, moderation, and RSS feeds. For now, though, feel free to play with the template system and get the blog looking exactly how you want it. A sample style sheet that implements the two-column layout is included with the sample code for this book, so feel free to try it out. To get Django to serve this as a plain file, add the following URL pattern in the root URLConf of the project (once again using the static file-serving view you saw in Chapter 3):

```
(r'^media/(?P<path>.*)$',
 'django.views.static.serve',
 { 'document_root': '/path/to/stylesheet/directory' }),
```

Simply fill in the path to the directory where the style sheet file is on your computer, and Django will serve it. (Though note that for production deployment of Django, it's best not to have Django serve static files like this.)

■ ■ ■

CHAPTER 7

Finishing the Weblog

Now that you've got a solid set of templates and, more important, a solid understanding of Django's template system, it's time to finish up the weblog with the final two features: a comment system with moderation and syndication feeds for entries and links.

Though Django provides applications—`django.contrib.comments` and `django.contrib.syndication`—that handle the basic functionality for both of these features, you're going to go beyond that a bit, customizing and extending their features as you go. This will involve a bit of Python code and a bit of templating, but as you'll see, it's nowhere near as much code as you'd have to write to implement these features from scratch. So let's dive right in.

Comments and `django.contrib.comments`

You've already seen that `django.contrib` contains some useful applications. Both the administrative interface and the authentication system you're using come from applications in `contrib`, as well as the flat pages application you used in your simple CMS. In general, it's a good idea to look there before starting to write something on your own. As I write this, `django.contrib` contains 17 applications, and there are plans to expand it to include more open source applications from the Django community. Even if something in `contrib` doesn't do exactly what you need, you'll often find something you can build on or that can make a tricky bit of code simpler.

Commenting is no exception to this. The baseline comment system you're going to build on is bundled as `django.contrib.comments`, and it supports either of two styles of commenting.

- **Free comments**: These can be posted by anyone, regardless of whether they have a user account on the site.

- **Registered comments**: These can only be posted by someone who has an account and is logged in.

For the weblog, you'll use the free comments system because you want anyone who reads the blog to be able to leave a comment.

Installing the Comments Application

Installing the comment system is easy. Open up your Django project's settings file (`settings.py`), and add the following line in the `INSTALLED_APPS` list:

```
'django.contrib.comments',
```

Next run `python manage.py syncdb`, and Django will install its models. If you fire up the development server and visit the administrative interface, you'll see a new Comments section with two items under it, one for each type of comment. The `Comment` model handles registered comments, and `FreeComment` handles free comments.

In the project's root `URLConf` file (`urls.py`), add one new URL pattern:

```
(r'^comments/', include('django.contrib.comments.urls.comments')),
```

You've seen this pattern several times now, and, in general, this is the hallmark of a well-built Django application. Installing it shouldn't involve any more work than the following:

1. Add it to `INSTALLED_APPS` and run `syncdb`.

2. Add a new URL pattern to route to its default URLConf.

3. Set up any needed templates.

Writing an application to work this way out of the box is an extremely powerful technique because it allows even very complex sites to be built quickly out of reusable applications, with each supplying one particular piece of functionality. Keeping this pattern in mind as you write your own applications will help you produce high-quality, useful applications. In Chapter 11, you'll look at some techniques for building in configurability and flexibility beyond this style of basic setup.

Basic Setup

To get started with the comments application, you'll only need to set up two templates, which will be used to preview a comment before posting it. But before you can preview a comment, you need to show a form for visitors to fill out. Let's start with that.

Open up the entry detail template—`coltrane/entry_detail.html`—and go to the main content block, which looks like this:

```
{% block content %}
<h2>{{ object.title }}</h2>
{{ object.body_html|safe }}
{% endblock %}
```

Go ahead and add a header that will distinguish the comment form:

```
{% block content %}
<h2>{{ object.title }}</h2>
{{ object.body_html|safe }}

<h2>Post a comment</h2>

{% endblock %}
```

Now you just need to display the form. The comments system includes a custom template tag library which, among other things, can do just that. The tag library is called `comments`, so you'll need to load it with the {% load %} tag:

```
{% block content %}
<h2>{{ object.title }}</h2>
{{ object.body_html|safe }}

<h2>Post a comment</h2>

{% load comments %}

{% endblock %}
```

Now, the tag you want is called {% free_comment_form %}, and its syntax looks like this:

```
{% free_comment_form for app_name.model_name object_id %}
```

In other words, it wants an application name and model name to identify the model the comment will be attached to—these will be fed into the get_model() function you saw in Chapter 6—and the id of the specific object it's going to be attached to, which will be available in the entry_detail template as the variable {{ object.id }}. So you can fill in the tag like so:

```
{% block content %}
<h2>{{ object.title }}</h2>
{{ object.body_html|safe }}

<h2>Post a comment</h2>

{% load comments %}

{% free_comment_form for coltrane.entry object.id %}

{% endblock %}
```

Note that you *don't* put the braces around object.id here. The braces, as in {{ object.id }}, are only used when you want to output the value of the variable. In a template tag, they're not needed and, in fact, will cause an error. Template tags can resolve variables on their own (as you'll see in Chapter 10 when you write a few tags that do that).

Now, go visit an entry, and you'll see the comment form show up. But if you fill in a comment and hit the Preview button, you'll see an ugly error telling you that the preview template doesn't exist. Since this will vary from site to site, Django can't provide it automatically. You will have to fill it in.

The template it wants is called comments/free_preview.html. So go to the project's template directory and create a new comments directory inside it, then place the following into a template inside of that called free_preview.html:

```
{% extends "base.html" %}

{% block title %}| Post a comment{% endblock %}

{% block content %}
<h2>Post a comment</h2>
```

```
<p>Here's how your comment will look:</p>

<p>On {{ comment.submit_date|date:"F j, Y" }}, {{ comment.person_name }} said:</p>

{{ comment.comment }}

<form action="/comments/postfree/" method="post">
<dl id="comment-form">
  <dt><label for="id_person_name">Your name:</label>
  {% if comment_form.person_name.errors %}
  <span class="error">{{ comment_form.person_name.errors|join:", " }}
  {% endif %}</dt>
  <dd>{{ comment_form.person_name }}</dd>
  <dt><label for="id_comment">Your Comment:</label>
  {% if comment_form.comment.errors %}
  <span class="error">{{ comment_form.comment.errors|join:", " }}
  {% endif %}</dt>
  <dd>{{ comment_form.comment }}
    <input type="hidden" name="options" value="{{ options }}" />
    <input type="hidden" name="target" value="{{ target }}" />
    <input type="hidden" name="gonzo" value="{{ hash }}" />
    </dd>
  <dd><input type="submit" name="post" value="Post comment" /></dd>
</dl>
</form>
{% endblock %}
```

The view that handles this (which lives in `django.contrib.comments.views`, if you'd like to have a look at it) is concerned with doing two things: letting users preview their comments and validating the submitted comment to make sure that, for example, all the required fields are present. The validation routine makes use of Django's form-handling system, which I'll cover in detail a bit later on, but for now you can probably guess what's going on in that part of the template. The remainder is simply showing a preview of the comment (each `FreeComment` object has fields named `submit_date`, `person_name`, and `comment`, representing the date the comment was posted, the name of the commenter, and the actual comment text).

It would be nice to have some safe way to let commenters use some basic HTML so that they can include things like links or text formatting in their comments. But Django's template system will automatically escape the contents of the comment in order to prevent malicious HTML from being displayed.

To solve this, you need to have some way to allow some basic formatting—say, the Markdown style of formatting you're using for the entries and links in the blog—but forbid any raw HTML from being passed through. The Python Markdown module supports this through a "safe mode" that will strip out raw HTML but process Markdown syntax normally, so that seems like an ideal way to solve it. The only question is how to apply it in the templates.

The answer is to use a template filter. Just as Django lets you define custom template tags, it will let you define custom filters as well. All you would need, then, is a filter that applies Markdown formatting, in safe mode, to a variable. The code for it would look like this:

```
from django import template
from markdown import markdown

def safe_markdown(value):
    return markdown(value, safe_mode=True)

register = template.Library()
register.filter(safe_markdown)
```

Note that this is much simpler than defining a custom tag. A filter is simply a function that gets passed a value and is expected to return another value, which will become part of the template's rendered output. Registering a filter uses `register.filter()`, as opposed to the `register.tag()` for custom template tags.

But you don't actually need to write this filter because a set of text-to-HTML formatting filters is bundled with Django in the `django.contrib.markup` application. This application doesn't provide any models, but it does include a library of custom template filters that know how to apply common text-to-HTML formatting systems like Markdown.

To use it, you'll need to do two things. First, add `django.contrib.markup` to the INSTALLED_APPS setting of your project. (There's no need to run `manage.py syncdb`, since this application doesn't provide any models to be installed in the database.) Next, load its library of custom filters, which is named `markup`. Here's how it will look in the template:

```
{% load markup %}
<h2>Post a comment</h2>

<p>Here's how your comment will look:</p>

<p>On {{ comment.submit_date|date:"F j, Y" }}, {{ comment.person_name }} said:</p>

{{ comment.comment|markdown:"safe" }}
```

This will apply Markdown formatting, using the safe mode that strips raw HTML, to the comment, which is precisely what you want.

One more template is required to complete the process. After a comment is successfully posted, the comment-submission view will issue an HTTP redirect to a second view, which uses the template `comments/posted.html`. This template will receive one variable, `object`, which is the content object the comment was attached to and which can be used to show a link back to that object. For example, you might place something like this in your `comments/posted.html` template:

```
<p>Your comment was posted successfully; you can see it by
<a href="{{ object.get_absolute_url }}">returning to the
discussion</a>.</p>
```

Retrieving Lists of Comments for Display

All you need to do now is retrieve the comments and display them. And just as it provides a custom template tag for showing the comment form, `django.contrib.comments` provides a tag that can handle comment retrieval. The syntax for it looks like this:

```
{% get_free_comment_list for app_name.model_name object_id as varname %}
```

So you can make use of it in your `entry_detail.html` template like so:

```
<h2>Comments</h2>
{% load markup %}
{% get_free_comment_list for coltrane.entry object.id as comment_list %}

{% for comment in comment_list %}

<p>On {{ comment.submit_date|date:"F j, Y" }},
{{ comment.person_name }} said:</p>

{{ comment.comment|markdown:"safe" }}
{% endfor %}
```

So the full content block of your `entry_detail.html` template now looks like this:

```
{% block content %}
<h2>{{ object.title }}</h2>
{{ object.body_html }}

<h2>Comments</h2>
{% load comments %}
{% load markup %}
{% get_free_comment_list for coltrane.entry object.id as comment_list %}

{% for comment in comment_list %}

<p>On {{ comment.submit_date|date:"F j, Y" }},
{{ comment.person_name }} said:</p>

{{ comment.comment|markdown:"safe" }}
{% endfor %}

<h2>Post a comment</h2>

{% free_comment_form for coltrane.entry object.id %}

{% endblock %}
```

If you'd like to add a line in the sidebar to show the number of comments on the entry, the `get_free_comment_count` tag will retrieve it for you. You might use it like this:

```
{% load comments %}
{% get_free_comment_count for coltrane.entry object.id as comment_count %}

<p>So far, there are {{ comment_count }}
comment{{ comment_count|pluralize }} on this entry.</p>
```

> ### ADMONITION: THE SCOPE OF THE {% load %} TAG
>
> Due to the way Django's template inheritance works, a custom tag or filter library loaded using the {% load %} tag will only be available in the block in which it was loaded. If you need to reuse the same tag library in a different block, you'll need to load it again.

Comment Moderation

Out of the box, this covers most of what you want for commenting: an easy way to let visitors post comments, and then pull out a list of the comments that are "attached" to a particular object. But given the proliferation of comment spam around the Web in recent years, you're still going to want some sort of automatic moderation system to screen incoming comments. For that, you'll need to write some code.

Both of the comment models in `django.contrib.comments` define a `BooleanField` called `is_public`, and that's what a moderation system should use. Now, there are a couple of very effective ways to filter comment spam:

- Whenever a comment is posted on an entry that's more than a certain number of days old (say, 30), automatically mark it nonpublic. The vast majority of comment spam targets old content, partly because most content is old and partly because it's less likely to be noticed by a site administrator.

- Use a statistical spam detection system. Akismet (`http://akismet.com/`) is the gold standard for this, with a history of over five billion spam comments to draw on for analysis. Best of all, they have a web-based API that will estimate whether a comment is spam or not.

On my personal blog, I get around six thousand spam comments a month. The combination of these two methods has, so far, prevented all but one or two of them from ever showing up publicly.

So you want to find some way to hook into the comment-submission system and automatically apply the two filtering methods previously mentioned to set `is_public=False` on the new comment whenever it looks like it'll be spam. There are a couple of obvious ways to do this:

- Just as you've defined a custom `save()` method on some of our own models, you could go to the comment models in Django and edit them to include a custom `save()` method that does the spam filtering.

- You could edit or replace the view that handles the comment submission and put the spam filtering there.

But both of these have major drawbacks. Either you're editing code that comes with Django (which will make it harder to upgrade down the road and may cause problems with debugging because you'll have a nonstandard Django codebase), or you're duplicating code Django has already provided in order to add a small modification.

Wouldn't it be nice if there was a way you could just write some of your own code, and then hook into Django somehow to make sure it runs at the right moment?

Signals and the Django Dispatcher

As it turns out, there is a way. Django includes a module—django.dispatch—which provides two things:

- A way for any piece of code in Django, or in one of your own applications, to advertise the fact that something happened.

- A way for any other piece of code to "listen" for a specific event happening and take some action in response.

The way the system works is pretty simple. Inside django.dispatch is a module called dispatcher, which defines several functions, but the two important ones are called send() and connect(). Here's how they work:

- django.dispatch.dispatcher.send(): This is used to send a *signal*— basically just a Python object that can be identified by the place it was imported from.

- django.dispatch.dispatcher.connect(): This is used to register a function as listening for a particular signal. When that signal is sent, the function you registered will be called.

For a simple example, go to the cms project directory, and start a Python interpreter by typing python manage.py shell. Then type the following:

```
>>> from coltrane.models import Entry
>>> from django.dispatch import dispatcher
>>> from django.db.models import signals
>>> def print_save_message(sender, instance):
...     print "An entry was just saved!"
>>> dispatcher.connect(print_save_message, signal=signals.post_save,➥
sender=Entry)
```

Now, query for an Entry and save it:

```
>>> e = Entry.objects.all()[0]
>>> e.save()
```

Your Python interpreter will suddenly print "An entry was just saved!" Here's what happened:

1. You imported the dispatcher and a module in `django.db.models`, which defines some signals.

2. You wrote a function that prints the message. The arguments it receives—`sender` and `instance`—will end up being the `Entry` model class (which is going to "send" the signal you're listening for) and the specific `Entry` object being saved. You're not doing anything with these arguments, but when you build the comment moderation system you'll see how they can be used.

3. You registered it using `dispatcher.connect()`, to be called when the post_save signal is sent by the `Entry` model.

4. When the `Entry` was saved, code within Django—built into the base `Model` class all your models inherit from—used `dispatcher.send()` to send the post_save signal.

5. The dispatcher called your custom function.

Django defines about a dozen signals you can use immediately, and it's easy to define and use your own as well. There are also some more-complex tricks you can do with the dispatcher, but what you've seen so far is all you'll actually need to build an effective comment moderator.

Building the Automatic Comment Moderator

To build your comment moderation system, you'll write a function that knows how to look at an incoming comment and figure out whether it's spam. Then you'll use the dispatcher to ensure that function is called each time a new comment is about to be saved. Just as you used the post_save signal in the previous example, there's a pre_save signal you can use to run code before an object is saved.

The first thing you want to do when you get a new comment is look at the entry it's being posted to. If that entry is more than, say, 30 days old, you'll just set its `is_public` field to `False` and not bother with any further checks. This is where the `instance` argument to your custom function comes into play. It will be the new comment object that's about to be saved, and from that you can get at the entry it's being posted on. Here's what the code looks like:

```
import datetime

def moderate_comment(sender, instance):
    if not instance.id:
        entry = instance.get_content_object()
        delta = datetime.datetime.now() - entry.pub_date
        if delta.days > 30:
            instance.is_public = False
```

So far, this function is pretty straightforward. You only check things if the comment—which will be the object in the `instance` argument—doesn't yet have an `id`, meaning it hasn't been saved to the database. If it does have an `id`, presumably it's already been checked. Checking it again would make it hard for a site administrator to ever manually approve a comment, since the comment would keep going through this process, being marked nonpublic on each save.

First you use the `instance` argument to find the entry the comment is being posted on. Both of Django's comment models define a method called `get_content_object()`, which returns the object the comment pertains to.

Next you subtract the entry's `pub_date` from the current date and time. Python's `datetime` class is set up so that this will work, and the result is an instance of a class called `timedelta`, which has attributes representing the number of days, hours, and so on between the two `datetime` objects involved.

Next you check the `days` attribute on that `timedelta` object. If it's greater than 30, you set the new comment's `is_public` field to `False`.

At this point you could already hook up the function, and it would do a good job of preventing spam:

```
from django.contrib.comments.models import FreeComment
from django.dispatch import dispatcher
from django.db.models import signals

dispatcher.connect(moderate_comment, signal=signals.pre_save,
                   sender=FreeComment)
```

Adding Akismet Support

Now let's add in the second layer of spam prevention: statistical spam analysis by the Akismet web service. The first thing you'll need is an Akismet API key—all access to Akismet's service requires this key. Luckily, it's free for personal, noncommercial use. Just follow the instructions on the Akismet web site (`http://akismet.com/personal/`) to get a key. Once you've got it, open up the Django settings file for the `cms` project and add the following line to it:

```
AKISMET_API_KEY = 'your API key goes here'
```

By making this a custom setting, you'll be able to reuse the Akismet spam filtering on other sites, even if they have different API keys.

Akismet is a web-based service. You send information about a comment to the service using an HTTP request, and it sends back an HTTP response telling you whether Akismet thinks that comment is spam. You could build up the code necessary to do this, but—as you'll often find when working with Python—someone else has already done it and made the code available for free.

In this case, it's a module called `akismet`, which is available from the author, Michael Foord, at his web site: `www.voidspace.org.uk/python/modules.shtml#akismet`. Go ahead and download and unpack it (it should come in a .zip file). This will give you a file named `akismet.py` that you can put on your Python import path (ideally, in the same location as the `coltrane` directory that holds the weblog application).

The `akismet` module includes a class called `Akismet` that handles the API. This class has two methods you'll be using: one called `verify_key()`, which ensures you're using a valid API key, and one called `comment_check()`, which submits a comment to Akismet and returns `True` if Akismet thinks the comment is spam.

So the first thing you'll need to do is import the `Akismet` class:

```
from akismet import Akismet
```

The Akismet API requires both the API key you've been assigned and the address of the site you're submitting the comment from. You could hard-code the URL of your site in here, but that would hurt the reusability of the code. A better option is to use Django's bundled sites framework (it lives in `django.contrib.sites`), which provides a model that represents a particular web site and knows which site is currently active.

You'll recall that back in Chapter 2, when you set up the simple CMS, you edited a `Site` object so it would "know" where you were running the development server. Whenever you're running with this database and settings file, you can get that `Site` object with the following:

```
from django.contrib.sites.models import Site
current_site = Site.objects.get_current()
```

This works because the `Site` model has a custom manager that defines the `get_current()` method. The `Site` object it returns has a field called `domain`, which you can use to fill in the information Akismet wants. This information is the keyword argument `blog_url` when creating an instance of the API (along with the API key, which comes from your settings file and is the keyword argument `key`):

```
from django.conf import settings
from django.contrib.sites.models import Site

akismet_api = Akismet(key=settings.AKISMET_API_KEY,
                      blog_url="http:/%s/" %➥
                      Site.objects.get_current().domain)
```

Then you can check your API key with the `verify_key()` method and, if it's valid, submit a comment for analysis with the `comment_check()` method. The `comment_check()` method is going to expect three arguments:

- The text of the comment to check.

- Some additional "metadata" about the comment, in a dictionary.

- A boolean (`True` or `False`) argument telling it whether to try to work out additional metadata on its own.

The text of the comment is easy enough to get, since it's a field on the comment itself. The dictionary of metadata needs to have at least four values in it, even if some of them are blank (because you don't necessarily know what they are). These values are the type of comment (which, for simple uses like this, is simply the string `comment`), the HTTP `Referer` header value, the IP address from which the comment was sent (also a field on the `comment` model), and the HTTP `User-Agent` of the commenter. Finally, you'll tell the `akismet` module to go ahead and work out any additional metadata it can find. More information means better accuracy, especially since the `akismet` module can, under some server setups, find some useful information automatically. The code looks like this:

```
from django.utils.encoding import smart_str

if akismet_api.verify_key():
    akismet_data = { 'comment_type': 'comment',
                     'referrer': '',
```

```
                        'user_ip': instance.ip_address,
                        'user-agent': '' }
    if akismet_api.comment_check(smart_str(instance.comment),
                                 akismet_data,
                                 build_data=True):
        instance.is_public = False
```

Remember that Django uses Unicode strings everywhere, so whenever you use an external API, you should convert Unicode strings to bytestrings by using the helper function django.utils.encoding.smart_str().

And note that since you don't know what the HTTP Referer and User-Agent headers are—that information is only available inside the view function that processes the submission, since it has access to the HTTP request—you simply leave them as empty strings.

Once you put it all together, the complete comment-moderation function, with both age-based and statistical Akismet filtering, looks like this:

```
import datetime
from akismet import Akismet
from django.conf import settings
from django.contrib.comments.models import FreeComment
from django.contrib.sites.models import Site
from django.db.models import signals
from django.dispatch import dispatcher
from django.utils.encoding import smart_str

def moderate_comment(sender, instance):
    if not instance.id:
        entry = instance.get_content_object()
        delta = datetime.datetime.now() - entry.pub_date
        if delta.days > 30:
            instance.is_public = False
        else:
            akismet_api = Akismet(key=settings.AKISMET_API_KEY,
                                  blog_url="http:/%s/" %➡
                                  Site.objects.get_current().domain)
            if akismet_api.verify_key():
                akismet_data = { 'comment_type': 'comment',
                                 'referrer': '',
                                 'user_ip': instance.ip_address,
                                 'user-agent': '' }
                if akismet_api.comment_check(smart_str(instance.comment),
                                             akismet_data,
                                             build_data=True):
                    instance.is_public = False

dispatcher.connect(moderate_comment,
                   signal=signals.pre_save,
                   sender=FreeComment)
```

The best place to put this is near the bottom of `coltrane/models.py` so that the `dispatcher.connect()` line will be read and executed when the weblog's models are imported. This also does away with the need for at least one of the imports—the `import datetime` line—because it's already been imported in that file.

ADMONITION: IMPORT PATHS AND MULTIPLE IMPORTS OF A SINGLE MODULE

When you import a Python module for the first time, all of the code inside it is parsed and executed. That's why the `dispatcher.connect()` line will be run whenever the weblog's models are first imported. But this opens up a subtle potential bug: Python does this once for each unique import path used to carry out the import. So, for example, if you were importing the search-oriented models you wrote for the CMS back in Chapter 3, the code in `cms/search/models.py` would be evaluated once if you did the import like this:

```
from cms.search import models
```

And it would be evaluated *again* if you later did another import like this:

```
from search import models
```

Django's `manage.py` utility changes your Python import path for convenience, and in so doing, makes it so that both of the preceding lines will work. So it's not unusual that a project ends up having imports in both forms like the ones shown. Unfortunately, this means that if you have a piece of code you want to run only once—like the `dispatcher.connect()` line, since you only want that function to register once—it will instead be run once for each different way the module gets imported.

It's best to pick a single style of import and use it consistently. As a general rule, I typically always stick to the way the application is listed in my `INSTALLED_APPS` setting. For example, if I have `cms.search` in `INSTALLED_APPS`, I always do the import as `from cms.search import models`.

E-mail Notification of Comments

A lot of weblogging and CMS systems that allow commenting also include a feature that automatically notifies site administrators whenever a new comment is posted. This is useful because it lets them keep up with active discussions, and also lets them spot any problems—a troublemaking commenter, arguments that get out of hand, or just the occasional bit of spam that slips through the filter. Since you've seen how easy it is to use Django's dispatcher to add extra functionality when a comment is posted, let's go ahead and add e-mail notifications as a finishing touch.

Sending e-mail from within Django is fairly easy to do, and breaks down into a few simple steps:

1. Fill in, at a minimum, the settings `EMAIL_HOST` and `EMAIL_PORT` in the Django settings file. These will be used to determine the e-mail (SMTP) server Django connects to in order to send mail. If your mail server requires a username and password to send mail, fill in `EMAIL_HOST_USER` and `EMAIL_HOST_PASSWORD` as well. If your mail server requires a secure TLS connection, set `EMAIL_USE_TLS` to `True`.

2. Fill in the setting `DEFAULT_FROM_EMAIL` to be the default From address used for automated e-mail sending.

3. Import an e-mail sending function from `django.core.mail` and call it. Most often you'll use `django.core.mail.send_mail()`, which takes a subject, message, From address, and list of recipients, in that order.

ADMONITION: VERIFYING E-MAIL–RELATED SETTINGS

Typically, your hosting provider or your Internet service provider (depending on who provides your e-mail service) will be able to give you the correct values to fill in for settings like `EMAIL_HOST`. To double-check them, you can use `django.core.send_mail()` manually in a Python interpreter (launched with `python manage.py shell` in your project directory) to send yourself a test message. If the settings are correct, you'll receive an e-mail. If anything goes wrong, Python will report the error message to you in the interpreter.

If you'd like to suppress the reporting of errors, you can pass the keyword argument `fail_silently=True` to any of Django's mail-sending functions. Keep in mind, however, that this will *completely* silence errors during the sending of the e-mail, which means you'll have no way of knowing whether any given message was sent successfully.

Now, you could use `send_mail()` and hard-code one or more recipients for comment notifications. But once again, this would hurt the reusability of your code. Two different sites using this application might want two different sets of people receiving comment notifications.

Fortunately, there's an easy solution. In the Django settings file are two settings—`ADMINS` and `MANAGERS`—that exist for dealing with situations like this. The `ADMINS` setting should be a list of programmers or other technical people who should receive notifications about problems with your site. When you deploy in production, Django will automatically e-mail debugging information to the people listed in `ADMINS` whenever a server error occurs. The `MANAGERS` setting, on the other hand, should be a list of people who aren't necessarily programmers, but who are involved in the management of the site. Each of these settings expects a format like the following:

```
MANAGERS = (('Alice Jones', 'alice@example.com'),
            ('Bob Smith', 'bob@example.com'))
```

In other words, it's a tuple, or list of tuples, where each tuple contains a name and an e-mail address. When these are filled in, two functions in `django.core.mail`—`mail_admins()` and `mail_managers()`—can be used as a shortcut to send an e-mail to those people.

So to add comment notification you can do something like the following:

```
from django.core.mail import mail_managers
email_body = "%s posted a new comment on the entry '%s'."
mail_managers("New comment posted",
              email_body % (instance.person_name,
                            instance.get_content_object()))
```

This will send an e-mail to everyone listed in the MANAGERS setting, notifying them of the new comment.

And so you have the final version of your function:

```
from akismet import Akismet
from django.conf import settings
from django.contrib.comments.models import FreeComment
from django.contrib.sites.models import Site
from django.core.mail import mail_managers
from django.db.models import signals
from django.dispatch import dispatcher
from django.utils.encoding import smart_str

def moderate_comment(sender, instance):
    if not instance.id:
        entry = instance.get_content_object()
        delta = datetime.datetime.now() - entry.pub_date
        if delta.days > 30:
            instance.is_public = False
        else:
            akismet_api = Akismet(key=settings.AKISMET_API_KEY,
                                  blog_url="http:/%s/" %➦
                                  Site.objects.get_current().domain)
            if akismet_api.verify_key():
                akismet_data = { 'comment_type': 'comment',
                                 'referrer': '',
                                 'user_ip': instance.ip_address,
                                 'user-agent': '' }
                if akismet_api.comment_check(smart_str(instance.comment),
                                             akismet_data,
                                             build_data=True):
                    instance.is_public = False
        email_body = "%s posted a new comment on the entry '%s'."
        mail_managers("New comment posted",
                      email_body % (instance.person_name,
                                    instance.get_content_object())))

dispatcher.connect(moderate_comment,
                   signal=signals.pre_save,
                   sender=FreeComment)
```

Dealing with Moderated Comments in Public-Facing Templates

The only thing left is to work out is how to deal with moderated comments in your templates. The tag that fetches the list of comments doesn't take the is_public field into account, and so it always fetches all the comments for a particular item, even if some of them have is_public set to `False`. The easiest way to deal with this is simply to check whether a comment is public before displaying it. Where you currently have this:

```
<h2>Comments</h2>
{% load markup %}
{% get_free_comment_list for coltrane.entry object.id as comment_list %}

{% for comment in comment_list %}

<p>On {{ comment.submit_date|date:"F j, Y" }}, {{
comment.person_name }} said:</p>

{{ comment.comment|markdown:"safe" }}
{% endfor %}
```

you can change it to this:

```
<h2>Comments</h2>
{% load markup %}
{% get_free_comment_list for coltrane.entry object.id as comment_list %}

{% for comment in comment_list %}
{% if comment.is_public %}

<p>On {{ comment.submit_date|date:"F j, Y" }}, {{
comment.person_name }} said:</p>

{{ comment.comment|markdown:"safe" }}
{% endif %}
{% endfor %}
```

And now any comments that aren't public won't be displayed.

It's also possible, if you're feeling adventurous, to write your own tag that mimics the behavior of `{% get_free_comment_list %}` but only retrieves comments with `is_public` set to `True`. If you'd like to study a ready-made version, I maintain an open source Django application, called `comment_utils`, which provides this and a few other comment-related features. You can browse the code or download it from `http://code.google.com/p/django-comment-utils/`.

Adding Feeds

The last features you want for your weblog is the ability to have RSS or Atom feeds of your entries and links. You also want to have custom feeds that handle, for example, entries in a specific category. Doing this from scratch—by writing view functions that retrieve a list of entries and render a template that creates the appropriate XML instead of an HTML page—wouldn't be too terribly hard. But because this is a common need for web sites, Django again provides some help to automate the process via the bundled application `django.contrib.syndication`. At its core, `django.contrib.syndication` provides two things:

- A set of classes that represent feeds and that can be subclassed for easy customization

- A view that knows how to work with these classes to generate and serve the appropriate XML

To see how it works, let's start by setting up an Atom feed for the latest entries posted to the weblog.

LatestEntriesFeed

Go into the `coltrane` directory and create a new empty file, called `feeds.py`. At the top, add the following lines:

```
from django.utils.feedgenerator import Atom1Feed
from django.contrib.sites.models import Site
from django.contrib.syndication.feeds import Feed
from coltrane.models import Entry

current_site = Site.objects.get_current()
```

Now you can start writing a feed class for the latest entries. Call it `LatestEntriesFeed`. It will be a subclass of the `django.contrib.syndication.feeds.Feed` class you're importing here.

First you need to fill in some required metadata. This is going to be an Atom feed, so several elements are required. (RSS feeds require less metadata, but it's a good idea to include this information anyway, since additional metadata is more useful for people who use feeds.) Here's an example:

```
class LatestEntriesFeed(Feed):
    author_name = "Bob Smith"
    copyright = "http://%s/about/copyright/" % current_site.domain
    description = "Latest entries posted to %s" % current_site.name
    feed_type = Atom1Feed
    item_copyright = "http://%s/about/copyright/" % current_site.domain
    item_author_name = "Bob Smith"
    item_author_link = "http://%s/" % current_site.domain
    link = "/feeds/entries/"
    title = "%s: Latest entries" % current_site.name
```

Go ahead and fill in appropriate information for your own name and relevant metadata. Note that while most of the items here will automatically vary according to the current site, I've hard-coded values into the two fields for authors and the `link` field.

For reusability across a wide variety of sites, this feed class can be subclassed to override only those values; or if you have a function that can determine the correct value for a given site, you can fill that in. (For example, you might use a reverse URL lookup to get the `link` field.) For a complete list of these fields and what you're allowed to put in each one, check the full documentation for `django.contrib.syndication`, which is online at www.djangoproject.com/documentation/syndication_feeds/.

Now you need to tell the feed how to find the items it's supposed to contain. This will be the latest 15 live entries. You do this by adding a method named `items()` to the feed class, which will return those entries:

```
def items(self):
    return Entry.live.all()[:15]
```

Each item needs to have a date listed in the feed. That's accomplished by a method called `item_pubdate()`, which will receive an object as an argument and should return a `date` or `datetime` object to use for that object. (The `Feed` class will automatically format this appropriately for the type of feed being used.) In the case of an `Entry`, that's just the value of the `pub_date` field:

```
def item_pubdate(self, item):
    return item.pub_date
```

Each item also needs to have a unique identifier, called a GUID (short for globally unique identifier). This can be the `id` field from the database, but it's generally better to use something less transient. If you ever migrated to a new server or a different database, the `id` values might change during the transition, and the GUID for a particular entry would change when that happened.

For a situation like this, the ideal solution is something called a *tag URI* (uniform resource identifier). Tag URIs are a standard way of generating a unique identifier for some Internet resource, in a way that won't change so long as that Internet resource continues to exist at the same address. If you're interested in the full details of the standard, tag URIs are specified by IETF RFC 4151 (`www.faqs.org/rfcs/rfc4151.html`), but the basic idea is that a tag URI for an item consists of three parts:

1. The `tag:` string.

2. The domain for the item, followed by a comma, followed by a relevant date for the item, followed by a colon.

3. An identifying string that is unique for that domain and date.

For the date, you'll use the `pub_date` field of each entry. For the unique identifying string, you'll use the result of its `get_absolute_url()` method, since that's required to be unique.

The result, for example, is that the entry at `www.example.com/2008/jan/12/example-entry/` would end up with a GUID of

```
tag:example.com,2008-01-12:/2008/jan/12/example-entry/
```

This meets all the requirements for a feed GUID. To implement this, you simply define a method on your feed class called `item_guid()`. Again, it receives an object as its argument:

```
def item_guid(self, item):
    return "tag:%s,%s:%s" % (current_site.domain,
                             item.pub_date.strftime('%Y-%m-%d'),
                             item.get_absolute_url())
```

One final thing you can add to your feed is a list of categories for each item. This will help feed aggregators to categorize the items you publish. You can do this by defining a method called item_categories:

```
def item_categories(self, item):
    return [c.title for c in item.categories.all()]
```

A full example feed class, then, looks like this:

```
class LatestEntriesFeed(Feed):
    author_name = "Bob Smith"
    copyright = "http://%s/about/copyright/" % current_site.domain
    description = "Latest entries posted to %s" % current_site.name
    feed_type = Atom1Feed
    item_copyright = "http://%s/about/copyright/" % current_site.domain
    item_author_name = "Bob Smith"
    item_author_link = "http://%s/" % current_site.domain
    link = "/feeds/entries/"
    title = "%s: Latest entries" % current_site.name

    def items(self):
        return Entry.live.all()[:15]

    def item_pubdate(self, item):
        return item.pub_date

    def item_guid(self, item):
        return "tag:%s,%s:%s" % (current_site.domain,
                                 item.pub_date.strftime('%Y-%m-%d'),
                                 item.get_absolute_url())

    def item_categories(self, item):
        return [c.title for c in item.categories.all()]
```

Now you can set up a URL for this feed. Go to the urls.py file in the cms project directory, and add two things. First, near the top of the file (above the list of URL patterns), add the following import statement and dictionary definition:

```
from coltrane.feeds import LatestEntriesFeed

feeds = { 'entries': LatestEntriesFeed }
```

Next, add a new pattern to the list of URLs:

```
(r'^feeds/(?P<url>.*)/$',
 'django.contrib.syndication.views.feed',
 { 'feed_dict': feeds }),
```

This will route any URL beginning with /feeds/ to the view in django.contrib.syndication, which handles feeds. The dictionary you set up maps between feed slugs, like entries, and specific feed classes.

One final thing you need to do is create two templates. `django.contrib.syndication` uses the Django template system to render the title and main body of each item in the feed so that you can decide how you want to present each type of item. So go to the directory where you've been keeping templates for this project, and inside it create a new directory called `feeds`. Inside that create two new files, called `entries_title.html` and `entries_description.html`. (The names to use come from the combination of the feed's slug—in this case, `entries`—and whether the template is for the item's title or its description.) Each of these templates will have access to two variables:

- `obj`: This is a specific item being included in the feed.

- `site`: This is the current `Site` object, as returned by `Site.objects.get_current()`.

So for item titles, you can simply use each entry's title. In the `entries_title.html` template, place the following:

```
{{ obj.title }}
```

For the description, you'll use the same trick as the entry archive templates you set up in the last chapter. Display the `excerpt_html` field if it has any content; otherwise, display the first 50 words of `body_html`. So in `entries_description.html`, fill in the following:

```
{% if obj.excerpt_html %}
{{ obj.excerpt_html|safe }}
{% else %}
{{ obj.body_html|truncatewords_html:"50"|safe }}
{% endif %}
```

Remember that Django's template system automatically escapes HTML in variables, so you still have to use the `safe` filter. With the templates in place, you can launch the development server and visit the URL `/feeds/entries/` to see the feed of latest entries in the weblog.

Writing a feed for the latest links should be easy at this point. Try writing the `LatestLinksFeed` class yourself and set it up correctly. (Remember that links don't have categories associated with them, so you should either leave out the `item_categories()` method or rewrite it to return a list of tags.) A full example is in the sample code you can download for this book, so refer to it if you get lost.

Entries by Category: A More Complex Feed Example

Now, you'd like to also offer categorized feeds so that readers who are interested in one or two specific topics can subscribe to feeds that only list entries from the categories they like. But this is a bit trickier because it raises two problems:

- The list of items in the feed should, of course, know how to figure out which `Category` it's looking at and ensure that it only returns entries from that category.

- Several of the metadata fields—the title of the feed, the link, and so on—will need to change dynamically based on the category.

Django's Feed class provides a way to deal with this, though. A Feed subclass can define a method called get_object(), which will be passed an argument containing the bits of the URL that came after the slug you registered the feed with, as a list. So, for example, if you registered a feed with the slug categories and visited the URL /feeds/categories/django/, your feed's get_object() would be passed an argument containing the single-item list ["django"]. From there you can look up the category.

Let's start by adding two items to the import statements at the top of your feeds.py file so that now it looks like this:

```
from django.core.exceptions import ObjectDoesNotExist
from django.utils.feedgenerator import Atom1Feed
from django.contrib.sites.models import Site
from django.contrib.syndication.feeds import Feed
from coltrane.models import Category, Entry
```

This gives you access to the Category model, as well as to an exception class Django defines—ObjectDoesNotExist. You can use this if someone tries to visit a URL for a nonexistent category's feed. (When you raise ObjectDoesNotExist, Django will return an HTTP 404 "File Not Found" response.)

Now you can begin writing your feed class. Since a lot of it is similar to the existing LatestEntriesFeed, you'll just subclass it and change the parts that need to be changed:

```
class CategoryFeed(LatestEntriesFeed):
    def get_object(self, bits):
        if len(bits) != 1:
            raise ObjectDoesNotExist
        return Category.objects.get(slug__exact=bits[0])
```

This will either raise ObjectDoesNotExist or return the Category you need to display entries for. Now you can set up the feed's title, description, and link, by defining methods with those names that receive the Category object as an argument (Django's feed system is smart enough to recognize that it needs to pass that object when calling them):

```
def title(self, obj):
    return "%s: Latest entries in category '%s'" % (current_site.name,
                                                    obj.title)


def description(self, obj):
    return "%s: Latest entries in category '%s'" % (current_site.name,
                                                    obj.title)


def link(self, obj):
    return obj.get_absolute_url()
```

"PLAIN" ATTRIBUTES VS. METHODS ON FEEDS

In general, any of the various bits of metadata for a feed—the title, description and link, and metadata for individual items in the feed—can either be hard-coded by a plain attribute of the correct name or generated dynamically by defining a method of that name. For feeds like `CategoryFeed` that need to look up some object (in this case a `Category`) through their `get_object()` method, you can define a method that expects to receive that object.

Again, for a full list of the different fields you can use on a feed—each of which will work like this— consult the full documentation for `django.contrib.syndication` online at `www.djangoproject.com/documentation/syndication_feeds/`.

You can change the `items()` method as well. Again, Django's feed system is smart enough to know that it needs to be passed the `Category` object, and it will make sure that happens:

```
def items(self, obj):
    return obj.live_entry_set()[:15]
```

Remember that you defined the `live_entry_set()` method on the `Category` model so that it would only return entries with "live" status.

And that's that. Now your `feeds.py` file should look like this:

```
from django.core.exceptions import ObjectDoesNotExist
from django.utils.feedgenerator import Atom1Feed
from django.contrib.sites.models import Site
from django.contrib.syndication.feeds import Feed
from coltrane.models import Category, Entry

current_site = Site.objects.get_current()

class LatestEntriesFeed(Feed):
    author_name = "Bob Smith"
    copyright = "http://%s/about/copyright/" % current_site.domain
    description = "Latest entries posted to %s" % current_site.name
    feed_type = Atom1Feed
    item_copyright = "http://%s/about/copyright/" % current_site.domain
    item_author_name = "Bob Smith"
    item_author_link = "http://%s/" % current_site.domain
    link = "/feeds/entries/"
    title = "%s: Latest entries" % current_site.name

    def items(self):
        return Entry.live.all()[:15]

    def item_pubdate(self, item):
        return item.pub_date
```

```
    def item_guid(self, item):
        return "tag:%s,%s:%s" % (current_site.domain,
                                 item.pub_date.strftime('%Y-%m-%d'),
                                 item.get_absolute_url())

    def item_categories(self, item):
        return [c.title for c in item.categories.all()]


class CategoryFeed(LatestEntriesFeed):
    def get_object(self, bits):
        if len(bits) != 1:
            raise ObjectDoesNotExist
        return Category.objects.get(slug__exact=bits[0])

    def title(self, obj):
        return "%s: Latest entries in category '%s'" % (current_site.name,
                                                        obj.title)

    def description(self, obj):
        return "%s: Latest entries in category '%s'" % (current_site.name,
                                                        obj.title)

    def link(self, obj):
        return obj.get_absolute_url()

    def items(self, obj):
        return obj.live_entry_set()[:15]
```

You can register this feed by changing the import line in your project's urls.py file from

```
from coltrane.feeds import LatestEntriesFeed
```

to

```
from coltrane.feeds import CategoryFeed, LatestEntriesFeed
```

and by adding one line to the feeds dictionary. Change it from

```
feeds = { 'entries': LatestEntriesFeed }
```

to

```
feeds = { 'entries': LatestEntriesFeed,
          'categories': CategoryFeed }
```

Finally, you'll want to set up the templates feeds/categories_title.html and feeds/
categories_title.html. Since they're just displaying entries, feel free to copy and paste the
contents of the two templates you used for the LatestEntriesFeed.

Writing feed classes that display entries or links by tag will follow the same pattern. Examples are included in the sample code you can download for this book, but again, I'd recommend giving it a try yourself before you peek to see how it's done.

Looking Ahead

And with that, you've implemented all the features you set out to have for your weblog. But, more important, you've covered a huge amount of territory within Django: models, views, URL routing, templating and custom template extensions, comments, and Django's dispatcher and syndication feeds. You should already be feeling a lot more comfortable working with Django and writing what would—if you were developing from scratch without Django's help—be some fairly complex features.

So give yourself a pat on the back because you've got a lot of useful Django knowledge under your belt now. Also take some time to work with the weblog application you've developed. Try to think of a feature or two you'd like to add, and then see if you can work out how to add them.

When you're ready, the next chapter will start a brand-new application: a code-sharing site with some useful social features, which will highlight Django's form-processing system for user-submitted content and show off some more advanced uses of the database API.

CHAPTER 8

■■■

A Social Code-Sharing Site

So far you've been using Django for the sorts of applications that are generally termed *content management*—in other words, applications in which an administrator logs in to a special interface and posts some content, then the system displays that content publicly with little or no interaction from general site visitors. While that covers a huge amount of common web-development tasks, it doesn't cover everything, and it's not the limit of what Django can do.

So for your third Django application, I'll show you how to build a user-driven application with much more interactivity and some social style features—in other words, a community-based repository of useful, reusable code.

A live version of this type of application, oriented toward Django users, is online at www.djangosnippets.org/, and in the next few chapters you'll see how to build a similar application that you can deploy any time you need a place for multiple users to share bits of code with each other.

Feature Checklist

As with the weblog application, the first thing you should do is get a rough idea of what you want to accomplish. Use this feature list as a starting point:

- Snippets of code with full descriptions of what they do

- Categorization by programming language, and full language-aware syntax highlighting of the rendered code

- A bookmark feature so that users can easily come back and find their favorite snippets

- A rating feature that lets users indicate whether a particular piece of code was useful to them

- Tagging for organizing snippets and finding related pieces of code

- Lists of the most popular snippets by overall rating and by the number of times they've been bookmarked

- A list of the most active authors (users who've submitted the most snippets)

In keeping with the tradition of naming applications after notable jazz musicians, I'm going to call this application cab, in honor of the singer/bandleader Cab Calloway. Cab was known for his skill at scat singing—singing with short syllables of sometimes nonsensical words—which seems appropriate for an application focused on lots of short bits of code.

Setting Up the Application

Once again, you'll need to create a new Python module to hold the application code. It should live directly on the Python import path, in the same directory as the `coltrane` application you built for the weblog. Now that you know how to do this manually, let's take a shortcut. Go into the directory where you want to create the application and type the following:

```
django-admin.py startapp cab
```

Remember that on some systems, you'll need to type out the full path to the `django-admin.py` command.

Previously, you've only encountered `startapp` in the context of a specific project, where it created a new application directory inside the project's directory. However, it works just fine for creating standalone application modules, and it takes some of the tedium out of starting out with a new application. Using the `django-admin.py startapp` command creates a new directory called `cab`. Populate it with an empty `__init__.py` and the basic `models.py` and `views.py` files for a new Django application.

In time, you'll end up replacing the `views.py` file with a `views` module containing several files, but for simpler applications, this setup will be all you'll need.

Before you go any further, you need to set up one other thing. For syntax highlighting of the code snippets, you'll be using a Python library called `pygments`. Its official site is at http:// pygments.org/, which has documentation and interactive examples, but to download it, visit http://pypi.python.org/pypi/Pygments, which is the page for the `pygments` project in the Python Package Index (formerly known, and sometimes still referred to, as the Python Cheese Shop, in honor of a famous Monty Python comedy sketch).

The Python Package Index is an incredibly useful resource for Python programmers. Right now it's tracking almost 4,000 third-party libraries and applications written in Python, all categorized and with a full history of releases. Any time you find yourself wondering if Python has a library for something you need to do, you should try a search there—the odds are good that someone's already written at least some of the code you'll need and listed it in the index.

As I'm writing this, the current version of `pygments` is 0.9, so you should be able to download a package labeled `Pygments-0.9.tar.gz`. Once you've downloaded the package, open it up; on most operating systems, you can just double-click on the file. This creates a directory called `Pygments-0.9`. On a command line, go into that directory and type:

```
python setup.py install
```

This installs the `pygments` library on your computer. Once it's done, you should be able to launch a Python interpreter and type `import pygments` without seeing any errors.

Building the Initial Models

Now that you've got your application module set up and the `pygments` library installed, you can start building your models. Logically, you're going to want a model to represent the snippets of code; let's call this model `Snippet`. You'll also want a model to represent the language in which a particular code snippet is written. This will make it much easier to store some extra metadata, handle the syntax highlighting, and sort snippets by language.

The Language Model

Open up the models.py file in the cab directory. The django-admin.py script has already filled in an import statement that pulls in Django's model classes, so you can start working immediately. Start with the model—let's call it Language—that represents the different programming languages. It'll need five fields:

- The name of the language

- A unique slug to identify it in URLs

- A language code that pygments can use to load the appropriate syntax-highlighting module

- A file extension to use when offering a snippet in this language for download

- A MIME type to use when sending a snippet file in this language

Based on what you already know about Django's model system, this is easy to set up:

```
class Language(models.Model):
    name = models.CharField(max_length=100)
    slug = models.SlugField(unique=True)
    language_code = models.CharField(max_length=50)
    mime_type = models.CharField(max_length=100)
```

Since the values (all strings) that go into these fields won't be very long, I've kept the field lengths fairly short.

Now, the most logical ordering for languages is alphabetical by name, so you can add that, activate the admin interface, and go ahead and set up the string representation of a Language to be its name:

```
class Meta:
    ordering = ['name']

class Admin:
    pass

def __unicode__(self):
    return self.name
```

You can also define a get_absolute_url() method, and even though you haven't yet set up any views or URLs, go ahead and write it using the permalink decorator, so it'll do reverse URL lookup when the time comes. When you do write the URLs, the name for the URL pattern that corresponds to a specific Language is going to be cab_language_detail, and it's going to take the Language's slug as an argument:

```
def get_absolute_url(self):
    return ('cab_language_detail', (), { 'slug': self.slug })
get_absolute_url = models.permalink(get_absolute_url)
```

ADMONITION: URL PATTERN NAMING

Technically, the only requirement Django imposes on the name of a URL pattern is that it must be a string and that it must be unique within a given project. However, as a general convention, I like to have the names of my URLs follow a predictable pattern based on the name of the application, the name of the model involved, and the action that the view will take. The detail view of a Language in the cab application, then, is cab_language_detail, while the view to add a Snippet, for example, is cab_snippet_add.

While you don't have to do this, I've found that it's a great help to other people who need to read the code, and sometimes even to me as I look back over a piece of my own code that I haven't worked with recently.

You'll want one more method on the Language model to help pygments with the syntax highlighting. pygments works by reading through a piece of text while using a specialized piece of code called a *lexer*, which knows the rules of the particular programming language the text is written in. The pygments download includes lexers for a large set of languages, each one identified by a code name, and pygments includes a function that, given the code name of a language, returns the lexer for that language.

Let's add a method to the Language model that uses that function to return the appropriate lexer for a given language. The function you want is pygments.lexers.get_lexer_by_name(), which means you'll need to add a new import statement at the top of your models.py file:

```
from pygments import lexers
```

Then you can write the method:

```
def get_lexer(self):
    return lexers.get_lexer_by_name(self.language_code)
```

Now the Language model is done, and your models.py file looks like this:

```
from django.db import models
from pygments import lexers

class Language(models.Model):
    name = models.CharField(max_length=100)
    slug = models.SlugField(unique=True)
    language_code = models.CharField(max_length=50)
    mime_type = models.CharField(max_length=100)

    class Meta:
        ordering = ['name']

    class Admin:
        pass
```

```
    def __unicode__(self):
        return self.name

    def get_absolute_url(self):
        return ('cab_language_detail', (), { 'slug': self.slug })
    get_absolute_url = models.permalink(get_absolute_url)

    def get_lexer(self):
        return lexers.get_lexer_by_name(self.language_code)
```

The Snippet Model

Now you can write the class that represents a snippet of code, which will need to have several fields:

- A title and description. You'll set up the description much the same way as the excerpt and body from the Entry model in your weblog, so that there are two fields: one to store the raw input, and one to store an HTML version.

- A foreign key pointing at the Language the snippet is written in.

- A foreign key to Django's User model to represent the snippet's author.

- A list of tags, for which you'll use the TagField you saw in the weblog application.

- The actual code, which, again, you'll store as two fields so that you can keep a rendered, syntax-highlighted HTML version separate from the original input.

- A bit of metadata that includes the date and time when the snippet was first posted, and the date and time when it was last updated.

To start, you'll need to import the TagField you've used previously:

```
from tagging.fields import TagField
```

You'll also need Django's User model:

```
from django.contrib.auth.models import User
```

Then you can build out the basic fields:

```
class Snippet(models.Model):
    title = models.CharField(max_length=255)
    language = models.ForeignKey(Language)
    author = models.ForeignKey(User)
    description = models.TextField()
    description_html = models.TextField(editable=False)
    code = models.TextField()
    highlighted_code = models.TextField(editable=False)
    tags = TagField()
    pub_date = models.DateTimeField(editable=False)
    updated_date = models.DateTimeField(editable=False)
```

Note that you've marked several of these as noneditable. They'll be filled in automatically by the custom `save()` method you'll write in a moment.

The logical ordering for snippets is by the descending order of the `pub_date` field. You'll want to activate the admin interface for the `Snippet` model and give it a string representation (which will use the title of the snippet):

```
class Meta:
    ordering = ['-pub_date']

class Admin:
    pass

def __unicode__(self):
    return self.title
```

Before you write the `save()` method, go ahead and add a method that knows how to apply the syntax highlighting. For this, you'll need two more items from `pygments`: the `formatters` module, which knows how to output highlighted code in various formats; and the `highlight()` function, which puts everything together to produce highlighted output. So change the `import` line from this:

```
from pygments import lexers
```

to this:

```
from pygments import formatters, highlight, lexers
```

The `pygments` highlight function takes three arguments: the code to highlight, the lexer to use, and the formatter to generate the output. The code comes from the `code` field on the `Snippet` model, and the lexer comes from the `get_lexer()` method you defined on the `Language` model. Then just use the HTML formatter built into `pygments` as the output formatter:

```
def highlight(self):
    return highlight(self.code,
                     self.language.get_lexer(),
                     formatters.HtmlFormatter(linenos=True))
```

The `linenos=True` argument to the formatter tells `pygments` to generate the output with line numbers so that it's easier to read the code and identify specific lines.

ADMONITION: WHY NOT HIGHLIGHT DIRECTLY IN `save()`?

It seems strange to be writing such a short method as this, when you could just put this code directly into the model's `save()` method. However, it's often a good idea to break things like this out into separate methods. Doing it this way means that you can highlight a `Snippet` without saving it, and it also reduces the coupling to a specific method of syntax highlighting. If you ever want to switch to a different syntax-highlighting system, for example, you would only have to rewrite this one method instead of potentially tracking down every place that uses syntax highlighting and changing them all.

Before you write the save() method, go ahead and import the Python Markdown module, and use that for generating the HTML version of the description:

```
from markdown import markdown
```

You're also going to need Python's datetime module:

```
import datetime
```

Now you can write the save() method, which needs to perform the following actions:

- Convert the plain-text description to HTML, and store that in the description_html field.

- Do the syntax highlighting, and store the resulting HTML in the highlighted_code field.

- Set the pub_date to the current date and time if this is the first time the snippet is being saved.

- Set the updated_date to the current date and time whenever the snippet is saved.

Here's the code:

```
def save(self):
    if not self.id:
        self.pub_date = datetime.datetime.now()
    self.updated_date = datetime.datetime.now()
    self.description_html = markdown(self.description)
    self.highlighted_code = self.highlight()
    super(Snippet, self).save()
```

Finally, add a get_absolute_url() method. The view that shows a particular Snippet is called cab_snippet_detail and takes the id of the Snippet as an argument:

```
def get_absolute_url(self):
    return ('cab_snippet_detail', (), { 'object_id': self.id })
get_absolute_url = models.permalink(get_absolute_url)
```

The finished model looks like this:

```
class Snippet(models.Model):
    title = models.CharField(max_length=255)
    language = models.ForeignKey(Language)
    author = models.ForeignKey(User)
    description = models.TextField()
    description_html = models.TextField(editable=False)
    code = models.TextField()
    highlighted_code = models.TextField(editable=False)
    tags = TagField()
    pub_date = models.DateTimeField(editable=False)
    updated_date = models.DateTimeField(editable=False)
```

```
    class Meta:
        ordering = ['-pub_date']

    class Admin:
        pass

    def __unicode__(self):
        return self.title

    def save(self):
        if not self.id:
            self.pub_date = datetime.datetime.now()
        self.updated_date = datetime.datetime.now()
        self.description_html = markdown(self.description)
        self.highlighted_code = self.highlight()
        super(Snippet, self).save()

    def get_absolute_url(self):
        return ('cab_snippet_detail', (), { 'object_id': self.id })
    get_absolute_url = models.permalink(get_absolute_url)

    def highlight(self):
        return highlight(self.code,
                         self.language.get_lexer(),
                         formatters.HtmlFormatter(linenos=True))
```

This handles the core of the application—code snippets organized by language—so now you can pause and start working on some initial views to get a feel for how things will look.

Testing the Snippets Application

As you build out these views and the rest of this application, I'm going to assume you've already got a Django project set up with a database and a template directory. If you'd like, you can keep using the existing project you've worked with for the two previous applications. However, this application isn't really related to either the simple CMS or the weblog, so if you'd like to start a new project now to work with this application, feel free to do so. In either case, you'll need to do three things:

1. **Add cab to the INSTALLED_APPS list of the project you'll use to test and work with this application**: If you're starting a new project, you'll also want to add django. contrib.admin and tagging to the list.

2. **Run manage.py syncdb to install the models you've written so far**: Later, when you write the rest of the models, you can run it again to install them. syncdb knows how to figure out which models are already installed and only sets up the new ones.

3. **Use the admin interface to create some Language objects and fill in some Snippets**:
For a list of the languages pygments supports, and the language codes for the lexers,
read pygments' lexer documentation online at http://pygments.org/docs/lexers/. In
the next chapter, you'll see how to set up public-facing views that let ordinary users
submit snippets without having to use the admin interface.

Initial Views for Snippets and Languages

As you wrote the weblog application, you relied heavily on Django's generic views to provide
the date-based archives and detail views of the entries and links. With this application, it
doesn't make as much sense to use date-based browsing, but you've already encountered
non–date-based generic views, and you can turn to them again for this application.

In the cab directory, create a new directory called urls, and in it create three files:

- __init__.py, to mark this directory as a Python module

- snippets.py, which will have the URLs for the snippet-oriented views

- languages.py, which will have the URLs for the language-oriented views

As you did with the weblog's URLs, you'll be keeping each group of URLs for this application in its own file. This means you'll have several files in cab/urls, but the benefit in flexibility
and reusability is worth it.

In urls/snippets.py, fill in the following code:

```
from django.conf.urls.defaults import *
from django.views.generic.list_detail import object_list, object_detail
from cab.models import Snippet

snippet_info = { 'queryset': Snippet.objects.all() }

urlpatterns = patterns('',
                        url(r'^$',
                            object_list,
                            dict(snippet_info, paginate_by=20),
                            name='cab_snippet_list'),
                        url(r'^(?P<object_id>\d+)/$',
                            object_detail,
                            snippet_info,
                            name='cab_snippet_detail'),
)
```

This sets up two things:

- **A list of snippets, in the order in which they were posted**: Note the extra argument
you've passed here: paginate_by. This tells the generic view that you'd like it to show only
20 snippets at a time. You'll see in a moment how to work with that in the templates.

- **A detail view for individual Snippet objects**: This is simply the object_detail generic
view.

You should be able to set up the templates for this pretty easily. The list view gets a variable called {{ object_list }}, which is a list of Snippet instances, and the detail view gets a variable called {{ object }}, which is a specific Snippet. The generic views look for the cab/snippet_list.html and cab/snippet_detail.html templates.

The only tricky thing is handling the pagination of snippets in the list view. The template only gets 20 snippets at a time, so you need to display Next and Previous links to navigate through them.

To handle this, the generic view provides two extra variables:

paginator: This is an instance of django.core.paginator.Paginator. It knows how many total pages of snippets there are and how many total snippets are involved.

page: This is an instance of django.core.paginator.Page. It knows its own page number and whether there's a next or previous page.

In the snippet_list template, you could use something like this:

```
<p>{{ page }};
{% if page.has_previous %}
<a href="?page={{ page.previous_page_number }}">Previous page</a>
{% endif %}
{% if page.has_next_page %}
<a href="?page={{ page.next_page_number }}">Next page</a>
{% endif %}</p>
```

You can download a full example in the Source Code/Download area of the Apress web site (www.apress.com).

The object_list generic view knows to look for the page variable in the URL's query string, and it adjusts the snippets it displays accordingly. Meanwhile, the Page object knows how to print itself smartly; in the template, {{ page }} displays something like "Page 2 of 6."

To set up these views, add a pattern like this to your project's root urls.py file:

```
(r'^snippets/', include('cab.urls.snippets')),
```

CSS for pygments Syntax Highlighting

You'll have noticed in the Snippet detail view that the code sample doesn't actually appear to be highlighted in any way. This is because pygments, by default, simply generates HTML with some class names filled in to mark things like language keywords. It expects that you'll use a style sheet to change the presentation appropriately.

To get a head start on styling the highlighted code, look through some of the samples in the online demo of pygments at http://pygments.org/demo/. pygments comes with several styles built in, and once you've found one you like, you can have it output the appropriate CSS. You can then save that to a file and use it as your style sheet.

Here's a simple example of how to get the appropriate CSS information from a pygments style. This assumes that you've created a pygments.css file that you'll write them into, and that you've decided you like the "murphy" style. Open a Python interpreter and type the following:

```
>>> from pygments import formatters, styles
>>> style = styles.get_style_by_name('murphy')
>>> formatter = formatters.HtmlFormatter(style=style)
>>> outfile = open('pygments.css', 'w')
>>> outfile.write(formatter.get_style_defs())
>>> outfile.close()
```

The pygments.css file now contains a list of CSS style rules for the "murphy" style. You can tweak them a bit if you like. You can also have pygments automatically add more specific information to the CSS selector it uses, if you know that the highlighted blocks will only appear inside certain elements in a page. Consult the documentation for the pygments HtmlFormatter class for full details on how the get_style_defs() method works.

Views for Languages

To show a list of the languages that snippets have been submitted in, you can use the object_list generic view again. However, displaying a list of snippets for a particular Language is going to require a little bit of code. You'll need to write a wrapper around a generic view, as you did in Chapter 5, to show the list of entries in a particular category.

Go ahead and delete the views.py file in the cab application's directory and create a views directory. In it, put these two files:

- __init__.py

- languages.py

languages.py is where you'll put your first handwritten view for this application.

In views/languages.py, add the following code to set up the wrapper around the generic view:

```
from django.shortcuts import get_object_or_404
from django.views.generic.list_detail import object_list
from cab.models import Language


def language_detail(request, slug):
    language = get_object_or_404(Language, slug=slug)
    return object_list(request,
                       queryset=language.snippet_set.all(),
                       paginate_by=20,
                       template_name='cab/language_detail.html',
                       extra_context={ 'language': language })
```

This returns a paginated list of snippets for a particular language. Now you can go to urls/languages.py and fill in a couple of URL patterns:

```
from django.conf.urls.defaults import *
from django.views.generic.list_detail import object_list
from cab.models import Language
from cab.views.languages import language_detail
```

```
language_info = { 'queryset': Language.objects.all(),
                  'paginate_by': 20 }

urlpatterns = patterns('',
                       url(r'^$',
                           object_list,
                           language_info,
                           name='cab_language_list'),
                       url(r'^(?P<slug>[-\w]+)/$',
                           language_detail,
                           name='cab_language_detail'),
)
```

Again, you should have no trouble setting up some basic templates to handle these views. The template names are cab/language_list.html and cab/language_detail.html.

To see these views in action, add a line like the following to your project's root urls.py file:

```
(r'^languages/', include('cab.urls.languages')),
```

An Advanced View: Top Authors

Since any user of the application will be allowed to submit a snippet of code, you'll want to have a way to show the users who've submitted the most snippets. Let's write a view to handle that.

Inside the cab/views directory, create a new file called popular.py. You'll use this file for this view, as well as for some others you'll write later on to list top-rated and most-often-bookmarked snippets.

Start the popular.py file with a couple of imports:

```
from django.contrib.auth.models import User
from django.views.generic.list_detail import object_list
```

It may seem a bit strange to import a generic view here, because it's hard to see any way you can use one for a query like this. In fact, even if you've been reading through the Django database API documentation, it might not be obvious how to do this query. So first, let's consider how the query will work.

One of the trickier features of Django's database API is a method called extra(), which takes several optional parameters. Its job is to provide a way to handle certain SQL constructs that don't necessarily fit easily into the standard API methods. It lets you specify custom bits of SQL to embed into each part of the query. You can add extra items to the SELECT clause and the WHERE clause, and you can specify extra tables to be joined along with their join conditions.

Using extra, then, you can create a Django QuerySet that queries for users and orders them by the number of snippets they've submitted. The query is going to look like this:

```
top_authors = User.objects.extra(select={ 'score':➡
  "SELECT COUNT(*) from cab_snippet WHERE cab_snippet.author_id =➡
  auth_user.id" },
                                  order_by=['score'])
```

This query adds a subquery, which counts the number of snippets users have submitted and orders the users by that count. As a convenience, each User object returned by the query also has an additional attribute, score, containing the number of snippets an individual user has submitted.

Since this is a Django QuerySet, you can pass it to the object_detail view:

```
def top_authors(request):
    top_authors_qs = User.objects.extra(select={ 'score':➥
    "SELECT COUNT(*) from cab_snippet WHERE cab_snippet.author_id =➥
    auth_user.id" },
                                    order_by=['score'])
    return object_list(request, queryset=top_authors_qs,
                    template_name='cab/top_authors.html',
                    paginate_by=20)
```

You'll end up with a paginated list of users ordered by their snippets. Then you can wire up a URL for it. Let's add a new file in the urls directory, popular.py, and use it for all of these top views. In it, you place the following:

```
from django.conf.urls.defaults import *
from cab.views import popular

urlpatterns = patterns('',
                    url(r'^authors/$',
                        popular.top_authors,
                        name='cab_top_authors'),
)
```

Once again, you can wire this up in your project's root urls.py file:

```
(r'^popular/', include('cab.urls.popular')),
```

After you've created the cab/top_authors.html template, you'll see some results. Of course, right now, it won't be that impressive, because the application only has one user—you. However, when deployed live on a site with multiple users, this will be a nice feature.

Improving the View of Top Authors

While this is a nice feature, it would be even better if you could encapsulate that query in a reusable way. Right now, it's a bit of a mouthful, and you wouldn't want to have to type it out over and over if you ever needed to reuse it.

Let's write a custom manager for the Snippet model and make this a method on the manager. Because you're going to end up writing several custom managers for this application, let's go ahead and create a file managers.py in the cab directory. Then, inside it, put the following code:

```
from django.db import models
from django.contrib.auth.models import User

class SnippetManager(models.Manager):
    def top_authors(self):
        return User.objects.extra(select={ 'score':➥
        "SELECT COUNT(*) from cab_snippet WHERE cab_snippet.author_id➥
        = auth_user.id" },
                                    order_by=['score'])
```

In cab/models.py, add a new import statement at the top:

```
from cab import managers
```

In the definition of the Snippet model, add the custom manager:

```
objects = managers.SnippetManager()
```

Now you can rewrite the top_user view like so:

```
from django.views.generic.list_detail import object_list
from cab.models import Snippet

def top_authors(request):
    return object_list(request, queryset=Snippet.objects.top_authors(),
                        template_name='cab/top_authors.html',
                        paginate_by=20)
```

That's much nicer.

While you're at it, you can make another improvement. Because Django works with several different database engines, it has to know how to handle the appropriate formatting of things like table and column names for each one. So let Django take care of that for you. The function you need to use is django.db.connection.ops.quote_name(), so in cab/managers, add a new import at the top of the file:

```
from django.db import connection
```

Now you can rewrite the top_authors() method and make it a bit clearer as well by using Python string formatting to build the subquery:

```
def top_authors(self):
    subquery = "SELECT COUNT(*) from %(snippets_table)s WHERE➥
    %(snippets_table)s.%(author_column)s = auth_user.id"
    params = { 'snippets_table': connection.ops.quote_name('cab_snippet'),
                'author_column': connection.ops.quote_name('author_id') }
    return User.objects.extra(select={ 'score': subquery % params },
                                order_by=['score'])
```

ADMONITION: DICTIONARY-BASED STRING FORMATTING

So far, you've been using fairly simple string formatting, where you write something like this:

```
select = "SELECT COUNT(*) FROM %s" % connection.ops.quote_name('cab_snippet')
```

Technically, the item on the right-hand side of the formatting operator (the % after the string) is a tuple, often a one-element tuple. But if you're going to be repeating a value multiple times in a string, as you are here with the table name, you can use an alternate syntax to give names to the formatting placeholders, and you can use a dictionary instead. The dictionary should have keys with those names, and their values are inserted into the string.

Let's make one final improvement. Instead of putting the database table name directly into the query, you can rely on the fact that each model class knows which database table it should use. The name of the database table is stored, along with a lot of other metadata, in an attribute on the class called _meta. (If you've been wondering where the things you define in the class Meta declaration end up, this is the answer.) The database table is in _meta.db_table. So you can use that and avoid hard-coding the table name into the query at all:

```
def top_authors(self):
    subquery = "SELECT COUNT(*) from %(snippets_table)s WHERE➡
    %(snippets_table)s.%(author_column)s = auth_user.id"
    params = { 'snippets_table': connection.ops.quote_name(➡
self.model._meta.db_table),
               'author_column': connection.ops.quote_name('author_id') }
    return User.objects.extra(select={ 'score': subquery % params },
                              order_by=['score'])
```

ADMONITION: USING _meta

The _meta attribute on a Django model class is mostly undocumented, because a lot of what it contains is there for Django's own internal use. Because of that, you should be careful about using things in _meta unless you've got a good idea of how they work. The best guide for knowing that is the source code; the _meta attribute is an instance of the class django.db.models.options.Options.

If, after you finish this book, you're looking for a way to start building a more advanced understanding of Django, reading through that code would be a good idea. Even if you never use the features available through _meta (and there are some useful things in there), you'll come away with a deeper understanding of how Django models work.

Adding a `top_languages` View

While you're adding these features, go ahead and add the ability to show the most popular languages. This will be a similar query to the "top authors" view, so it'll be easy to write now.

One important design decision, though, is where to put the method to do this query. You could put it on the `SnippetManager` and probably even rework the `top_authors()` method into a `top_objects()` method, which could return the top authors, the top languages, or (later on when you've built out the models for them) the most-bookmarked or highest-rated snippets according to an argument passed to it. That would cut down on the number of times you have to write methods to do this sort of query. However, a disadvantage to this approach is that, logically, the list of top languages doesn't "belong" with the `Snippet` model; it belongs with the `Language` model. Since it's better to present a logical API for your application's users than to be lazy about writing code, go ahead and give `Language` a custom manager and put this query there.

In `cab/managers.py`, add the following:

```
class LanguageManager(models.Manager):
    def top_languages(self):
        from cab.models import Snippet
        subquery = "SELECT COUNT(*) from %(snippets_table)s WHERE➡
        %(snippets_table)s.%(language_column)s = cab_language.id"
        params = { 'snippets_table': connection.ops.quote_name(➡
Snippet._meta.db_table),
                    'language_column': connection.ops.quote_name('language_id') }
        return self.extra(select={ 'score': subquery % params },
                          order_by=['score'])
```

> **ADMONITION: AVOIDING CIRCULAR DEPENDENCIES**
>
> You'll notice that the `import` statement for the `Snippet` model is *inside* the `top_languages()` method. This is necessary because `cab/models.py` imports from `cab/managers.py`. If you placed `from cab.models import Snippet` at the top of `cab/managers.py`, you'd get an infinite loop of each file trying to import the other.
>
> Putting the `import` statement inside the `top_languages` method ensures that the import of the `Snippet` model waits until the method is actually called, at which point there's no chance of a loop.

In `cab/models.py`, you can add the manager in the definition of the `Language` model:

```
objects = managers.LanguageManager()
```

In `cab/views/popular.py`, you can change the `import` statement from:

```
from cab.models import Snippet
```

to:

```
from cab.models import Language, Snippet
```

Write this view:

```
def top_languages(request):
    return object_list(request,
                       queryset=Language.objects.top_languages(),
                       template_name='cab/top_languages.html',
                       paginate_by=20)
```

and change `cab/urls/popular.py` to the following:

```
from django.conf.urls.defaults import *
from cab.views import popular

urlpatterns = patterns('',
                       url(r'^authors/$',
                           popular.top_authors,
                           name='cab_top_authors'),
                       url(r'^languages/$',
                           popular.top_languages,
                           name='cab_top_languages'),
)
```

Now you can create the `cab/top_languages.html` template and add some snippets in various languages to see the results change.

Looking Ahead

Now that you've got the core of this application in place, the next chapter will look at some of the user interactions, including an introduction to Django's form-processing system, so you can see how to let users submit snippets without going through the admin interface.

If you'd like a little challenge before moving on to form handling, try writing a view that lists tags in order by the number of snippets that use them. Take a look in the tagging application to see how the tags work, and check out the Django content types framework documentation (`www.djangoproject.com/documentation/contenttypes/`) to get a feel for how to use the generic relations that the tags use. If you get stumped, a working example is in the Source Code/Download area of the Apress web site (`www.apress.com`).

CHAPTER 9

Form Processing in the Code-Sharing Application

All of your Django applications so far—with the exception of the comments system for the weblog—have been focused exclusively on systems where trusted members of a site's staff will enter content through Django's administrative interface, rather than on interactive features that let ordinary users submit content to be displayed. For this new application, though, you're going to need a way to allow users to submit their snippets of code. You'll also want to make sure that their submissions are in a format that works with the data models you've set up.

Fortunately, Django is going to make this fairly easy through the use of a simple but powerful system for displaying and processing web-based forms. In this chapter you'll get a thorough look at the form-handling system and use it to build the forms people will use to submit and edit their code samples.

A Brief Tour of Django's Form System

Django's form-handling code lives in the module `django.newforms` and provides three key components that, taken together, cover every aspect of constructing, displaying, and processing a form:

- A set of *field* classes, similar to the types of fields available for Django data models, which represent a particular type of data and know how to validate that data.

- A set of *widget* classes, which know how to render various types of HTML form controls (text inputs, check boxes, and so on) and read out the corresponding data from an HTTP form submission.

- A `Form` class that ties these concepts together and provides a unified interface for defining the data to be collected and high-level rules for validating it.

ADMONITION: WHY "NEW" FORMS?

If you take a look at the Django codebase, you'll notice two form-oriented packages: `newforms` and `oldforms`. `django.oldforms` is the original form-handling system Django shipped with at the time of its first public release, and it has been officially deprecated. The `oldforms` system worked and has been used in plenty of production-quality applications. However, it was rather cumbersome to work with and sometimes resulted in fairly tedious or repetitive code—two things Django aims to eliminate whenever possible.

The `django.newforms` package is its replacement, and it is a significant improvement in terms of the ease with which forms can be constructed and handled. By the time Django 1.0 is released, all of Django's own internal systems and bundled applications will have switched to using it, and eventually the `oldforms` package will be removed (at which point `django.newforms` will simply become `django.forms`). Therefore, you should always use `django.newforms` for new applications.

A Simple Example

To get a feel for how this works, let's take a look at a simple but common requirement: user signups.

ADMONITION: WHERE DOES THIS CODE GO?

This specific code doesn't logically belong to the `cab` application you're developing, and if you ever do develop code for handling user signups it would be best to place that code in its own separate application. For now, though, don't worry about saving this code into Python files. It's just a useful example that shows off as many parts of Django's form-handling system as possible.

If you ever do need to implement a user signup system, however, feel free to refer to this code and adapt it to suit your needs.

Basic signups will require a registration form that collects three pieces of data:

- A username

- An e-mail address to associate with the new account

- A password the user will use to log in

Additionally, you'll want to do a little bit of custom validation work:

- You'll want to make sure that the username isn't already in use because you can't have two users with the same username.

- It's always a good idea to show two password fields and have the user type the same password twice. This will catch typos and provide a little extra safety to make sure new users get the password they're expecting.

Logically, this works out to an HTML `<form>` element with four fields: one each for the username and e-mail address and two to handle the repeated password. Here's how you might start out building the form:

```
from django import newforms as forms


class SignupForm(forms.Form):
    username = forms.CharField(max_length=30)
    email = forms.EmailField()
    password1 = forms.CharField(max_length=30)
    password2 = forms.CharFIeld(max_length=30)
```

Aside from the use of classes from `django.newforms` instead of `django.db.models`, this starts out looking similar to the way you define model classes in Django: simply subclass the appropriate base class and add the appropriate fields.

ADMONITION: IMPORTING THE newforms PACKAGE

You'll notice that the `import` statement that pulls in the `django.newforms` package is written as `from django import newforms as forms`, and you reference everything as being attached to the `forms` namespace. This is a good habit to get into because (as previously mentioned) `django.newforms` will eventually become simply `django.forms`. If you import and reference the `newforms` package in this fashion, then when the switch happens, you'll only need to change one line—the `import` statement—and the rest of your code will continue to work normally.

But it's not quite perfect. HTML provides a special form input type for handling passwords—`<input type="password">`—and that would be a more appropriate way to render the password fields. You can do that by changing those two fields slightly:

```
password1 = forms.CharField(max_length=30,
                            widget=forms.PasswordInput())
password2 = forms.CharField(max_length=30,
                            widget=forms.PasswordInput())
```

The `PasswordInput` widget will render itself as an `<input type="password">`, which is exactly what you want. This also shows off one major strength of the way Django's form system separates the validation of data—which is handled by the field—from the presentation of the form, which is handled by the widgets. It's fairly common to run into situations where you have a single underlying validation rule that needs to work with multiple fields that all become different types of HTML inputs. This separation makes it easy: you can reuse a single field type and just change the widget.

While you're at it, let's make one more change:

```
password1 = forms.CharField(max_length=30,
                            widget=forms.PasswordInput(render_value=False))
password2 = forms.CharField(max_length=30,
                            widget=forms.PasswordInput(render_value=False))
```

The `render_value` argument to the `PasswordInput` tells it that even if it has some data, it shouldn't show it. An error entering the password should completely clear the field to make sure the user types it in correctly the next time.

Validating the Username

The fields you've specified so far all have some implicit validation rules associated with them. The `username` field and the two password fields both have maximum lengths specified, and the `EmailField` will check that its input looks like an e-mail address (by applying a regular expression). But you also need to make sure that the username isn't already in use, so you'll need to define some custom validation for the `username` field.

You can do this by defining a method on the form called `clean_username()`. During the validation process, Django's form system automatically looks for any method whose name starts with `clean_` and ends in the name of a form on the field, then calls it after the field's built-in validation rules have been applied.

Here's what the `clean_username()` method looks like (assuming that the Django user model has already been imported using `from django.contrib.auth.models import User`):

```
def clean_username(self):
    try:
        User.objects.get(username=self.cleaned_data['username'])
    except User.DoesNotExist:
        return self.cleaned_data['username']
    raise forms.ValidationError("This username is already in use.➥
    Please choose another.")
```

This code packs a lot into a few lines. First of all, this method is only called if the `username` field has already passed its built-in requirement of being fewer than 30 characters of text. In that case, the value submitted for the `username` field is in `self.cleaned_data['username']`. The attribute `cleaned_data` is a dictionary of any submitted data that's made it through validation so far.

You query for a user whose username exactly matches the value submitted to the `username` field. If there is no such user, Django will raise the exception `User.DoesNotExist`. You'll know that the username isn't in use and so the value for the `username` field is valid. In this case, you simply return that value.

If there is a user with this username, you raise an exception: `ValidationError`. Django's form-handling code will catch this exception and turn it into an error message that you can display. (You'll see how to do this in a moment, when you look at the template that shows this form.)

Validating the Password

Validating the password is a bit trickier because it involves looking at two fields at once and making sure they match. You could do this by defining a method for one of the fields and having it look at the other, like so:

```
def clean_password2(self):
    if self.cleaned_data['password1'] != self.cleaned_data['password2']:
        raise forms.ValidationError("You must type the same password each time")
    return self.cleaned_data['password2']
```

But there's a better way to do this. Django lets you define a validation method—simply called clean()—which applies to the form as a whole. Here's how you could write it:

```
def clean(self):
    if 'password1' in self.cleaned_data and 'password2' in self.cleaned_data:
        if self.cleaned_data['password1'] != self.cleaned_data['password2']:
            raise forms.ValidationError("You must type the same password each time")
    return self.cleaned_data
```

Note that in this case you manually check that there are values in cleaned_data for the two password fields. If there were any errors raised during individual field validation, cleaned_data will be empty. So you need to check this before referring to anything you expect to find in it.

ADMONITION: FORM FIELDS ARE REQUIRED BY DEFAULT

All of the field types built in to Django's form system are required by default and so cannot be left blank. If either of the password fields was left blank, a ValidationError would be raised before the clean() method is called, and so you don't need to raise an additional error to require a value.

To mark a form field as optional, pass it the keyword argument required=False.

Creating the New User

At this point you could stop writing form code and move on to a view that processes the form. You could write the view so that it creates and saves the new User object. But if you ever needed to reuse this form in other views, you'd have to write out that code again and again. So it's better to write a method on the form itself that knows what to do with the valid data. Since it's saving a new User object to the database, the obvious name to give this method is save().

ADMONITION: save() ISN'T JUST FOR THE DATABASE

Most of the time, forms are used to create and update model objects, in which case save() is the natural choice. But forms can be used for other purposes (for example, a contact form might send an e-mail message instead of saving an object).

The general convention in the Django community is that any time a form class has a method that "knows" what action to take with the valid data, that method should be called save(), even when it doesn't save any data to your database. The advantage of giving this type of method a consistent and recognizable name outweighs any initial confusion it might cause.

In the save() method, you need to create a User object from the username, e-mail, and password submitted to your form. Assuming you've already imported the User model, you can do it like this:

```
def save(self):
    new_user = User.objects.create_user(username=self.cleaned_data['username'],
                                          email=self.cleaned_data['email'],
                                          password=self.cleaned_data['password1'])
    return new_user
```

ADMONITION: USERS AND PASSWORDS

One big problem with a database of users and passwords is that anyone who can get access to the database can see all of the passwords. Since many people tend to reuse the same passwords on multiple web sites, this can pose a significant security risk.

To help you protect your users, Django avoids storing the "plain" password that the user will actually use to log in. Instead, Django uses a mathematical trick called a *hash function*, which transforms the password into a random-looking (but not actually random) string of letters and numbers. That result is then stored in the database instead of the actual password. The advantage is that a hash function only works one way: if you know the password, you can apply the hash function and always get the same result, but if you only know the result you can't work backward to get the password.

This provides a reasonably secure way to store passwords. When you try to log in, Django's authentication system applies the hash function to the password you've entered and compares the result to the value in the database. This means that the "plain" password never has to be permanently stored anywhere. But because this is a bit tricky to work with, Django's User model has a custom manager that defines the create_user() method you're using here. This method handles the work of applying the hash function to the password and storing the correct value.

And here's the finished form:

```
from django.contrib.auth.models import User
from django import newforms as forms


class SignupForm(forms.Form):
    username = forms.CharField(max_length=30)
    email = forms.EmailField()
    password1 = forms.CharField(max_length=30,
    widget=forms.PasswordInput(render_value=False))
    password2 = forms.CharField(max_length=30,
    widget=forms.PasswordInput(render_value=False))

    def clean_username(self):
        try:
            User.objects.get(username=self.cleaned_data['username'])
        except User.DoesNotExist:
            return self.cleaned_data['username']
        raise forms.ValidationError("This username is already in use.➡
        Please choose another.")

    def clean(self):
        if 'password1' in self.cleaned_data and 'password2' in self.cleaned_data:
            if self.cleaned_data['password1'] != self.cleaned_data['password2']:
                raise forms.ValidationError("You must type the same➡
 password each time")
        return self.cleaned_data

    def save(self):
        new_user = User.objects.create_user(username=self.cleaned_data['username'],
                                    email=self.cleaned_data['email'],
                                    password=self.cleaned_data['password1'])
        return new_user
```

How Form Validation Works

The method you'll use in views to determine whether submitted data is valid or not is called is_valid() and is defined on the base Form class that all Django forms derive from. Inside the Form class, is_valid() touches off the form's validation routines, in a specific order, by calling full_clean() (another method defined in the base Form class in django.newforms; see Figure 9-1).

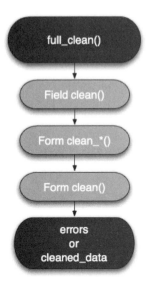

Figure 9-1. *The order in which validation methods are applied to a Django form*

The order of validation goes like this:

1. First, `full_clean()` loops through the fields on the form. Each field class has a method named `clean()`, which implements that field's built-in validation rules, and each of these methods will either raise a `ValidationError` or return a value. If a `ValidationError` is raised, no further validation is done for that field (since the data is already known to be invalid). If a value is returned, it goes into the form's `cleaned_data` dictionary.

2. If a field's built-in `clean()` method didn't raise a `ValidationError`, then any available custom validation method—a method whose name starts with `clean_` and ends with the name of the field—is called. Again, these methods can either raise a `ValidationError` or return a value; if they return a value it goes into `cleaned_data`.

3. Finally, the form's `clean()` method is called. It can also raise a `ValidationError`, albeit one that's not associated with any specific field. If `clean()` finds no new errors, it should return a complete dictionary of data for the form, usually by doing `return self.cleaned_data`.

4. If no validation errors were raised, the form's `cleaned_data` dictionary will be fully populated with the valid data. If there were validation errors, however, `cleaned_data` will not exist, and a dictionary of errors (`self.errors`) will be filled with validation errors. Each field knows how to retrieve its own errors from this dictionary, which is why you can do things like `{{ form.username.errors }}` in a template.

5. Finally, `is_valid()` either returns `False` if there were validation errors or `True` if there weren't.

Understanding this process is key to getting the most out of Django's form-handling system. It may seem a bit complex at first, but having multiple places where validation rules can be attached to a form results in a huge amount of flexibility and makes it easier to write reusable code. For example, if you find yourself needing to use a particular type of validation over and over again, you'll notice that writing a custom method on each form gets tedious. It'll probably be a good idea to just write your own field class, define a custom `clean()` method on it, and then reuse that field.

Similarly, the distinction between methods that go with a specific field, and the "form-level" `clean()` method, opens up a lot of useful tricks with validating multiple fields together, which wouldn't necessarily make sense if viewed entirely from the perspective of a single field.

Processing the Form

Now, let's take a look at a view you might use to display and process this form:

```
from django.http import HttpResponseRedirect
from django.shortcuts import render_to_response

def signup(request):
    if request.method == 'POST':
        form = SignupForm(data=request.POST)
        if form.is_valid():
            new_user = form.save()
            return HttpResponseRedirect("/accounts/login/")
    else:
        form = SignupForm()
    return render_to_response('signup.html',
                                { 'form': form })
```

Let's break this down step by step:

1. First you check the method of the incoming HTTP request. Usually, this will be GET or POST. (Though there are other HTTP methods, they're not as commonly used, and web browsers typically only support GET and POST for form submissions.)

2. If, and only if, the request method is POST, you instantiate a SignupForm and pass it request.POST as its data. Back in Chapter 3, when you wrote a simple search function, you saw that request.GET is a dictionary of data sent with a GET request, and similarly request.POST is the dictionary of data (in this case, the form submission) sent along with a POST request.

3. You check whether the submitted data is valid by calling the form's is_valid() method. Under the hood, this matches up the submitted data with the fields on the form and checks against each field's validation rules. If the data passes validation, is_valid() will return True, and the form's cleaned_data dictionary will be populated with the correct values. Otherwise, is_valid() will return False, and the cleaned_data dictionary will not exist.

4. If the data was valid, you call the form's save() method, which you previously defined. Then you return an HTTP redirect—using django.http.HttpResponseRedirect—to a new page, which, presumably, would be wired up to a view to let the new user log in. Whenever you accept data from an HTTP POST, you should *always* redirect after successful processing. By taking the user to a new page, you avoid a common pitfall where refreshing or clicking the Back button in a web browser accidentally resubmits a form.

5. If the request method was anything other than POST, you instantiate a SignupForm without any data. Technically speaking, this is called an *unbound* form (one that has no data to work with), as opposed to a *bound* form, which does have some data to validate.

6. You render a template, passing the form as a variable into it, and return a response. Note that because of the way this view is written, you'll never get to this step if the user submitted valid data. In that case, the if statements farther up would already have ensured that a redirect was returned. Also, note that this step is the same regardless of whether there was invalid data or no data at all—the SignupForm object doesn't have to be treated specially according to the different cases.

Finally, let's take a look at how you might display this in the signup.html template used by this view:

```
<html>
  <head>
    <title>Sign up for an account</title>
  </head>
  <body>
    <h1>Sign up for an account</h1>
    <p>Use the form below to register for your new account; all
        fields are required.</p>
    <form method="post" action="">
      {% if form.non_field_errors %}
      <p><span class="error">
      {{ form.non_field_errors|join:", " }}
      </span></p>
      {% endif %}
      <p>{% if form.username.errors %}
      <span class="error">{{ form.username.errors|join:", " }}</span>
      {% endif %}</p>
      <p><label for="id_username">Username:</label>
          {{ form.username }}</p>
      <p>{% if form.email.errors %}
      <span class="error">
      {{ form.email.errors|join:", " }}
      </span>
      {% endif %}</p>
      <p><label for="id_name">Your e-mail address:</label>
          {{ form.email }}</p>
      <p>{% if form.password1.errors %}
      <span class="error">
```

```
        {{ form.passsword1.errors|join:", " }}
        </span>
        {% endif %}</p>
        <p><label for="id_password1">Password:</label>
            {{ form.password1 }}</p>
        <p>{% if form.password2.errors %}
        <span class="error">
        {{ form.passsword2.errors|join:", " }}
        </span>
        {% endif %}</p>
        <p><label for="id_password2">Password (again, to catch
            typos): </label>
            {{ form.password2 }}</p>
        <p><input type="submit" value="Submit"></p>
    </form>
  </body>
</html>
```

Most of the HTML here is pretty simple: a standard `<form>` tag with `<label>` tags for each field and a button to submit. But notice how you actually show the fields. Each one is accessed as an attribute of the `{{ form }}` variable. You can check each one to see if it had any errors and display the error messages (which will be in a list, even if there's only one message—hence you use the `join` template filter, which can join a list of items using a specified string as a separator).

Note, though, that at the top of the form you use `{{ form.non_field_errors }}`. This is because the error raised from the `clean()` method doesn't "belong" to any one field (since it comes from comparing two fields to each other). Whenever you have a potential validation error from the `clean()` method, you'll need to check for `non_field_errors` and display it if present.

A Form for Adding Code Snippets

So now you have a pretty good idea of how to write a form for adding instances of your `Snippet` model. You'll simply set up fields for the things you want users to fill in, and then give it a `save()` method, which creates and saves the new snippet.

But there's one new thing you have to handle here. The `author` field on your `Snippet` model has to be filled in, and it has to be filled in correctly, but you don't want to show it to your users and let them choose a value. If you did that, any user could effectively pretend to be any other by filling in someone else's name on a snippet. So you need some way to fill in that field without making it a public part of the form.

Luckily, this is easy to do: a form is just a Python class. So you can add your own custom `__init__()` method to it and trust that the view function that processes the form will pass in the correct, authenticated user, which you can store and refer back to when it's time to save the snippet. So let's get started.

Go into the `cab` directory and create a file called `forms.py`. In it you can start writing your form as follows:

```
from django import newforms as forms
from cab.models import Snippet
```

```
class AddSnippetForm(forms.Form):
    def __init__(self, author, *args, **kwargs):
        super(AddSnippetForm, self).__init__(*args, **kwargs):
        self.author = author
```

Note that, aside from accepting an extra argument—author, which you store for later use—you're doing two important things here:

- In addition to the author argument, you specify that this method accepts *args and **kwargs. This is a Python shorthand for saying that it will accept any combination of positional and keyword arguments.

- You use super() to call the parent class's __init__() method, passing the other arguments your custom __init__() accepted. This ensures that the __init__() from the base Form class gets called and sets everything else up properly on your form.

Using this form—accepting *args and **kwargs and passing them on to the parent method—is a useful shorthand when the method you're overriding accepts a lot of arguments, especially if a lot of them are optional. The __init__() method of the base Form class actually accepts up to seven arguments, all of them optional, so this is a handy trick.

Now you can add the fields you care about:

```
title = forms.CharField(max_length=255)
description = forms.CharField(widget=forms.Textarea())
code = forms.CharField(widget=forms.Textarea())
tags = forms.CharField(max_length=255)
```

Note that once again you're relying on the fact that you can change the widget used by a field to alter its presentation. Where Django's model system uses two different fields—CharField and TextField—to represent different sizes of text-based fields (and has to, because they work out to different data types in the underlying database columns), the form system only has a CharField. To turn it into a <textarea> in the eventual HTML, you simply change its widget to a Textarea, in much the same way that you used the PasswordInput widget in the example user signup form.

And that takes care of everything except the language, which is suddenly looking a little bit tricky. What you'd like to do is show a drop-down list (an HTML <select> element) of the available languages and validate that the user picked one of those. But none of the field types you've seen so far can handle that, so you'll need to turn to something new.

One way you could handle this is with a field type called ChoiceField. It takes a list of choices (in the same format as a model field that accepts choices—you've seen that already in, for example, the status field on the weblog's Entry model) and ensures that the submitted value is one of them. But setting that up properly so that the form queries for the set of languages each time it's used (in case an administrator has added new languages to the system) would require some more hacking in the __init__() method. And representing a model relationship like this is an awfully common situation, so you'd expect Django to provide an easy way to handle this.

As it turns out, Django does provide an easy solution: a special field type called ModelChoiceField. Where a normal ChoiceField would simply take a list of choices, a ModelChoiceField takes a Django QuerySet, and dynamically generates its choices from the result of the query (executed fresh each time). To use it, you'll need to change the model import at the top of the file to also bring in the Language model:

```
from cab.models import Snippet, Language
```

And then you can simply write:

```
language = forms.ModelChoiceField(queryset=Language.objects.all())
```

For this form, you don't need any special validation beyond what the fields themselves give you, so you can just write the save() method and be done:

```
def save(self):
    snippet = Snippet(title=self.cleaned_data['title'],
                      description=self.cleaned_data['description'],
                      code=self.cleaned_data['code'],
                      tags=self.cleaned_data['tags'],
                      language=self.cleaned_data['language'])
    snippet.save()
    return snippet
```

Since creating an object and saving it all in one step is a common pattern in Django, you can actually shorten that a bit. The default manager class Django provides will include a method called create(), which creates, saves, and returns a new object. Using that, your save() method is a couple lines shorter:

```
def save(self):
    return Snippet.objects.create(title=self.cleaned_data['title'],
                                  description=self.cleaned_data['description'],
                                  code=self.cleaned_data['code'],
                                  tags=self.cleaned_data['tags'],
                                  language=self.cleaned_data['language'])
```

And now your form is complete:

```
from django import newforms as forms
from cab.models import Snippet, Language


class AddSnippetForm(forms.Form):
    def __init__(self, author, *args, **kwargs):
        super(AddSnippetForm, self).__init__(*args, **kwargs):
        self.author = author

    title = forms.CharField(max_length=255)
    description = forms.CharField(widget=forms.Textarea())
    code = forms.CharField(widget=forms.Textarea())
```

```
        tags = forms.CharField(max_length=255)
        language = forms.ModelChoiceField(queryset=Language.objects.all())

        def save(self):
            return Snippet.objects.create(title=self.cleaned_data['title'],
                                description=self.cleaned_data['description'],
                                code=self.cleaned_data['code'],
                                tags=self.cleaned_data['tags'],
                                language=self.cleaned_data['language'])
```

Writing a View to Process the Form

Now you can write a short view to handle submissions. In the cab/views directory, create a file called snippets.py, and in it place the following code:

```
from django.http import HttpResponseRedirect
from django.shortcuts import render_to_response
from cab.forms import AddSnippetForm

def add_snippet(request):
    if request.method == 'POST':
        form = AddSnippetForm(author=request.user, data=request.POST)
        if form.is_valid():
            new_snippet = form.save()
            return HttpResponseRedirect(new_snippet.get_absolute_url())
    else:
        form = AddSnippetForm(author=request.user)
    return render_to_response('cab/add_snippet.html',
                            { 'form': form })
```

This will instantiate the form, validate the data, save the new Snippet, and return a redirect (again, always redirect after a successful POST) to the detail view of that snippet.

At first this looks great, but there's a problem lurking here. You're referring to request.user, which will be the currently logged in user (this is automatically set up by Django when the authentication system has been properly activated). But what happens if the person filling out this form isn't logged in?

The answer is that your data won't really be valid. When the current user isn't logged in, request.user is a "dummy" object representing an anonymous user, and it can't be used as the value of a snippet's author field. So what you need is some way to ensure that only logged-in users can fill out this form.

Fortunately, Django provides an easy way to handle this, via a decorator in the authentication system called login_required. You can simply import it and apply it to your view function, and anyone who's not logged in will be redirected to a login page:

```
from django.http import HttpResponseRedirect
from django.shortcuts import render_to_response
from django.contrib.auth.decorators import login_required
from cab.forms import AddSnippetForm
```

```
def add_snippet(request):
    if request.method == 'POST':
        form = AddSnippetForm(author=request.user, data=request.POST)
        if form.is_valid():
            new_snippet = form.save()
            return HttpResponseRedirect(new_snippet.get_absolute_url())
    else:
        form = AddSnippetForm(author=request.user)
    return render_to_response('cab/add_snippet.html',
                              { 'form': form })
add_snippet = login_required(add_snippet)
```

ADMONITION: SETTING UP LOGIN/LOGOUT VIEWS

Django's authentication system, bundled in `django.contrib.auth`, includes the views and forms you'll need to properly authenticate users and log them in. So long as you're just testing an application on your own computer, you can log in through Django's admin interface, and then visit any views you've marked with `login_required`. But for a live public deployment, you'll want to set up public-facing login/logout views for ordinary users.

To see how to use the built-in authentication views, consult the documentation for Django's authentication system online at www.djangoproject.com/documentation/authentication/.

From here you could write the cab/add_snippet.html template like so:

```
<html>
  <head>
    <title>Add a snippet</title>
  </head>
  <body>
    <h1>Add a snippet</h1>
    <p>Use the form below to submit your snippet; all fields are
       required.</p>
    <form method="post" action="">
      <p>{% if form.title.errors %}
      <span class="error">
      {{ form.title.errors|join:", " }}
      </span>
      {% endif %}</p>
      <p><label for="id_title">Title:</label>
      {{ form.title }}</p>
      <p>{% if form.language.errors %}
      <span class="error">
      {{ form.language.errors|join:", " }}
      </span>
      {% endif %}</p>
```

```
        <p><label for="id_languages">Language:</label>
        {{ form.language }}</p>
        <p>{% if form.description.errors %}
        <span class="error">
        {{ form.description.errors|join:", " }}
        </span>
        {% endif %}</p>
        <p><label for="id_description">Description:</label></p>
        <p>{{ form.description }}</p>
        <p>{% if form.code.errors %}
        <span class="error">
        {{ form.code.errors|join:", " }}
        </span>
        {% endif %}</p>
        <p><label for="id_code">Code:</label></p>
        <p>{{ form.code }}</p>
        <p>{% if form.tags.errors %}
        <span class="error">
        {{ form.tags.errors|join:", " }}
        </span>
        {% endif %}</p>
        <p><label for="id_tags">Tags:</label>
      {{ form.tags }}</p>
        <p><input type="submit" value="Submit"></p>
      </form>
    </body>
</html>
```

Automatically Generating a Form for Adding Snippets

Although Django's form system lets you be pretty concise about writing and using this form, you still haven't arrived at an ideal solution. Setting up a form for adding or editing instances of a model is a pretty common thing, and it would be awfully annoying to have to keep writing these sorts of boilerplate forms over and over (especially when you've already specified most or all of the relevant information once in the definition of the model class).

Fortunately, there's a way to drastically reduce the amount of code you have to write. Provided you don't need too much in the way of custom behavior from your form, Django provides a shortcut class, called ModelForm, which can automatically generate a moderately customizable form from a model definition, including all the relevant fields and the necessary save() method. At its most basic, here's how it works:

```
from django.newforms import ModelForm
from cab.models import Snippet


class SnippetForm(ModelForm):
    class Meta:
        model = Snippet
```

Subclassing ModelForm and supplying an inner Meta class that specifies a model will set up this form class to automatically derive its fields from the specified model. And ModelForm is smart enough to ignore any fields in the model defined with editable=False, so fields like the HTML version of the description won't show up in this form. The only thing that's lacking here is that the author field will show up. Luckily, ModelForm supports some customizations, including a list of fields to specifically exclude from the form, so you can simply change the definition to the following:

```
class SnippetForm(ModelForm):
    class Meta:
        model = Snippet
        exclude = ['author']
```

And it'll leave the author field out. Now you can simply delete cab/forms.py and rewrite cab/views/snippets.py like so:

```
from django.http import HttpResponseRedirect
from django.newforms import ModelForm
from django.shortcuts import render_to_response
from django.contrib.auth.decorators import login_required
from cab.models import Snippet


class SnippetForm(ModelForm):
    class Meta:
        model = Snippet
        exclude = ['author']


def add_snippet(request):
    if request.method == 'POST':
        form = SnippetForm(data=request.POST)
        if form.is_valid():
            new_snippet = form.save()
            return HttpResponseRedirect(new_snippet.get_absolute_url())
    else:
        form = SnippetForm()
    return render_to_response('cab/add_snippet.html',
                                { 'form': form })
add_snippet = login_required(add_snippet)
```

However, this isn't quite right. The Snippet needs to have an author filled in, but you've left that field out of the form. You could go back and define a custom __init__() method again and pass in request.user, but ModelForm has one more trick up its sleeve. You can have it create the Snippet object and return it without saving by passing an extra argument—commit=False—to its save() method. When you do this, save() will still return a new Snippet object, but it will *not* save it to the database. This will leave you free to add the user yourself and manually insert the new Snippet into the database:

```python
from django.http import HttpResponseRedirect
from django.newforms import ModelForm
from django.shortcuts import render_to_response
from django.contrib.auth.decorators import login_required
from cab.models import Snippet


class SnippetForm(ModelForm):
    class Meta:
        model = Snippet
        exclude = ['author']


def add_snippet(request):
    if request.method == 'POST':
        form = SnippetForm(data=request.POST)
        if form.is_valid():
            new_snippet = form.save(commit=False)
            new_snippet.author = request.user
            new_snippet.save()
            return HttpResponseRedirect(new_snippet.get_absolute_url())
    else:
        form = SnippetForm()
    return render_to_response('cab/add_snippet.html',
                              { 'form': form })
add_snippet = login_required(add_snippet)
```

ADMONITION: commit=False AND MANY-TO-MANY RELATIONSHIPS

If the model you're working with has a ManyToManyField (which will be represented in a form by a field type called ModelMultipleChoiceField), you'll need to take one additional step when you use the save() method of a ModelForm with commit=False. Many-to-many relationships can't be set up until after the primary object is saved (since they need to know its id in the database). So any time you use commit=False on a form that had a many-to-many relation, the form will have a method named save_m2m(), which stores the data for the eventual many-to-many relationships, and you'll need to call that method manually (with no arguments) after you've saved the primary object.

Now you can open up `cab/urls/snippets.py` and add a new import:

```
from cab.views.snippets import add_snippet
```

and a new URL pattern:

```
url(r'^add/$', add_snippet, name='cab_snippet_add'),
```

Simplifying Templates That Display Forms

The template outlined previously will continue to work because the form's fields haven't changed. But again, it would be nice if Django provided an easy way to show a form in a template without having to write out all the repetitive HTML and checks for field errors. You've eliminated the tedium of defining the form class itself, so why not eliminate the tedium of templating it?

To deal with this, every Django form has a few methods attached to it that know how to render the form into different types of HTML:

`as_ul()`: Renders the form as a set of HTML list items (`<li>` tags), with one item per field.

`as_p()`: Renders the form as a set of paragraphs (HTML `<p>` tags), with one item per paragraph.

`as_table()`: Renders the form as an HTML table, with one `<tr>` per field.

So, for example, you could replace the templating you've been doing so far (a set of HTML paragraph elements) with only the following:

```
{{ form.as_p }}
```

But there are a few things to note when using these methods:

- None of them output the enclosing `<form>` and `</form>` tags because the form doesn't "know" how or where you plan to have the form submitted. You'll need to fill in these tags yourself, with appropriate `action` and `method` attributes.

- None of them output any buttons for submitting the form. Again, the form doesn't know how you want it to be submitted, so you'll need to supply one or more `<input type="submit">` tags yourself.

- The `as_li()` method doesn't output the surrounding `<ul>` and `</ul>` tags, and the `as_table()` method doesn't output the surrounding `<table>` and `</table>` tags. This is in case you want to add more HTML yourself (which is a common need for form presentation), so you'll need to remember to fill in these tags.

- Finally, these methods are not easily customizable. When you just need a basic presentation for a form (especially for rapid prototyping so you can test an application), they're extremely handy, but if you need custom presentation you'll probably want to switch back to manually templating the form.

Editing Snippets

Now you have a system in place for users to submit their code snippets, but what happens if someone wants to go back and edit one? It's inevitable that someone will accidentally submit some code that has a typo or a minor error, or find a better solution, and it would be nice to let users edit their own snippets in those cases. So let's go ahead and set up snippet editing.

Fortunately, this is going to be easy. ModelForm also knows how to edit an existing object, which takes care of most of the heavy lifting. All you have to do, then, is handle two things:

- Figure out which Snippet object to edit.

- Make sure that the user who's trying to edit the Snippet is its original author.

You can handle the first part fairly easily by having your snippet-editing view receive the id of the Snippet in the URL, and then looking it up in the database. Then you can compare its author field to the currently logged-in user to ensure that they match. So let's start by adding a couple more imports to cab/views/snippets.py:

```
from django.shortcuts import get_object_or_404
from django.http import HttpResponseForbidden
```

The HttpResponseForbidden class represents an HTTP response with the status code 403, which indicates that the user doesn't have permission to do whatever they were trying to do. You'll use it when someone tries to edit a snippet they didn't originally submit. Here's the view:

```
def edit_snippet(request, snippet_id):
    snippet = get_object_or_404(Snippet, pk=snippet_id)
    if request.user.id != snippet.author.id:
        return HttpResponseForbidden()
    if request.method == 'POST':
        form = SnippetForm(instance=snippet, data=request.POST)
        if form.is_valid():
            snippet = form.save()
            return HttpResponseRedirect(snippet.get_absolute_url())
    else:
        form = SnippetForm(instance=snippet)
    return render_to_response('cab/edit_snippet.html',
                              { 'form': form })
edit_snippet = login_required(edit_snippet)
```

To tell a ModelForm subclass that you'd like it to edit an existing object, you simply pass that object as the keyword argument instance; the form will handle the rest. And note that since the Snippet already has an author, and that value won't be changing, you don't need to use commit=False and then manually save the Snippet. The form won't change that value, so you can simply let it save as is.

Now you can add a URL pattern for it. First you change the import line in cab/urls/snippets.py to also import this view:

```
from cab.views.snippets import add_snippet, edit_snippet
```

and then you add the URL pattern:

```
url(r'^edit/(?P<snippet_id>\d+)/$', edit_snippet, name='cab_snippet_edit'),
```

Since the form for both this and the add_snippet view will have the same fields, you can simplify the templating a bit by using only one template and passing a variable that indicates whether you're adding or editing (so that things like the page title can change accordingly). So let's change the add_snippet view's final line to pass an extra variable called add, set its value to True, and change the template name to cab/snippet_form.html:

```
return render_to_response('cab/snippet_form.html',
                          { 'form': form, 'add': True })
```

Then you can change the same line in edit_snippet to use cab/snippet_form.html and set the add variable to False:

```
return render_to_response('cab/snippet_form.html',
                          { 'form': form, 'add': False })
```

Now you can simply have one template—cab/snippet_form.html—which can look like this:

```
<html>
  <head>
    <title>{% if add %}Add a{% else %}Edit your{% endif %} snippet</title>
  </head>
  <body>
    <h1>{% if add %}Add a{% else %}Edit your{% endif %} snippet</h1>
    <p>Use the form below to {% if add %}add{% else %}edit {% endif %}
      your snippet; all fields are required</p>
    <form method="post" action="">
      {{ form.as_p }}
      <p><input type="submit" value="Send"></p>
    </form>
  </body>
</html>
```

Now you have views, forms, and templates, which let users both add and edit their code snippets. Here's the finished cab/views/snippets.py file, for reference:

```
from django.http import HttpResponseForbidden, HttpResponseRedirect
from django.newforms import ModelForm
from django.shortcuts import get_object_or_404, render_to_response
from django.contrib.auth.decorators import login_required
from cab.models import Snippet


class SnippetForm(ModelForm):
    class Meta:
        model = Snippet
        exclude = ['author']
```

```
def add_snippet(request):
    if request.method == 'POST':
        form = SnippetForm(data=request.POST)
        if form.is_valid():
            new_snippet = form.save(commit=False)
            new_snippet.author = request.user
            new_snippet.save()
            return HttpResponseRedirect(new_snippet.get_absolute_url())
    else:
        form = SnippetForm()
    return render_to_response('cab/snippet_form.html',
                              { 'form': form, 'add': True })
add_snippet = login_required(add_snippet)

def edit_snippet(request, snippet_id):
    snippet = get_object_or_404(Snippet, pk=snippet_id)
    if request.user.id != snippet.author.id:
        return HttpResponseForbidden()
    if request.method == 'POST':
        form = SnippetForm(instance=snippet, data=request.POST)
        if form.is_valid():
            snippet = form.save()
            return HttpResponseRedirect(snippet.get_absolute_url())
    else:
        form = SnippetForm(instance=snippet)
    return render_to_response('cab/snippet_form.html',
                              { 'form': form, 'add': False })
edit_snippet = login_required(edit_snippet)
```

Looking Ahead

Before moving on, I would suggest taking a little time to work with Django's form system. Though you should have a good understanding by now of the basics, you'll probably want to spend some time looking over the full documentation for the django.newforms package (online at www.djangoproject.com/documentation/newforms/) to get a feel for all of its features (including the full range of field types and widgets, as well as some more advanced tricks for customizing form presentation).

When you're ready to come back, the next chapter will wrap up this application by adding the bookmarking and rating features, including lists of the most popular snippets and the necessary template extensions to determine whether a user has already bookmarked or rated a snippet.

CHAPTER 10

■■■

Finishing the Code-Sharing Application

With the addition of the forms for user submissions, your code-sharing application is nearly complete. Only three features are left to implement from the original list. Then you can wrap up by rounding out the application with a few final views. Let's get started.

Bookmarking Snippets

Currently, your application's users can keep track of their favorite snippets by bookmarking them in a web browser or posting bookmarks to a service like del.icio.us. However, it would be nice to give each user the ability to track a personalized list of snippets directly on the site. This will cut down on the amount of clutter in each user's general-purpose bookmarks, and it will provide a useful social metric—most-bookmarked snippets—that you can track and display publicly.

The first thing you need to support this is, obviously, a model representing a user's bookmark. This is a pretty simple model, because all it needs to do is track a few pieces of information:

- The user the bookmark belongs to

- The snippet the user bookmarked

- The date and time when the user bookmarked the snippet

You can manage this by opening up cab/models.py and adding a new model with three fields for this information:

```
class Bookmark(models.Model):
    snippet = models.ForeignKey(Snippet)
    user = models.ForeignKey(User, related_name='cab_bookmarks')
    date = models.DateTimeField(editable=False)

    class Meta:
        ordering = ['-date']
```

```
def __unicode__(self):
    return "%s bookmarked by %s" % (self.snippet, self.user)

def save(self):
    if not self.id:
        self.date = datetime.datetime.now()
    super(Bookmark, self).save()
```

There's only one new feature in use here, and that's the related_name argument to the foreign key pointing at the User model. The fact that you've created a foreign key to User means that Django will add a new attribute to every User object, which you'll be able to use to access each user's bookmarks. By default, this attribute would be named bookmark_set based on the name of your Bookmark model. For example, you might query for a user's bookmarks like so:

```
from django.contrib.auth.models import User

u = User.objects.get(pk=1)
bookmarks = u.bookmark_set.all()
```

However, this can create a problem: if you ever use any other application with a bookmarking system, and if that application names its model Bookmark, you'll get a naming conflict, because the bookmark_set attribute of a User can't simultaneously refer to two different models.

The solution to this is the related_name argument to ForeignKey, which lets you manually specify the name of the new attribute on User, which you'll use to access bookmarks. In this case, you use cab_bookmarks, so once this model is installed and you have some bookmarks in your database, you'll be able to run queries like this:

```
from django.contrib.auth.models import User

u = User.objects.get(pk=1)
bookmarks = u.cab_bookmarks.all()
```

Generally, it's a good idea to use related_name any time you're creating a relationship from a model with a common name.

Also, note that since users will manage their bookmarks entirely through public-facing views, you don't need to activate the admin interface for the Bookmark model, so there is no inner Admin class here.

Go ahead and run manage.py syncdb to install this model into your database. Again, syncdb is smart enough to realize that it only needs to create one new table.

Basic Bookmark Views

Now you can add a couple of views to let users bookmark snippets and remove their bookmarks later if they wish. Create a file in cab/views called bookmarks.py, and start with the add_bookmark view:

```
from django.http import HttpResponseRedirect
from django.shortcuts import get_object_or_404, render_to_response
from django.contrib.auth.decorators import login_required
from cab.models import Bookmark, Snippet

def add_bookmark(request, snippet_id):
    snippet = get_object_or_404(Snippet, pk=snippet_id)
    try:
        Bookmark.objects.get(user__pk=request.user.id,
                             snippet__pk=snippet.id)
    except Bookmark.DoesNotExist:
        bookmark = Bookmark.objects.create(user=request.user,
                                           snippet=snippet)
    return HttpResponseRedirect(snippet.get_absolute_url())
add_bookmark = login_required(add_bookmark)
```

The logic here is pretty simple. You look to see if the user already has a bookmark for this snippet, and if not—in which case the `Bookmark.DoesNotExist` exception will be raised—you create one. Either way, you return a redirect back to the snippet, and, of course, you ensure that the user has to be logged in to do this.

Deleting a bookmark is similarly easy:

```
def delete_bookmark(request, snippet_id):
    if request.method == 'POST':
        snippet = get_object_or_404(Snippet, pk=snippet_id)
        Bookmark.objects.filter(user__pk=request.user.id,
                                snippet__pk=snippet.id).delete()
        return HttpResponseRedirect(snippet.get_absolute_url())
    else:
        return render_to_response('cab/confirm_bookmark_delete.html',
                                  { 'snippet': snippet })
delete_bookmark = login_required(delete_bookmark)
```

Here you're using two important techniques:

- Instead of querying to see if the user has a bookmark for this snippet and then deleting it manually (which incurs the overhead of two database queries), you simply use `filter()` to create a `QuerySet` of any bookmarks that match this user and this snippet. You then call the `delete()` method of that `QuerySet`. This issues only one query—a `DELETE` query, whose `FROM` clause limits it to the correct rows, if any exist.

- You're requiring that bookmark deletion use an HTTP `POST`. If the request method isn't `POST`, you display a confirmation page instead.

This last point bears emphasizing, because requiring HTTP `POST` and a confirmation screen for anything that deletes content—even trivial-seeming content like a bookmark—is an extremely important habit to get into. Not only does it prevent accidental deletion by a user who clicks the wrong link on a page, but it also adds a small measure of security against a common type of web-based attack: cross-site request forgery (CSRF). In a CSRF attack, a hacker lures a user of your site to a page that contains a hidden link or form pointing back to your application. The hacker exploits the fact that because the HTTP requests are coming from the user, many applications allow modification or deletion of content.

Additionally, it's generally good practice to require POST for any operation that alerts or deletes data on the server. The HTTP specification states that certain methods, including GET, should be considered safe and generally should not have side effects.

ADMONITION: SAFE AND IDEMPOTENT HTTP METHODS

The view you've written for adding a bookmark can be accessed via an HTTP GET, which seems to contradict the idea that this type of view should be safe.

The HTTP specification uses two different but related terms to describe request methods: *safe* and *idempotent.* A safe request is one that has no side effects and simply retrieves some information, while an idempotent request is one in which the effect of multiple identical requests is the same as the effect of one request. HTTP requires GET requests to be idempotent, but it doesn't strictly require them to be safe.

The add_bookmark view is idempotent, because multiple requests from the same user to bookmark the same snippet don't create multiple Bookmark objects. The net effect is the same as if there was only one request, because only one Bookmark object gets created.

The add_bookmark view isn't safe in this sense, though, because it can have a side effect (creating a Bookmark object). This doesn't violate the HTTP specification, but in general, you should be careful when allowing a GET request to have side effects. In this case, creating a bookmark doesn't really pose a risk. If someone were to be tricked into clicking a link to bookmark a snippet, for example, the worst thing that could happen would be that they'd need to delete the bookmark. So it's generally acceptable to allow bookmark creation to happen via a GET request.

Templating the confirmation page is easy enough. You can display some information about the snippet the user is about to "unbookmark," and then you can include a simple form that submits the confirmation via POST:

```
<form method="post" action="">
    <p><input type="submit" value="Delete bookmark"></p>
</form>
```

ADMONITION: FURTHER PROTECTION AGAINST CSRF

Requiring an HTTP POST helps somewhat against CSRF, because it means that an attacker can't merely display a link to a particular page and have that trigger deletion of content. However, for full protection, you'll want to refer to and enable django.contrib.csrf, an application bundled with Django that provides some stronger measures. It automatically inserts and checks for a randomly generated string in an incoming POST submission, and it returns an HTTP 403 (Forbidden) response if that string is not posted back by the user's browser.

You can find full documentation for this system online at www.djangoproject.com/documentation/csrf/.

It's easy enough to set up URLs for adding and deleting bookmarks. You can create cab/urls/bookmarks.py and start filling it in:

```
from django.conf.urls.defaults import *
from cab.views import bookmarks

urlpatterns = patterns('',
                       url(r'^add/(?P<snippet_id>\d+)/$',
                           bookmarks.add_bookmark,
                           name='cab_bookmark_add'),
                       url(r'^delete/(?P<snippet_id>\d+)/$',
                           bookmarks.delete_bookmark,
                           name='cab_bookmark_delete'),
)
```

Now that you've got views in place for managing bookmarks, go ahead and write one to show a list of the current user's bookmarks. This is just a wrapper around the object_list generic view:

```
from django.views.generic.list_detail import object_list

def user_bookmarks(request):
    return object_list(queryset=Bookmark.objects.filter(user__pk=request.user.id),
                       template_name='cab/user_bookmarks.html',
                       paginate_by=20)
```

You can set up a URL for it so that the root of the bookmark URLs simply shows the user's bookmarks:

```
url(r'^$', bookmarks.user_bookmarks, name='cab_user_bookmarks'),
```

Finally, to round out the bookmark-oriented views, add one that queries for the most-bookmarked snippets. Since this query returns Snippet objects, place it on the SnippetManager in cab/managers.py:

```
def most_bookmarked(self):
    from cab.models import Bookmark
    subquery = "SELECT COUNT(*) from %(bookmarks_table)s WHERE➡
      %(bookmarks_table)s.%(snippet_column)s = snippet.id"
    params = { 'bookmarks_table':➡
 connection.ops.quote_name(Bookmark._meta.db_table),
               'snippet_column': connection.ops.quote_name('snippet_id') }
    return self.extra(select={ 'score': subquery % params,
                      order_by=['-score'])
```

Write the view in cab/views/popular.py:

```
def most_bookmarked(request):
    return object_list(queryset=Snippet.objects.most_bookmarked(),
                       template_name='cab/most_bookmarked.html',
                       paginate_by=20)
```

Then add the URL pattern in cab/urls/popular.py:

```
url(r'^bookmarks/$', popular.most_bookmarked, name='cab_most_bookmarked'),
```

A New Template Tag: {% if_bookmarked %}

To go with the add/delete views, it would be nice when viewing a snippet to have some way of telling whether a user has already bookmarked it or not. That way, you could either hide any links to bookmarking views you might otherwise show or switch to showing a link or button to delete the bookmark.

You could set this up to be part of the detail view of a snippet, but that's not necessarily the only place you might want this functionality. If you're showing a list of snippets, for example, you might want a quick and easy way to determine where to show a link for bookmarking and where not to. The ideal solution would be a template tag, which can tell whether a user has already bookmarked a specific snippet. Something that works like this would be ideal:

```
{% if_bookmarked user object %}
    <form method="post" action="{% url cab_bookmark_delete object.id %}">
      <p><input type="submit" value="Delete bookmark"></p>
    </form>
{% else %}
    <p><a href="{% url cab_bookmark_add object.id %}">Add bookmark</a></p>
{% endif_bookmarked %}
```

ADMONITION: WIRING UP THE URLS

Because you're using the {% url %} tag to generate the link to the add_bookmark view, you need to add the URLs for the cab application to your project's root URLConf module (via include() calls). If you use the {% url %} tag with a URL name that you haven't yet set up in your project, it won't be able to find the correct URL and will simply return an empty string instead of a URL.

But how can you write this? So far, all of your custom template tags have been pretty simple. They typically just read their arguments and spit something back out into the context. Writing this tag requires two new techniques:

- The ability to write a tag that reads ahead a bit in the template to find, for example, the {% else %} clause and the closing tag, and keeps track of what to display

- The ability to resolve arbitrary variables from the template context, as in the case of a variable such as object

Fortunately, both of these are easy enough to accomplish.

Parsing Ahead in a Django Template

You'll recall from Chapter 6 when you wrote your first custom template tags that the compilation function for a tag receives two arguments, conventionally called parser and token. At the time, you were only concerned with the token portion because it contained the arguments you were interested in. However, now you're in a situation where parser—which is the actual object that's parsing the template—is going to come in handy.

Before diving in too deeply, let's go ahead and lay out the infrastructure for the custom tag. In the cab directory, create a new directory called templatetags, and in that directory, create two new files: __init__.py and snippets.py. Then, open up cab/templatetags/snippets.py and fill in a couple of necessary imports:

```
from django import template
from cab.models import Bookmark
```

Now, you can start writing the compilation function for the {% if_bookmarked %} tag:

```
def do_if_bookmarked(parser, token):
    bits = token.contents.split()
    if len(bits) != 3:
        raise template.TemplateSyntaxError("%s tag takes two arguments" % bits[0])
```

This looks at the syntax used to call the tag—which is of the form {% if_bookmarked user snippet %}—and verifies that it has the right number of arguments, bailing out immediately with a TemplateSyntaxError if it doesn't.

Now you can turn your attention to the parser argument and see how it can help you out. You want to read ahead in the template until you find either an {% else %} or an {% endif_bookmarked %} tag. You can do just that by calling the parse() method of the parser object and passing a list of things you'd like it to look for. The result of this parsing will be an instance of the class django.template.NodeList, which is—as the name implies—a list of template nodes:

```
nodelist_true = parser.parse(('else', 'endif_bookmarked'))
```

You're storing this result in a variable called nodelist_true because—in terms of the if/else-style behavior of this tag—it corresponds to the output you want to display if the condition (the user has bookmarked the snippet) is true.

The call to parser.parse() moves ahead in the template to just *before* the first item in the list you told it to look for. This means you now want to look at the next token and find out if it's an {% else %}. If it is, you'll need to do a bit more parsing:

```
token = parser.next_token()
if token.contents == 'else':
    nodelist_false = parser.parse(('endif_bookmarked',))
    parser.delete_first_token()
else:
    nodelist_false = template.NodeList()
```

If the first thing the parser finds from your list is indeed an {% else %}, then you want to read ahead again to {% endif_bookmarked %} to get the output to display when the user *hasn't* bookmarked the snippet. This is another NodeList, which you store in the variable nodelist_false.

If, on the other hand, the parser finds an `{% endif_bookmarked %}` with no `{% else %}`, then you simply create an empty `NodeList`. If the user hasn't bookmarked the snippet, then you shouldn't display anything when there's no `{% else %}` clause.

Finally, you return a `Node` class, passing the two arguments gathered from the tag and the two `NodeList` instances. Although you haven't defined it yet, the `Node` class you're going to use will be called `IfBookmarkedNode`:

```
return IfBookmarkedNode(bits[1], bits[2], nodelist_true, nodelist_false)
```

Resolving Variables Inside a Template Node

Now you can begin writing the `IfBookmarkedNode`. Obviously, it needs to subclass `template.Node`, and it needs to accept four arguments in its __init__() method. You'll simply store the two `NodeList` instances for later use when you render the template:

```
class IfBookmarkedNode(template.Node):
    def __init__(self, user, snippet, nodelist_true, nodelist_false):
        self.nodelist_true = nodelist_true
        self.nodelist_false = nodelist_false
```

But what about the `user` and `snippet` variables? Right now, they're the raw strings from the template, and you don't yet know what values they'll actually resolve to when you get a look at the context. You need some way of saying that these are actually template variables that you need to resolve later on. Fortunately, that's easy enough to do:

```
self.user = template.Variable(user)
self.snippet = template.Variable(snippet)
```

The `Variable` class in `django.template` handles the hard work for you. When given the template context to work with, it knows how to resolve the variable and gives you back the actual value it corresponds to.

Now you can start to write the `render()` method:

```
def render(self, context):
    user = self.user.resolve(context)
    snippet = self.snippet.resolve(context)
```

Each `Variable` instance has a method called `resolve()`, which handles the actual business of resolving the variable. If the variable turns out not to correspond to anything, it'll even handle raising an exception—`django.template.VariableDoesNotExist`—automatically for you. Of course, you've seen that it's usually a good idea for custom template tags to fail silently when possible, so catch that exception and just have the tag return nothing when one of the variables is invalid:

```
def render(self, context):
    try:
        user = self.user.resolve(context)
        snippet = self.snippet.resolve(context)
    except template.VariableDoesNotExist:
        return ''
```

If you get past this point, then you know that these variables resolved successfully, and you can use them to query for an existing Bookmark. The only tricky thing now is what to return in each case. You have two NodeList instances, and you want to render one or the other according to whether the user has bookmarked the snippet. Fortunately, that's easy. Just as a Node must have a render() method that accepts the context and returns a string, so too must NodeList:

```
if Bookmark.objects.filter(user__pk=user.id,
                           snippet__pk=snippet.id):
    return self.nodelist_true.render(context)
else:
    return self.nodelist_false.render(context)
```

Now you have a finished tag. After you register it, cab/templatetags/snippets.py looks like this:

```
from django import template
from cab.models import Bookmark

def do_if_bookmarked(parser, token):
    bits = token.contents.split()
    if len(bits) != 3:
        raise template.TemplateSyntaxError("%s tag takes two arguments" % bits[0])
    nodelist_true = parser.parse(('else', 'endif_bookmarked'))
    token = parser.next_token()
    if token.contents == 'else':
        nodelist_false = parser.parse(('endif_bookmarked',))
        parser.delete_first_token()
    else:
        nodelist_false = template.NodeList()
    return IfBookmarkedNode(bits[1], bits[2], nodelist_true, nodelist_false)


class IfBookmarkedNode(template.Node):
    def __init__(self, user, snippet, nodelist_true, nodelist_false):
        self.nodelist_true = nodelist_true
        self.nodelist_false = nodelist_false
        self.user = template.Variable(user)
        self.snippet = template.Variable(snippet)

    def render(self, context):
        try:
            user = self.user.resolve(context)
            snippet = self.snippet.resolve(context)
        except template.VariableDoesNotExist:
            return ''
        if Bookmark.objects.filter(user__pk=user.id,
                                   snippet__pk=snippet.id):
            return self.nodelist_true.render(context)
```

```
        else:
            return self.nodelist_false.render(context)

register = template.Library()
register.tag('if_bookmarked', do_if_bookmarked)
```

Now you can simply do {% load snippets %} in a template and use the {% if_bookmarked %} tag.

Using `RequestContext` to Automatically Populate Template Variables

But you can only use the {% if_bookmarked %} tag if the template you're using the tag in has an available variable that represents the currently logged-in user. This is a slightly trickier proposition because so far you haven't been writing your views to pass the current user as a variable to the templates they use. Mostly that's because you haven't had much need to do so. Everything you've been doing with the logged-in user has happened at the view level by accessing `request.user`, so you haven't really run into a case—until now—where you genuinely needed to have a variable for the user available in templates.

You could simply go back at this point and make the necessary change in all your handwritten views, but that immediately brings up two disadvantages:

- **It's tedious and repetitive**. Generally, Django encourages you to avoid anything that can be described in that fashion.

- **It doesn't help for views you didn't write yourself**. In a lot of cases, you're simply wrapping a generic view, and short of manually passing the `extra_context` argument each and every time you use a generic view, there doesn't seem to be any way to solve this. Plus, this might not help any if you need to use views from someone else's application. If that person hasn't written views to accept an argument similar to `extra_context`, you won't be able to do anything.

Fortunately, there's an easier solution. As you'll recall from the first handwritten views back in Chapter 3, the dictionary of variables and values passed to a template is an instance of `django.template.Context`. Because this is an ordinary Python class, you can subclass it to add customizable behavior. Django includes one very useful subclass of `Context`—`django.template.RequestContext`—which can automatically populate some extra variables each time it's used *without* needing to have those variables explicitly declared and defined in each view.

`RequestContext` gets its name from the fact that it makes use of functions called *context processors* (which I mentioned briefly in Chapter 6). Each context processor is a function that receives a Django `HttpRequest` object as an argument and returns a dictionary of variables based on that `HttpRequest`. `RequestContext` then automatically adds those variables to the context, in addition to any variables explicitly passed to the context during the process of executing a view function.

In normal use, `RequestContext` reads its list of context processor functions from the setting `TEMPLATE_CONTEXT_PROCESSORS`. The default set happens to include a context processor that reads `request.user` to get the current user and adds it to the context as the variable `{{ user }}`. This just happens to be exactly what you want here. As long as a view uses `RequestContext`, its template can rely on the fact that the variable `{{ user }}` will be available and will correspond to the currently active user.

Using `RequestContext` is trivially easy; you simply import it:

```
from django.template import RequestContext
```

You can use it anywhere you need a context for a template. The only difference between a normal `Context` and `RequestContext` is that the latter must receive the `HttpRequest` object as an argument. For example, in a view, you might write:

```
context = RequestContext(request, { 'foo': 'bar' })
```

It works with the `render_to_response()` shortcut as well, though the usage is slightly different. For example, where you'd normally write this:

```
return render_to_response('example.html',
                          { 'foo': 'bar' })
```

you instead write this:

```
return render_to_response('example.html',
                          { 'foo': 'bar' },
                          context_instance=RequestContext(request))
```

And for cases where you're wrapping a generic view, you don't even have to do anything—Django's generic views default to using `RequestContext`. So far, you've only written three views in this application that don't use generic views—the `delete_bookmark`, `add_snippet`, and `edit_snippet` views, to be precise—so it's not too hard to go back and add the use of `RequestContext` to them. Because the rest are generic views or wrap generic views, they're already using `RequestContext`.

ADMONITION: USING RequestContext REPETITIVELY

Even though `RequestContext` obviously makes it a lot easier to handle situations where you want to have certain variables globally available to your templates, it still feels a little bit repetitive to have to manually state that you want it each time. And if the generic views use `RequestContext` automatically, why shouldn't a shortcut such as `render_to_response()` use it as well? In fact, why isn't it just the default context class?

One good reason is the fact that `RequestContext` requires access to the `HttpRequest` object, and there's no way for it to get that access automatically. Unless the `HttpRequest` is passed to it explicitly, `RequestContext` won't be able to do anything. Another good reason is that in a lot of cases, you'll want to render a template independently of any HTTP request being processed. It's not unusual at all for the Django template system to be used to generate e-mail messages, files that are written to disk, and all manner of other things that have little to do directly with the HTTP request/response cycle.

If you do find yourself aching for a shortcut, though, it's easy to write one like so:

```
from django.shortcuts import render_to_response
from django.template import RequestContext

def render_response(request, *args, **kwargs):
    kwargs['context_instance'] = RequestContext(request)
    return render_to_response(*args, **kwargs)
```

Personally, I tend to avoid doing this, and as a matter of style, I prefer to simply write out the use of RequestContext each time. I find that doing so serves as a reminder to me that I'm setting up a view to have the extra variables RequestContext will populate, and the extra bit of code to set it up makes it easy to spot when I come back later and read over a view function. Handling RequestContext manually also avoids the problem of writing code that relies heavily on a shortcut function that might not be distributed along with a particular application, which in turn improves the reusability of your code.

Adding the User Rating System

The only thing left to implement from the feature list is a rating system that lets users mark particular snippets they found useful (or not useful, as the case may be). Once again, start with a data model. As with the bookmarking system, it's fairly simple. You need to collect four pieces of information:

- The snippet being rated

- The user doing the rating

- The value of the rating—in this case, either a +1 or -1, for a simple "up or down" voting system

- The date of the rating

You can easily build out the model in cab/models.py:

```
class Rating(models.Model):
    RATING_UP = 1
    RATING_DOWN = -1
    RATING_CHOICES = ((RATING_UP, 'useful'),
                      (RATING_DOWN, 'not useful'))
    snippet = models.ForeignKey(Snippet)
    user = models.ForeignKey(User, related_name='cab_rating')
    rating = models.IntegerField(choices=RATING_CHOICES)
    date = models.DateTimeField()
```

```
def __unicode__(self):
    return "%s rating %s (%s)" % (self.user, self.snippet,
                                  self.get_rating_display())

def save(self):
    if not self.id:
        self.date = datetime.datetime.now()
    super(Rating, self).save()
```

As with the Bookmark model, you're setting related_name explicitly on the relationship to the User model in order to avoid any potential name clashes with other applications that might define rating systems. The rating value, meanwhile, uses an integer field, with appropriately named constants, to handle the actual "up" and "down" rating values, in much the same fashion as the status field on the weblog's Entry model. There is one new item, though: in the __unicode__() method, you're calling a method named get_rating_display(). Any time a model has a field with choices like this, a method—whose name is derived from the name of the field—will be automatically added by Django, which will return the human-readable value for the currently selected value.

While you're in the cab/models.py file, you can also add a method to the Snippet model that calculates a snippet's total score by summing all of the ratings attached to it. If you've had much experience with SQL-based databases, your first instinct will probably be to look for a way to run a SELECT SUM(rating) query against the ratings table. From a database perspective, that's certainly the obvious way to do it. Unfortunately, as of this writing, Django's object-relational mapper doesn't directly support these types of aggregate queries (SUM(), AVG(), MAX(), and so on), which means that you have two options:

- Run the query manually by writing and executing the SQL yourself.

- Find a different way to run the query.

Doing it manually isn't terribly hard; you can access the underlying database connection; use a standardized, lower-level API to run queries directly against your database; and read the raw results. You've already encountered the module django.db.connection in the context of your various popularity-based queries, though so far you've only used it for the ability to format pieces of a query correctly.

However, manually performing this query is going to be fairly tedious. It would be nicer if there were some cleaner way to handle it, and as it turns out, there is: Python has a built-in function, sum(), that returns the sum of the items in a list. All you need to do is get a list of the rating values for a particular Snippet and call sum() on them. Here's one way you might handle it:

```
def get_score(self):
    return sum([r.rating for r in self.rating_set.all()])
```

This is short and sweet, but unfortunately, it's also extremely inefficient. Under the hood, it's querying the full rows from the ratings table and instantiating a Rating object for each row.

A more efficient way to do this would be to only select the single field you care about—rating—and sum the results. Django provides an easy way to do this, via a method (which is available on all default managers and on every QuerySet) called values(). Rather than select every column and instantiate a model object (which involves a bit of overhead), values()

returns a list of dictionaries. You can pass a list of field names to limit the columns it selects (and, as a result, the keys in the returned dictionaries). For example, you might see the following in a Python interpreter:

```
>>> from cab.models import Rating
>>> Rating.objects.values('rating')
[{'rating': 1}, {'rating': 1}, {'rating': 1}, {'rating': -1}]
```

which leads to a slightly better version of the get_score() method:

```
def get_score(self):
    return sum([r['rating'] for r in self.rating_set.values('rating')])
```

This is more efficient, but having to access the dictionary key each time makes it a bit less elegant to write. There's one more way you can do this, though. values() returns a dictionary, but there's a similar method named values_list() that returns a list of tuples containing only the fields you've told it to select. This method takes an optional argument—flat=True—which, if you only select a single field, flattens the result into a single list of the values from that field. This leads to the following code:

```
def get_score(self):
    return sum(self.rating_set.values_list('rating', flat=True))
```

This provides a nice balance between efficiency and clean code. It's slightly slower than manually running a SELECT SUM() directly against the database, but it's much shorter and far more readable than the equivalent code to execute that manual query.

ADMONITION: EXECUTING RAW SQL

Sometimes there won't be an alternate way to run a query that the Django object-relational mapper doesn't support directly. Other times, performance considerations will absolutely require that the query run as raw SQL that you can hand-tune. In such cases, you'll want to look at the function django.db.connection. cursor(), which returns a database cursor object compliant with the standard Python Database API specified by Python Enhancement Proposal (PEP) 249 (available online at www.python.org/dev/peps/ pep-0249/). You can use this cursor object to execute any query your database is capable of supporting.

Finally, in cab/managers.py, you can add one more method on the SnippetManager for calculating the top-rated snippets:

```
def top_rated(self):
    from cab.models import Rating
    subquery = "SELECT SUM(%(rating_column)s) from %(rating_table)s WHERE➥
    %(rating_table)s.%(snippet_column)s = snippet.id"
    params = { 'rating_column': connection.ops.quote_name('rating'),
               'rating_table': connection.ops.quote_name(Rating._meta.db_table),
               'snippet_column': connection.ops.quote_name('snippet_id') }
    return self.extra(select={ 'score': subquery % params },
                      order_by=['-score'])
```

This takes care of all the custom queries you'll need, so go ahead and run manage.py syncdb to install the Rating model.

Rating Snippets

Letting users rate snippets is pretty easy. All you need is a view that gets a snippet ID and an "up" or "down" rating, then adds a new Rating object. The view logic is simple. Go ahead and create one more view file—cab/views/ratings.py—to place this code in:

```python
from django.http import HttpResponseRedirect
from django.shortcuts import get_object_or_404
from django.contrib.auth.decorators import login_required
from cab.models import Rating, Snippet

def rate(request, snippet_id):
    snippet = get_object_or_404(Snippet, pk=snippet_id)
    if 'rating' not in request.GET or request.GET['rating'] not in ('1', '-1'):
        return HttpResponseRedirect(snippet.get_absolute_url())
    try:
        rating = Rating.objects.get(user__pk=request.user.id,
                                    snippet__pk=snippet.id)
    except Rating.DoesNotExist:
        rating = Rating(user=request.user,
                        snippet=snippet)
    rating.rating = int(request.GET['rating'])
    rating.save()
    return HttpResponseRedirect(snippet.get_absolute_url())
rate = login_required(rate)
```

Only two moderately tricky things are going on here:

- You're going to expect this view to be accessed with a query string like ?rating=1 or ?rating=-1, so you verify that this is present and has an acceptable value; if not, you simply redirect back to the snippet.

- To avoid ballot stuffing by a user trying to rate the same snippet over and over, you ensure that the view simply changes the value of an existing rating if one is found.

Setting up the URL for this should be fairly easy. You can simply add a cab/urls/ratings.py file and set up the necessary URL pattern:

```python
from django.conf.urls.defaults import *
from cab.views.ratings import rate

urlpatterns = patterns('',
                       url(r'^(?P<snippet_id>\d+)$', rate, name='cab_snippet_rate'),
)
```

Adding an {% if_rated %} Template Tag

Go ahead and add an {% if_rated %} template tag similar to the {% if_bookmarked %} tag you developed earlier in this chapter. The compilation function for it should look familiar (once again, this goes into cab/templatetags/snippets.py):

```python
def do_if_rated(parser, token):
    bits = token.contents.split()
    if len(bits) != 3:
        raise template.TemplateSyntaxError("%s tag takes two arguments" % bits[0])
    nodelist_true = parser.parse(('else', 'endif_rated'))
    token = parser.next_token()
    if token.contents == 'else':
        nodelist_false = parser.parse(('endif_rated',))
        parser.delete_first_token()
    else:
        nodelist_false = template.NodeList()
    return IfRatedNode(bits[1], bits[2], nodelist_true, nodelist_false)
```

Once again, you use the ability to parse ahead in the template to work out the structure of the if/else possibilities for the tag and store a pair of NodeList instances to pass as arguments to the Node class, which you can call IfRatedNode. First, you need to change the import statement at the top of the file from:

```python
from cab.models import Bookmark
```

to:

```python
from cab.models import Bookmark, Rating
```

Then you can write the IfRatedNode:

```python
class IfRatedNode(template.Node):
    def __init__(self, user, snippet, nodelist_true, nodelist_false):
        self.nodelist_true = nodelist_true
        self.nodelist_false = nodelist_false
        self.user = template.Variable(user)
        self.snippet = template.Variable(snippet)

    def render(self, context):
        try:
            user = self.user.resolve(context)
            snippet = self.snippet.resolve(context)
        except template.VariableDoesNotExist:
            return ''
        if Rating.objects.filter(user__pk=user.id,
                                 snippet__pk=snippet.id):
            return self.nodelist_true.render(context)
        else:
            return self.nodelist_false.render(context)
```

At the bottom of the file, you can register the tag:

```
register.tag('if_rated', do_if_rated)
```

Retrieving a User's Rating

Now that you have the {% if_rated %} tag, you can add a second, complementary tag, to retrieve the user's rating for a particular snippet. That lets you set up a template like so:

```
{% load snippets %}
{% if_rated user snippet %}
  {% get_rating user snippet as rating %}
  <p>You rated this snippet <strong>{{ rating.get_rating_display }}</strong>.</p>
{% endif_rated %}
```

When a user has rated a snippet, this should end up displaying something like, "You rated this snippet **useful**."

The compilation function is straightforward:

```
def do_get_rating(parser, token):
    bits = token.contents.split()
    if len(bits) != 5:
        raise template.TemplateSyntaxError("%s tag takes four arguments" % bits[0])
    if bits[3] != 'as':
        raise template.TemplateSyntaxError("Third argument to➥
 %s must be 'as'" % bits[0])
    return GetRatingNode(bits[1], bits[2], bits[4])
```

The Node class is also easy. You just need to resolve the two variables, retrieve the Rating, and put it into the context:

```
class GetRatingNode(template.Node):
    def __init__(self, user, snippet, varname):
        self.user = template.Variable(user)
        self.snippet = template.Variable(snippet)
        self.varname = varname

    def render(self, context):
        try:
            user = self.user.resolve(context)
            snippet = self.snippet.resolve(context)
        except template.VariableDoesNotExist:
            return ''
        rating = Rating.objects.get(user__pk=user.id,
                                    snippet__pk=snippet.id)
        context[self.varname] = rating
        return ''
```

Next, you register the tag:

```
register.tag('get_rating', do_get_rating)
```

Then you can use the tag like so (in the detail view of a snippet, for example):

```
{% load snippets %}
{% if_rated user object %}
  {% get_rating user snippet as rating %}
  <p>You rated this snippet {{ rating.get_rating_display }}.</p>
{% else %}
    <p>Rate this snippet:
        <a href="{% url cab_snippet_rate object.id %}?rating=1">useful</a> or
        <a href="{% url cab_snippet_rate object.id %}?rating=-1">not useful</a>.</p>
{% endif_rated %}
```

Looking Ahead

At this point, you've implemented everything on your original feature list. You have user-submittable and user-editable snippets, with tagging and with sorting by language. You also have bookmarking and rating features as well as some aggregate views to display things like the top-rated and most-bookmarked snippets and the most-used languages. Along the way, you've learned how to work with Django's form system, and you've picked up some advanced tricks for working with the object-relational mapper and the template engine.

Of course, you could still add a lot more features at this point:

- Following up on your experiences with the weblog application, you could easily add comments (with moderation) and feeds.

- You could borrow the content-retrieving template tags you wrote for the weblog and use them to retrieve the latest snippets or adapt them to perform some of the custom queries you've written for this application.

- You could build out a whole lot of new views and queries; even with the simple set of models you have here, there's a lot of room for interesting ways to explore this application, and what you've set up so far just scratches the surface.

- You could explore ways of integrating this application with some of the others you've written and used (perhaps a code-sharing site with a weblog that points out the site staff's favorite snippets).

By now, you've reached a point where you can start building out these features on your own and tailor this application to work precisely the way you want it to. Consider some of these ideas and think about how you'd implement them, then sit down and write the code. Then start brainstorming some things you'd like that *aren't* listed above, and try your hand at them too, because if you've made it this far, you're ready to make use of your knowledge and put Django to work for you.

In recognition of that, I'm not going to dictate any more feature lists or implementations to you. Instead, in the next (and final) chapter, I'll change gears a bit and talk about some general best practices for developing your Django applications and getting the most out of them.

CHAPTER 11

■■■

Writing Reusable Django Applications

So far, this book has mostly been concerned with covering various aspects of Django in the context of building a set of specific applications. Through the process of writing the code for those applications, you've seen Django's major components in action and learned how they can drastically reduce the amount of work needed to build useful web applications. But that's really just a small part of what Django can do to help you cut down on the time and effort needed to build out an application. By encouraging certain best practices and by making it easier to follow them as you write, Django also helps you to improve the quality, flexibility, and reusability of your code. And in the long run, that's a much larger gain.

Time and time again, you've seen how components included in Django, or applications bundled along with it, can help you kick-start the process of developing a new application by handling common tasks for you. When you're developing with Django, you don't need to worry about writing lots of code to handle your database queries. It's easy to route specific URLs to parts of your application or to generate HTML through templating. And when you use the applications bundled with Django, you can get a lot of functionality for "free." For instance, you've seen how Django provides features such as user accounts and authentication, RSS feed generation, user-submitted comments, and even a dynamic administrative interface for site content.

From there, the natural next step is to consider ways to write new applications that you can reuse over and over, just the same way you reuse Django's own components and the bundled applications in `django.contrib`. The applications in `django.contrib` provide good examples to look at, because—aside from the fact that they're included in the Django download—there's nothing special or magical about them. All of them, even the administrative interface, are simply applications that have been written with flexibility and reusability in mind, and so are no different from any other well-designed Django application.

As you gain experience with Django and start building up a library of applications you've written on your own, you'll find that developing your own reusable applications is surprisingly easy and provides a powerful resource. Instead of reimplementing a particular feature each time you need it, you can simply write it once and reuse it again and again, giving you an impressive head start on each new project you work on.

In this chapter, I'll take an in-depth look at some practical guidelines for developing these sorts of reusable applications, and I'll show you some specific techniques that can make the process easier.

One Thing at a Time

A popular adage in software development states that a particular program should "do one thing, and do it well." This dates back to the early days of the UNIX operating system, which consisted, in part, of a collection of small, simple programs that users could chain together to create powerful effects. Because of this, UNIX is often contrasted with operating systems that tend to use large, complex applications packed with lots of features.

While complex applications do have their place, the philosophy of building up a system from a collection of smaller, self-contained parts opens up a lot of flexibility. Instead of having to make changes to a large and complicated piece of software when you need new features and keep track of how all of its features interact with each other, you can build up different arrangements of simpler applications and only write new code when you don't yet have the necessary pieces to build what you need.

Although UNIX originally applied this idea to tasks like text processing, this approach is just as powerful when applied to web development. By keeping a library of small, self-contained applications that each handle some particular feature, you gain the ability to reuse them over and over, in different combinations and configurations, as building blocks for new sites.

Staying Focused

One of the greatest dangers in software development is the process of *feature creep* or *scope creep*. Let's say you have an idea for an interesting feature that's at least somewhat related to what you're working on, so you go ahead and add it. But once that feature is in place, you start coming up with ideas for ways to build on it and enhance it with even more features and capabilities, and you start writing more and more code to support these features. Eventually, you end up with a huge tangled mess that's strayed significantly from its original purpose.

However, when you're writing code for a modular system like Django, it's often a bit easier to spot the warning signs of feature creep and get back on track. A complex site with a lot of features but only a small number of applications listed in INSTALLED_APPS often indicates that one or more of the applications it's using is trying to do too much.

Similarly, the relatively simple structure of a Django application—models, views, URLs, and maybe some custom forms or template tags—will quickly start to feel cluttered if you're trying to pack too many features into a single application. Sometimes you'll genuinely need to maintain a large number of model classes or logical groups of views and URL patterns in a single application, but often the amount of bookkeeping work you'll need to do to keep that much code organized will hint that your application isn't as tightly focused as it could be.

As a general rule, the easiest way to stay on track is to answer a simple question: "What does this application do?" Rather than listing out every feature, just try to summarize the application's purpose. For example, with the weblog application, the answer to this question would be, "Give the site staff an easy interface for posting entries and links into a weblog, and keep these entries organized by using tags and topical categories." For django.contrib.auth, the answer would be, "Provide a mechanism for storing user account information and for authenticating users so they can interact with the site."

If you find that your answer to this question is getting long—more than a sentence or two, in a lot of cases—it may be time to step back and evaluate whether your application is trying to do too many things at once.

Once you're in this mindset, you'll find that you approach new feature ideas with skepticism. Rather than thinking of features solely in terms of how cool they'd be to have on your site, you'll also start thinking in terms of how they relate to your application's purpose. This makes it a lot easier to weed out things that don't belong and either reject them or file them away to be implemented somewhere else.

Advantages of Tightly Focused Applications

Once you're developing applications with this sort of tight focus, you'll find that it's a lot easier to reuse them. For example, a well-focused application is often a lot simpler to set up and install, because you usually don't have to worry about setting up large numbers of templates or keeping track of (and possibly training your site staff to use) lots of new data models.

You'll also find that it's much easier to adapt a tightly focused application when you run into new situations where you really do need to add a new feature or build in a little bit more flexibility, because you usually have less code to look through and edit, and it's usually organized in a fairly simple fashion. Many extremely useful Django applications consist of only three or four short files of code.

Finally, you'll notice that you suddenly have a much easier time dealing with the real, specific problems your application is trying to solve. When you're no longer maintaining large numbers of unrelated features in a single application, you're free to examine its particular problem domain in much greater detail and come up with much more thorough and flexible solutions.

A good real-world example of this would be to expand the simple user-signup system I used as an example (in Chapter 9) to teach you about Django's form-processing system. It would be tempting to simply go from the basic signup form and view you looked at and start adding features that don't have as much to do with the process of user signups. For example, you could add the ability for users to fill out a site-specific user profile or set up preferences to control how the site is presented to a specific user. However, that's the beginning of feature creep. Although user profiles and preference systems are important and useful things to have, they don't have a whole lot to do with the user signup process, and just getting that process right can be complicated enough on its own. Signups should, at least optionally, be able to require an explicit activation step by sending an e-mail to the new user to confirm the account. Also, if you need to have user signups on multiple sites, you'll probably need to specify different ways to collect the initial account information. For example, some sites might need new users to read and agree to terms of service or other policies, while others might have restrictions on who can sign up. Finally, many sites also want some way of preventing automated signups by spambots. Many spambots can navigate automatically through an e-mail–based activation system, so you might want to add additional wrinkles to the signup process, such as optionally generating an image with some text in it and requiring the new user to read it and type the text into a field in the form.

This is a common scenario in application development: even something that seems simple at first glance can have a lot of complexity lurking just below the surface. Keeping your applications tightly focused will help you keep your attention on dealing with that complexity, so you don't end up with only a partial solution to the problem you originally set out to solve.

Developing Multiple Applications

The idea that any given application should do one thing and do it well is only one half of the process of building complex systems from small, self-contained parts. The other half is the idea that it's a good thing to start out from an initial idea and end up developing several applications that implement different parts of it.

To a certain extent, this is a natural consequence of developing tightly focused applications. If you don't let yourself fall into feature creep within a given application, you'll naturally end up with a list of features you'd like to have but that don't logically belong to that application. The obvious next step, then, is to develop a separate application with an appropriate focus for the features you want to implement.

Getting into the habit of "spinning off" new applications whenever you have a new set of features to implement can be tricky at first, not only because it's easy to fall victim to feature creep, but also because it's extremely tempting to view web development in a way that equates an application with a web site.

Now, sometimes this isn't a bad idea. For example, many popular off-the-shelf weblogging tools take this approach and provide not only basic features like entries and links, but also their own administrative interfaces, their own user and authentication systems, their own templating systems, and many other things. For cases in which a particular application is being developed for nontechnical or only moderately technical users who simply want to download and install a single package and have their site running immediately, this can be an extremely useful way to work.

However, when you're writing applications that are meant to be used and reused by other developers, or just by you as you work on different projects, this can be a disastrous method of developing an application. You'll quickly lose the ability to mix and match specific features as you build new sites, and typically the only way to compensate is by adding systems that let you develop plug-ins or other additions to a single large application. This just increases the complexity of the code and the amount of work you have to do each time you need to add or reuse a feature.

The alternative—viewing a web site as a collection of tightly focused applications, each providing some particular feature or set of features—results in far more flexibility and often encourages better code within each application, as you've already seen. Django is designed to accommodate this style of development:

- **Rather than handling everything through a single, monolithic application, Django has you specify a list of applications to use (the INSTALLED_APPS setting)**: You can also designate which applications are responsible for which functionality by setting up the root URL configuration.

- **Instead of forcing all the code for a particular site to exist within a single specific directory, Django uses the standard Python import path to look for the applications you list in INSTALLED_APPS**: This avoids tying your code to any specific directory structure, and it lets you reuse a single copy of an application in multiple projects rather than having to endlessly copy it into new project directories.

- Through abstractions such as the Site model in `django.contrib.sites`, Django encourages you to think in terms of reusing applications across multiple sites, even when those sites share a database and possibly even a single instance of the administrative interface: `django.contrib.admin` can easily provide administration for multiple sites through a setting called `ADMIN_FOR`, which lists the settings modules of all the sites to administer.

The net effect of this is that, although you can do so if you're really determined, trying to build all of your features into one large application will often give you the feeling that you're swimming against the current. As soon as you start splitting things up logically according to function, you'll find development to be a lot easier.

Drawing the Lines Between Applications

Of course, this raises the question of how to tell when you should split off a feature or set of features and start developing one or more new, separate applications. To some extent, learning how to recognize the need to spin off new applications is something that comes with experience, but you can follow some good general guidelines to help with the decision-making process.

The most obvious sign that you need to start developing a new, separate application is when you find that there's a particular feature, or some related features, that you want to have but that doesn't logically belong to the application you're working on. For example, you'd probably want to have some form of publicly accessible user signup system to accompany the code-sharing snippets application you developed in the last few chapters, but that system obviously doesn't belong in that application, so you should develop it separately.

This gets somewhat trickier when you're considering sets of features that are at least somewhat related. The discussion in the previous section of adding user profiles and preferences along with the signup system is a good example of this, because all of the features involved relate in some way to handling user accounts. A case can be made for handling them together, because they'll almost always be used together. Most of the time, a site that has users signing up through a public registration system will also have some sort of profile features or preferences that they can take advantage of.

In these cases, it's often useful to think in terms of *orthogonality*. Generally, in software development, two features are orthogonal if a change to one doesn't affect the other. User preferences, then, are orthogonal to user signups, because you could, for example, change the way the signup process works (say, by adding an explicit activation step or building in measures to defeat spambots) without changing the way users configure their preferences. When features are clearly orthogonal to each other like this, they almost always belong in separate applications.

Finally, reuse can be a good criterion for determining whether some particular feature deserves to be split out into its own application. If you can imagine a case where you'd want to use that feature, and *just* that feature, on another site, the odds are good that it ought to be in a separate application to make that reuse easier.

Splitting Up the Snippets Application

For an instructive example of applying these guidelines, consider the code-sharing application you developed over the last few chapters. You developed it as a single application, but you might have noticed that it contained several features that could just as easily be split out into separate applications (although they'd be necessary if you were to deploy an actual code-sharing site publicly).

For example, the rating system you developed was useful and necessary for the social features you wanted to have, but under all three of the guidelines listed previously (unrelated features, orthogonality, and reuse), it would be a strong candidate for becoming its own application for these reasons:

- **Unrelated features**: Providing a mechanism for users to rate code snippets isn't all that closely related to the core purpose of the application, which is providing the means for users to submit and edit the snippets in the first place.

- **Orthogonality**: The rating system is largely orthogonal to the rest of the application. For example, you could change it from a simple "up" or "down" rating to a numeric score or to a system where users give ratings such as "three stars out of four," without affecting the way people submit, edit, and bookmark snippets.

- **Reuse**: It's easy to imagine other sites or projects where you'd want to have a system for users to rate content, but where you wouldn't necessarily want to have the code-snippet features along with it.

The same is true of the bookmarking system and for almost precisely the same reasons: it's not related to the core "purpose" of the application (which, again, is the code-snippet functionality). It's orthogonal to the other features. Providing the ability for users to bookmark their favorite pieces of site content is something that'd be useful on a lot of different types of sites.

Building for Flexibility

Logically splitting functionality up into multiple applications is only part of the process of making that functionality reusable. As you've already seen, it's easy to imagine a case where even a seemingly "simple" feature can vary quite a bit from one project to the next. One good example of this would be a contact form. Many different types of sites need some sort of function that lets visitors fill out a form and submit some information to site staff, but the use cases can vary wildly. For example, some sites might want a form that lets visitors send a message to the site owner(s) to provide feedback or report problems. Other sites, often business sites, will probably want to collect more information and might even want different types of forms for different situations. For example, one form might handle sales inquiries, while another could handle customer-service requests. Still other sites might want to supplement the form's validation rules with spam checks (perhaps by using Akismet or some other form of automated analysis).

At first it seems like there'd be no way to develop a single application that can handle all these cases (and this is just a small sample of the use cases for a contact form). You might suspect that you'll just have to bite the bullet and write a different version of the application each time you use it. However, with a bit of planning and a little bit of code, a Django application can become flexible enough to handle all of these variations on the underlying theme, and more.

Flexible Form Handling

If you're going to write a contact-form application, you might start out by defining a simple contact form like so:

```
from django import newforms as forms
from django.core.mail import mail_managers


class ContactForm(forms.Form):
    name = forms.CharField(max_length=255)
    email = forms.EmailField()
    message = forms.CharField(widget=forms.Textarea())

    def save(self):
        message = "%s (%s) wrote:\n\n%s" % (self.cleaned_data['name'],
                                            self.cleaned_data['email'],
                                            self.cleaned_data['message'])
        mail_managers(subject="Site feedback", message=message)
```

A simple view could process this form:

```
from django.http import HttpResponseRedirect
from django.shortcuts import render_to_response
from django.template import RequestContext


def contact_form(request):
    if request.method == 'POST':
        form = ContactForm(data=request.POST)
        if form.is_valid():
            form.save()
            return HttpResponseRedirect("/contact/sent/")
    else:
        form = ContactForm()
    return render_to_response('contact_form.html',
                              { 'form': form },
                              context_instance=RequestContext(request))
```

For the simplest cases, this would be fine. But how could you handle a situation in which you need to use a different form—one with additional fields, for example, or additional validation rules?

The easiest solution is to remember that a Django view is simply a function and that you can define it to take any additional arguments you want to handle. You can add a new argument to the view that specifies the form class to use, and you can reference that argument whenever you need to instantiate a form from within the view:

```
def contact_form(request, form_class):
    if request.method == 'POST':
        form = form_class(data=request.POST)
        if form.is_valid():
            form.save()
            return HttpResponseRedirect("/contact/sent/")
    else:
        form = form_class()
    return render_to_response('contact_form.html',
                              { 'form': form },
                              context_instance=RequestContext(request))
```

You can improve this slightly by supplying a default value for the new argument:

```
def contact_form(request, form_class=ContactForm):
```

This is how many of the optional parameters to Django's generic views work: the view function accepts a large number of arguments and supplies sensible default values. Then, if you need to change the behavior slightly, you simply pass the appropriate argument.

If you're developing a business site that wants to handle sales inquiries through a form, you could define a form class to handle that—perhaps called SalesInquiryForm—and then set up a URL pattern like so:

```
url(r'^inquiries/sales/$',
    contact_form,
    { 'form_class': SalesInquiryForm },
    name='sales_inquiry_form'),
```

The form_class argument you pass here overrides the default in the contact_form view, and—as long as you remember to define a save() method on your SalesInquiryForm class—it simply works. If you need multiple forms of different types, you can reuse the contact_form view multiple times, passing a different form_class argument each time, in much the same way you previously reused generic views by passing different sets of arguments.

Flexible Template Handling

Of course, simply changing the form class might not help very much, because the view will always use the same template—contact_form.html—to render it. But once again, you can make a small change to the view and add some flexibility to the template handling; in this case, you can directly emulate Django's generic views, which all accept an argument called template_name to override the default template they'd use:

```
def contact_form(request, form_class=ContactForm,
                 template_name='contact_form.html'):
    if request.method == 'POST':
        form = form_class(data=request.POST)
        if form.is_valid():
            form.save()
            return HttpResponseRedirect("/contact/sent/")
    else:
```

```
        form = form_class()
    return render_to_response(template_name,
                              { 'form': form },
                              context_instance=RequestContext(request))
```

Then you can change the URL pattern to specify a different template:

```
url(r'^inquiries/sales/$',
    contact_form,
    { 'form_class': SalesInquiryForm,
      'template_name':  'sales_inquiry.html' },
    name='sales_inquiry_form'),
```

Being able to change both the form that the view uses and the template it uses to display that form gives you a huge amount of flexibility for reusing this view. Now you can easily set up multiple forms and customize the templates for each one with any specific presentation or instructions you want to add.

Flexible Post-Form Processing

There's one more thing missing here: no matter what arguments you pass to the view, it will always redirect to the URL /contact/sent/ after successful submission. Let's fix that by adding one final argument, called success_url:

```
def contact_form(request, form_class=ContactForm,
                 template_name='contact_form.html',
                 success_url='/contact/sent/'):
    if request.method == 'POST':
        form = form_class(data=request.POST)
        if form.is_valid():
            form.save()
            return HttpResponseRedirect(success_url)
    else:
        form = form_class()
    return render_to_response(template_name,
                              { 'form': form },
                              context_instance=RequestContext(request))
```

Now you have full control over the entire process of displaying, validating, and processing the form:

```
url(r'^inquiries/sales/$',
    contact_form,
    { 'form_class': SalesInquiryForm,
      'template_name':  'sales_inquiry.html',
      'success_url': 'inquiries/sales/sent/' },
    name='sales_inquiry_form'),
```

You can now handle all of the cases listed previously—different combinations of forms, additional fields, and additional validation—by nothing more complicated than passing the right arguments to the `contact_form` view, in exactly the same way you've been passing arguments to Django's generic views. You could add even more flexibility to this view by emulating some other common arguments accepted by generic views. For example, the `extra_context` argument would be handy to support so that additional custom template variables could be made available.

Of course, it's important not to go overboard and add so many arguments that the view becomes too complex to use or to write. Supporting large numbers of optional arguments can be tricky. The right balance between flexibility and complexity will vary from one situation to the next, but you should try to support at least a few arguments. While you don't have to use the following names for them, picking a standard set of argument names and sticking to them will greatly improve the readability of your code. Also, when you're writing a view to take a similar argument, using the same argument names as Django's generic views is often a good idea. In my own applications, I generally try to support at least the following arguments:

- `form_class`, when I'm writing a view that handles a form
- `success_url`, when I'm writing a view that redirects after successful processing (of a form, for example)
- `template_name`, as in generic views
- `extra_context`, also as in generic views

Also, I always make sure to use `RequestContext` for template rendering. This enables both the standard set of context processors, which add things like the currently logged-in user to the context, as well as any custom context processors that have been added to the site's settings.

Flexible URL Handling

In the previous examples, the default value for the `success_url` argument was a hard-coded URL. In the applications you've developed in this book, though, you've worked hard to stay away from ever doing that. For example, in the models, when you defined `get_absolute_url()`, you always used the `permalink()` decorator to ensure that it uses a reverse URL lookup based on the current URL configuration. And in your templates, you saw how to use the `{% url %}` tag to perform a similar reverse URL lookup and make sure we you always output the correct URLs for links.

You haven't encountered this in a view, however, and neither of the solutions you've seen so far will work in this context. However, there is another function that will do what you want: `django.core.urlresolvers.reverse()`. This is actually the underlying mechanism for both the `permalink()` decorator and the `{% url %}` tag. Using `reverse`, you can easily refer to any URL pattern and have it automatically look up and generate the correct URL. So if you set up a URL pattern with a name of, say, `contact_form_sent`, you could rewrite the `contact_form` view's argument list like so (after importing `reverse()`, of course):

```
def contact_form(request, form_class=ContactForm,
                 template_name='contact_form.html',
                 success_url=reverse('contact_form_sent')):
```

And the proper URL would be filled in by a reverse lookup at your live URLConf.

Whenever you need to refer to or return a URL, you should always use the reverse lookup utility that's appropriate for what you're writing:

- `django.db.models.permalink()`: Use this decorator when you're writing a model's `get_absolute_url()` method or other methods on a model that return a URL.

- `{% url %}`: Use this tag when you're writing a template.

- `django.core.urlresolvers.reverse()`: Use this in any other Python code.

To make the reverse lookups easier to use, any URLConf module included in your application should give sensible names to all of its URL patterns (preferably prefixed with the name of the application to avoid name clashes, as you've been doing previously with URL pattern names like `cab_snippet_detail`).

Taking Advantage of Django's APIs

It's also worth noting that many of Django's own APIs work the same way, or in extremely similar ways, with many different types of models. For example, a Django `QuerySet` has the same methods—`all()`, `filter()`, `get()`, and so on—regardless of which model it ends up querying against. This means that you can often write code that accepts a `QuerySet` as an argument and simply applies standard methods to it.

ADMONITION: QuerySet EVALUATION

Keep in mind that each individual `QuerySet` object only evaluates and performs its query once. After that, it simply stores a copy of its results. In many cases, this won't be a problem, because your code calls methods such as `filter()`, which modify the original `QuerySet` and force a new query when you ask for results. However, if you're not modifying the `QuerySet`, you'll want to call its `all()` method and work with the new `QuerySet` object it returns. This will avoid any potential problems from an already evaluated `QuerySet` with stale results.

Similarly, you can use the `ModelForm` helper you saw in Chapter 9 as a way to quickly and easily generate a form for adding or editing any type of object. Since `ModelForm` works the same way for any model (though customizations such as the `exclude` feature are typically filled in on a per-model basis), you can use it with any of multiple models, even if you don't know in advance what model you'll be working with.

Staying Generic

In addition to writing views that take optional arguments to customize their behavior, you can also build flexibility into your nonview code by avoiding tying it to specific models or specific ideas of how it ought to work. For example, when you added comment moderation features to your weblog, you made some assumptions that can limit its flexibility. For example, you used the `pub_date` field of the `Entry` model to determine whether a comment was being posted on an older entry. However, you might want to use comment moderation later on with a different model that doesn't have this field. You also hard-coded the moderation rules you wanted:

comments on entries older than 30 days are automatically nonpublic, comments on newer entries go through Akismet, and all new comments generate a notification e-mail. However, if you ever needed comment moderation somewhere else, you might want a different set of rules.

Again, for the limited purposes of the weblog application, this was fine. However, since comment moderation is a useful feature that you might want to deploy later with other types of sites, a better option might be to write an application that does nothing but moderation, and write it so that it can allow each different model to specify rules for moderating its comments.

One common pattern for handling this sort of situation is to write a pair of classes. One represents a set of rules (which are implemented by reading attributes or calling methods on the class), and the other is a registry class that keeps track of different sets of rules and knows how to apply them. For example, you might represent comment moderation by starting with a class called CommentModerator and defining a set of moderation options:

```
class CommentModerator(object):
    akismet = False
    moderate_after = False
    moderate_date_field = None
    enable_field = None
    email_notification = False
```

Then you could tell users to subclass it and change the options—setting akismet to True to turn on Akismet filtering, for example, or filling in moderate_after = 30 and moderate_date_field = "pub_date" to specify that comments go into automatic moderation 30 days after the date in the pub_date field. Then you could write a second class, called Moderator, that allows you to register a given model with an associated CommentModerator subclass:

```
from django.dispatch import dispatcher
from django.db.models import signals
from django.contrib.comments.models import FreeComment

class Moderator(object):
    def __init__(self):
        self.registry = {}
        dispatcher.connect(self.pre_save, sender=FreeComment,
                           signal=signals.pre_save)
        dispatcher.connect(self.post_save, sender=FreeComment,
                           signal=signals.post_save)

    def register(self, model, moderation_class):
        self.registry[model] = moderation_class
```

The pre_save() and post_save() methods on this class (not shown here) would look to see if a new comment is being posted to a model in the registry. They would then apply the appropriate moderation rules to it based on the associated CommentModerator subclass.

This system is a bit more complex than the comment moderation feature you wrote for the weblog, but it pays off in incredible flexibility. You could set up a different set of moderation rules for each model you allow comments on, and if you needed to support custom moderation rules that aren't covered by the code in the Moderator class, you could simply sub-class it, write the appropriate code for your custom moderation rules, and then use that subclass to handle your comment moderation.

Distributing Django Applications

Once you've written an application so that you can reuse it easily, the final step is to make it easily distributable. Even if you never intend to publicly release an application you've written, going through this step can still be useful. You'll end up with a nice, packaged version of your application that you can easily copy from one computer to another, and a simple mechanism for installing it, which ensures that the application will end up in a location that's on the Python import path.

The first step in creating an easily distributed Django application is to make sure you're developing your application as a module that can live directly on the Python import path, rather than one that needs to be placed inside a project directory. Developing in this fashion makes it much easier to move a copy of an application from one computer to another, or to have multiple projects using the same application. You'll recall that the last two applications you built in this book have followed this pattern, and in general, you should always develop standalone applications in this fashion.

ADMONITION: CODE THAT'S TIGHTLY COUPLED TO A PROJECT

Sometimes you will have code that's tightly coupled to a particular project. For example, it's somewhat common to write a view that handles the home page of a site, and have that handle requirements that are so site-specific that it wouldn't make sense to reuse that view on other projects.

If you'd like, you can place code like this in an application that's directly inside the project directory, but keep in mind that for common cases like this, there's no need for an application. Django doesn't require that view functions be within an application module (Django's own generic views aren't, for example). So you can simply put project-specific views directly inside the project. You only need to create an application if you're also defining models or custom template tags.

Python Packaging Tools

Since a Django application is just a collection of Python code, it's best to simply use standard Python packaging tools to distribute it. The Python standard library includes the module distutils, which provides the basic functionality you'll need, including creating and installing packages and (if you want to distribute your application to the public) registering with the Python Package Index.

The primary way you'll use distutils is by writing a script—conventionally called setup.py—that contains some information about your package. Then you'll use that script to generate the package. In the simplest case, this is a three-step process:

1. In a temporary directory (not one on your Python import path), create an empty `setup.py` file and a copy of your application's directory, containing its code.

2. Fill out the `setup.py` script with the appropriate information.

3. Run `python setup.py sdist` to generate the package; this creates a directory called `dist` that contains the package.

ADMONITION: A SETUP FOR CONTINUOUS PACKAGING

One minor annoyance with this process is that, as the developer of a package, you have to have a copy of the application code in the same directory as the `setup.py` file; otherwise, you won't be able to generate the package. (If you're simply installing a package someone else has produced, you don't need to do this.)

While it's easy enough to temporarily make a copy of your application's code so that you can create the package, this can be tedious to do over and over. Instead, I often maintain a permanent directory structure that has one directory for each package I maintain. Inside each directory is the `setup.py` script and any other files related to the packaging, and the actual application code. Then I place a link (a symlink on UNIX systems, or a shortcut on Windows) to the application code in a directory on my Python import path.

I've found this to be a much easier way to work with an application that evolves over time (and hence needs to be packaged several times for different versions). You should feel free to use a similar technique or experiment to find a setup that suits you.

The other common method of distributing Python packages uses a system called `setuptools`. Though it has some similarities to `distutils` (both use a script called `setup.py`, and the way you use that script to create and install packages is the same), `setuptools` adds a large number of features on top of the standard `distutils`, including ways to specify dependencies between packages and automatically download and install packages and all of their dependencies. You can learn more about `setuptools` online at http://peak.telecommunity.com/DevCenter/setuptools. However, let's use `distutils` for the example here, since it's part of Python's standard library and thus doesn't require you to install any additional tools to generate packages.

Writing a `setup.py` Script with `distutils`

To see how Python's standard `distutils` library works, let's walk through packaging a simple application. Go to a directory that's *not* on your Python import path, and in it place the following:

- An empty file named `setup.py`

- An empty file named `hello.py`

In `hello.py`, add the following code:

```
print "Hello! I'm a packaged Python application!"
```

Obviously, this isn't the most useful Python application ever written, but now that you have a bit of code, you can see how to write the packaging script in `setup.py`:

```
from distutils.core import setup

setup(name="hello",
      version="0.1",
      description="A simple packaged Python application",
      author="Your name here",
      author_email="Your e-mail address here",
      url="Your website URL here",
      py_modules=["hello"],
      download_url="URL to download this package here")
```

Now you can run `python setup.py sdist`, which creates a `dist` directory containing a file named `hello-0.1.tar.gz`. This is a Python package, and you can install it on any computer that has Python available. The installation process is simple: open up the package (the file is a standard compressed archive file that most operating systems can unpack), and it will create a directory called `hello-0.1` containing a `setup.py` script. Running `python setup.py install` in that directory installs the package on the Python import path.

Of course, this is a very basic example, but it shows most of what you'll need to know to create Python packages. The various arguments to the `setup` function in your `setup.py` file provide information about the package, and `distutils` does the rest. This only gets tricky if your application consists of several modules or submodules, or if it also includes non-Python files (such as documentation files) that need to be included in the package.

To handle multiple modules or submodules, you simply list them in the `py_modules` argument. For example, if you have an application named `foo`, which contains a submodule `foo.templatetags`, you'd use this argument to tell `distutils` to include them:

```
py_modules=["foo", "foo.templatetags"],
```

The setup script expects the `foo` module to be alongside it in the same directory, so it looks inside `foo` to find `foo.templatetags` for inclusion.

Standard Files to Include in a Package

When you created the previous example package, the `setup.py` script probably complained about some standard files not being found. Though they're not technically required, several files are typically included with a Python package, and `distutils` warns you when they're not present. At a minimum, you should include two files in any package you plan to distribute:

- **A file named LICENSE or LICENSE.txt**: This should contain copyright information. For many Python packages, this is simply a copy of a standard open source license with the author's name filled in appropriately.

- **A file named README or README.txt**: This should provide some basic human-readable information about the package, its contents, and pointers to documentation or further information.

You may also find these other common files in many packages:

- **AUTHORS or AUTHORS.txt**: For software developed by a team of contributors, this is often a list of everyone who's contributed code. For large projects, this can grow to an impressive size. Django's AUTHORS file, for example, lists everyone who's contributed code to the project and runs several hundred lines long.

- **INSTALL or INSTALL.txt**: This often contains installation instructions. Even though Python packages all offer the standard setup.py install mechanism, some packages may also offer alternate installation methods or include detailed instructions for specialized cases.

- **CHANGELOG or CHANGELOG.txt**: This usually includes a brief summary of the application's history, noting the changes between each released version.

Including these sorts of files in a Python package is fairly easy. While the setup.py script specifies the Python modules to be packaged, additional files like these can be listed in a file (in the same directory as setup.py) named MANIFEST.in. The format of this file is extremely simple and often looks something like this:

```
include LICENSE.txt
include README.txt
include CHANGELOG.txt
```

Each include statement goes on a separate line and names a file to be included in the package. For advanced use, such as packaging a directory of documentation files, you can use a recursive-include statement. For example, if there are documentation files in a directory called docs, you could use this to include them in the package:

```
recursive-include docs *
```

Documenting an Application

Finally, one of the most important parts of a distributable, reusable Django application is good documentation. I haven't talked much about documentation so far, because I've mostly been focused on code, but any time you're writing code that someone else might end up using (or that you might need to pick up again and use after not looking at it for a while), documentation is essential.

One thing you can and often should do is include some documentation files in your application's package. You can generally assume that other developers will know how Python and Django work, so you don't need to document things like using setup.py install or adding the application to the INSTALLED_APPS list of a Django project. However, you should explain what your application does and how it works, and you should give at least an outline of each of the following items:

- Any models provided by your application, their intended uses, and any custom managers or useful custom methods you've set up for them

- A list of views in your application, along with the template names they expect and any variables they make available in the template context

- A list of any custom template tags or filters you've provided and what they do

- A list of any custom forms you've provided and what purposes they serve

- A list of any third-party Python modules or Django applications your application relies on and information on how to obtain them

In addition to this or, more often, as a precursor to this, you should also include documentation directly in your code. Python makes it easy to provide documentation alongside the code you're writing by giving *docstrings* to your Python modules, classes, and functions. A docstring is simply a literal string of text, included as the first thing in the definition of a module, class, or function. To see an example of how this works, launch a Python interpreter and type:

```
>>> def add(n1, n2):
...     """
...     Add two numbers and return the result.
...
...     """
...     return n1 + n2
...
```

This defines a simple function and gives it a docstring. You use triple quotes (the """ at the beginning and end of the docstring) because Python allows triple-quoted strings to run over multiple lines.

Docstrings end up being useful in three primary ways:

- **Anyone who's reading your code can also see the docstrings and pick up additional information from them**: This is possible because they're included directly in the code.

- **Python's automated help tool knows how to read a docstring and show you useful information**: In the previous example, you could type help(add) in the interpreter, and Python would show you the function's argument signature and print its docstring.

- **Other tools can read docstrings and assemble them automatically into documentation in a variety of formats**: Several standard or semistandard tools can read through an entire application, for example, and print out organized documentation, in HTML or PDF formats, from the docstrings.

Documentation Displayed Within Django

This last point is particularly important, because Django can read through your code looking for docstrings and use them to display useful documentation to users. The administrative interface usually contains a link (in the upper right-hand corner of the main page) labeled "Documentation", which (if the necessary Python documentation tools are available; see the next section for details) takes the user to a page listing all of the documentation Django can produce. This includes:

- **A list of all the installed models, organized by the applications they belong to**: For each model, Django shows a table listing the fields defined on the model and any custom methods, as well as the docstring of the model class.

- **A list of all the URL patterns and the views they map to**: For each view, Django displays the docstring.

- **Lists of all available template tags and filters, both from Django's own built-in set and from any custom tag libraries included in your installed applications**: For each tag or filter, Django shows the docstring.

Finally, giving your code good docstrings gives you a head start on producing standalone documentation for your application. It's a good practice to write useful docstrings anyway, since so many tools in Python make use of them. Once you have them, you can copy them into files to use as standalone reference documentation to distribute with your applications.

What to Document

In general, you should be liberal about giving docstrings to classes and functions in your code. It's better to have documentation when you don't need it than to need documentation when you don't have it. Generally, the only time you shouldn't worry about giving something a docstring is when you're writing something that's standard and well known. For example, you don't need to supply a docstring for the get_absolute_url() method of a model, because that's a standard method to define on models, and you can trust that people reading your code will know why it's there and what it's doing. However, if you're providing a custom save() method, you often *should* document it, because an explanation of any special behavior it provides will be useful to people reading your code.

Typically, a good docstring provides a short overview of what the associated code is doing. The docstring for a class should explain what the class represents, for example, and how it's intended to be used, while the docstring for a function or method should explain what it does and mention any constraints on the arguments or the return value.

Additionally, you should keep in mind the following items, which are specific to Django, when writing docstrings:

- **Model classes should include information about any custom managers attached to the model**: However, they don't need to include a list of fields in their docstrings, because that's generated automatically.

- **Docstrings for view functions should always mention the template name that will be used**: In addition, they should give a list of variables that are made available to the template.

- **Docstrings for custom template tags should explain the syntax and arguments the tags expect**: Ideally, they should also give at least one example of how the tag works.

Within the admin interface, Django can automatically format much of this documentation for you if you have the Python docutils module installed (you can obtain it from http://docutils.sourceforge.net/ if it's not already installed on your computer). The docutils package includes a lightweight syntax called reStructuredText (commonly abbreviated as reST), and Django knows how to transform this into HTML. If you'd like, you can use this syntax in your docstrings to get nicely formatted documentation.

Django also makes use of a couple of customized extensions to the reST syntax to allow you to easily refer to Django-specific things such as model classes or view functions. To see how this works, consider a simple view that might go into your weblog application:

```
def latest_entries(request):
    return render_to_response('coltrane/entry_archive.html',
                              { 'latest': Entry.objects.all()[:15] })
```

Now, you wouldn't ever need to write this, because Django provides a generic view to handle it, but you can use it to show off some documentation tricks. Here's the same view with a useful docstring:

```
def latest_entries(request):
    """
    View of the latest 15 entries published. This is similar to
    the :view:`django.views.generic.date_based.archive_index`
    generic view.

    **Template:**'

    ``coltrane/entry_archive.html``

    **Context:**

    ``latest``
        A list of :model`coltrane.Entry` objects.

    """
    return render_to_response('coltrane/entry_archive.html',
                              { 'latest': Entry.live.all()[:15] })
```

A lot of what's going on here is fairly simple: line breaks become paragraph breaks in the HTML-formatted documentation, double asterisks become bold text for headings, and the list of context variables become an HTML definition list, with the variable name latest (surrounded by backticks) in a monospaced font.

ADMONITION: LEARNING reStructuredText

For most uses, you won't need to know much more about reST syntax than what's covered in the example. If you'd like to learn more about it, though, a full primer and extensive documentation (as you'd expect from a tool that's designed to make documentation easy) is available online at http://docutils.sourceforge. net/docs/user/rst/quickstart.html. The docutils package also includes tools for reading files written using reST syntax and generating nicely formatted output in HTML and other formats. It's an extremely useful tool to be familiar with, and it scales up to large documentation projects. For example, I originally wrote and edited the text of this book in reST syntax before translating it into other formats for publication.

However, two specialized things are going on here: the mention of a generic view and the mention of the `Entry` model. These make use of the Django-specific extensions and are transformed into a link to the generic view's documentation and a link to the `Entry` model's documentation, respectively.

In addition to the `:view:` and `:model:` shortcuts shown in the previous example, three others are available:

- `:tag:`: This should be followed by the name of a template tag. It links to the tag's documentation.

- `:filter:`: This should be followed by the name of a template filter. It links to the filter's documentation.

- `:template:`: This should be followed by a template name. It links to a page that either shows locations in your project's `TEMPLATE_DIRS` setting where that template can be found or shows nothing if the template can't be found.

Looking Ahead

A lot more that can be said about developing Django applications to get the maximum possible use and reuse out of them, but what I've covered here is a good start.

Learning when to apply these general principles to specific applications—and, just as importantly, when *not* to apply them (there are no universal rules of software development)—is best accomplished through the experience of writing and using Django applications. Consider making up a list of application ideas that interest you, and try your hand at a few of them, even if you never end up using them in any serious situation. Feel free to go back and tinker with the applications you've built in this book. There's a lot of room to expand them and add new features or even to spin off entire new applications from them. Also, keep in mind that there's a whole ecosystem of Django applications already written and available online, providing a large base of code you can study.

Always remember that Django has a large and friendly community of developers and users who answer questions on mailing lists and in chat rooms, so whenever you get stumped (and we all get stumped once in a while), you can turn to them for help.

Above all, remember what I mentioned back in Chapter 1, when you got your first look at Django: Django's job is to make web development *fun* again, by relieving you of all the tedium and repetitive busy work that's traditionally been part of the process. So find an idea or two that you like, let Django take care of the heavy lifting for you, and just have fun writing your code.

Index

You Need the Companion eBook

Your purchase of this book entitles you to buy the companion PDF-version eBook for only $10. Take the weightless companion with you anywhere.

We believe this Apress title will prove so indispensable that you'll want to carry it with you everywhere, which is why we are offering the companion eBook (in PDF format) for $10 to customers who purchase this book now. Convenient and fully searchable, the PDF version of any content-rich, page-heavy Apress book makes a valuable addition to your programming library. You can easily find and copy code—or perform examples by quickly toggling between instructions and the application. Even simultaneously tackling a donut, diet soda, and complex code becomes simplified with hands-free eBooks!

Once you purchase your book, getting the $10 companion eBook is simple:

❶ Visit **www.apress.com/promo/tendollars/**.

❷ Complete a basic registration form to receive a randomly generated question about this title.

❸ Answer the question correctly in 60 seconds, and you will receive a promotional code to redeem for the $10.00 eBook.

THE EXPERT'S VOICE™

2855 TELEGRAPH AVENUE | SUITE 600 | BERKELEY, CA 94705

All Apress eBooks subject to copyright protection. No part may be reproduced or transmitted in any form or by any means, electronic or mechanical, including photocopying, recording, or by any information storage or retrieval system, without the prior written permission of the copyright owner and the publisher. The purchaser may print the work in full or in part for their own noncommercial use. The purchaser may place the eBook title on any of their personal computers for their own personal reading and reference.

Offer valid through 11/08.